VALLEY OF SHINING STONE

VALLEY OF
SHINING STONE

THE STORY OF ABIQUIU

Lesley Poling-Kempes

The University of Arizona Press   Tucson

The University of Arizona Press
© 1997 Lesley Poling-Kempes
All Rights Reserved

♾ This book is printed on acid-free, archival-quality
paper.
Manufactured in the United States of America
Second printing 1999

Library of Congress Cataloging-in-Publication Data
Poling-Kempes, Lesley.
Valley of shining stone: the story of Abiquiu/
Lesley Poling-Kempes.
   p. cm.
   "The oral histories collected for this book were
   conducted for the Ghost Ranch history project."
   Includes bibliographical references and index.
   ISBN 0-8165-1421-6 (alk. paper).—
   ISBN 0-8165-1446-1 (pbk.: alk. paper)
     1. Abiquiu Region (N.M.)—History.
I. Title
F804.A (Abiquiu)
978.9′52—dc21   97-4621
                                        CIP

British Cataloguing-in-Publication Data
A catalogue record for this book is available from the
British Library.

Publication of this book was made possible in part by
grants from the Pack Foundation and Bahti Indian
Arts.

This book is dedicated to my parents, Ann and David Poling, who brought me to the valley of the Piedra Lumbre when I was just a child; their love and support have kept my feet on the road and my eyes on the horizon for more than four decades.

This book is also dedicated to my children, Christopher and Marianne, who have patiently and cheerfully endured my commitment to this project; and to my husband, Jim, my greatest friend, with whom I have shared this beautiful, faraway country for more than twenty years.

CONTENTS

ILLUSTRATIONS

ACKNOWLEDGMENTS

The following individuals graciously shared their time and memories of Abiquiu and the region of the Piedra Lumbre in formal interviews, casual conversations, or personal correspondence. Without their help this book would not have been possible. I am deeply indebted to each and every one of them: Elizabeth Bode Allred, Edward H. Bennett, Jr., Karl Bode, Lillian Bode, Derek Bok, Martha Cox Boyle, Jim Breese, Ed Brousseau, Roberta Brousseau, Maria Chabot, Edwin H. Colbert, Mary Jean Cook, Cordelia Coronado, John Crosby, John Dancy, Criselda Dominguez, Tom Dozier, Florence Hawley Ellis, Reginaldo Espinoza, John Fife, Joe Fitzgibbon, Dorthy Burnham Fredericks, Juanita Gallegos, Sophie Garcia, Carl Glock, Miguel Gonzales, Caroline Grant, Robert Grant, Ed Groesbeck, James W. Hall, James W. Hall, Jr., Jon Hall, Ruth Hall, Tim Hall, Jane Harris, Will Harris, John Hayden, Eleanor Hibben, Frank C. Hibben, Vic Jameson, Dennis Jaramillo, Ophelia Jaramillo, Robert H. Kempes, Robert D. Kilmarx, Father Robert Kirsh, John Pen La Farge, Margery Lambert, Eleanor Pack Liddell, Anne Morrow Lindbergh, Alfredo Lopez, Alice Lopez, Agueda Martinez, Molly Martinez, Rebecca Martinez, Thomas D. Martinez, Henry McKinley, Peggy Pack McKinley, Aubrey Owen, Yuvonnia Owen, Phoebe Pack, Vernon Pack, Henry Peabody, John C. Purdy, Mary Purdy, Robert Radnitz, Georgia Salazar, Herman Salazar, Joe I. Salazar, Elizabeth Seals, Jim Shibley, David Sholin, Margery Fowler Spelletich, Myrtle Stedman, Peggy Terrell, Jim Thorpe, Dexter Trujillo, Floyd Trujillo, Virgil Trujillo, Virginia Trujillo, Uvaldo

Valasquez, Edmundo E. Vasquez, Henrietta C. Waring, Samuel Welles, Richard Wells, Ann Breese White, and Roger White.

Special assistance in their various areas of expertise was given by Ann Baldwin of the U.S. Forest Service, Ghost Ranch Living Museum; Lynett Gillette, Ruth Hall Museum of Paleontology, Ghost Ranch; Elizabeth Glassman and Pita Lopez, Georgia O'Keeffe Foundation; Lynette Miller, Wheelwright Museum of the American Indian; Cheryl Muceus, Florence Hawley Ellis Museum of Anthropology, Ghost Ranch; Arthur L. Olivas, photographic archivist, Richard Rudisill, curator of photographic history, and Orlando Romero, librarian, Museum of New Mexico; and Richard Salazar, New Mexico State Records and Archives.

Charles M. Carrillo, Gilberto Benito Córdova, John L. Kessell, Frances Leon Quintana, Marc Simmons, and John R. Van Ness graciously shared with me their considerable professional and personal knowledge of Abiquiu and the Piedra Lumbre's formidable story.

Edgar W. Davy, Ghost Ranch librarian, was ever ready to assist me in my research explorations and placed the Ghost Ranch library's valuable collection of historic books and reference materials at my disposal. Judy Shibley donated considerable hours of personal time to the archival excavation of several of the valley's poorly documented old-timers, notably Carol Bishop Stanley and Juan de Dios Gallegos. Sarah Noss, under the auspices of the Ghost Ranch History Project, transcribed dozens of taped interviews.

With patience, grace, and good humor, Esther Martinez of San Juan Pueblo and Tessie Naranjo of Santa Clara Pueblo edited and translated the Tewa place-names used in this book.

The oral histories collected for this book were conducted for the Ghost Ranch History Project. I am grateful for the continuing support of the Ghost Ranch Conference Center for this research program: former Ghost Ranch director Dr. James W. Hall initiated the project in 1988, and his successor, the Reverend Joseph Keesecker, has given continued endorsement to this effort to collect and preserve material of importance to the history of the Piedra Lumbre basin and the Pueblo of Abiquiu.

In ways too numerous to count, the office and library staff at Ghost

Ranch graciously assisted me in my work on this book. Special thanks are due to Joan Boliek, who guided me through the labyrinth of the Ghost Ranch archives, and to Jim Shibley, who served as my personal guide and chief storyteller through the vast lands and voluminous legends of the Piedra Lumbre basin.

The skull motif used throughout this book is based on a drawing done by Georgia O'Keeffe and given to Arthur Pack in the 1930s. This skull has been the symbol of Ghost Ranch since that time and is used here with the generous permission of the Ghost Ranch Conference Center, Abiquiu, New Mexico.

INTRODUCTION

The moment comes: we intersect a history, a long existence, offering it our fresh discovery as regeneration.　　　·

Shirley Hazzard quoted in William Least Heat Moon, *PrairyErth*

The Pueblo people of New Mexico believe that the earth is imbued with the breath, thoughts, and feelings of every person that has ever placed a foot upon it. They say that the earth is alive with the spirits of those who have walked across its body: the faraway past vibrates in the soil, and the stories of the long-ago people lie scattered like stones upon the places that once harbored them.

Standing upon the wide, luminous space of earth that is the Piedra Lumbre basin in northern New Mexico one is privy to the whispers of a thousand years of stories. A chorus of voices—prehistoric Native American, historic Tewa, Ute, Navajo, Hopi, Apache, Hispanic, and Anglo—echoes from the rock walls whose gleaming, unworldly color gave the region its name.

The Piedra Lumbre is connected physically and culturally with the lower Chama River Valley of northern New Mexico, specifically with Abiquiu, the ancient village located five miles to the southeast of the high-desert basin. The Pueblo of Abiquiu—and Abiquiu was, in every sense of the word, a Native American pueblo centuries before it was a Spanish village—is unlike any community in the Southwest: it is an Indian community whose ancestral trails reached hundreds of miles to the Anasazi, Tewa, Hopi, and nomadic Native American tribes of the Great Plains and West; it is also a Hispanic community whose residents proudly trace the branches of their family trees directly to the first Spanish New World colonists. Because of its dual heritage, Abiquiu may be the only community in the Southwest ever given the choice between legal designation as an Indian pueblo or a Hispanic village. Although the two cultures have merged over the centuries, deep in the warp and woof of the pueblo's old cloth the individual threads and varying hues and dyes of both the Indian and Hispano cultures remain strong and vibrant.

The region of Abiquiu and the Piedra Lumbre has been a pivotal and prominent locale for human stories since the time before recorded time, its soil the home for the famous and infamous of very nearly every era in Southwestern history. American painter Georgia O'Keeffe is the much-heralded headliner of the valley's notable citizens list. But she is, in fact and in legend, a latecomer whose story is the icing on an already rich and multilayered cake of characters who in their own time exerted considerable and remarkable influence on the story of the Southwest.

Historians have loved Abiquiu and the Piedra Lumbre from afar. The valley's story has been told in fits and starts, usually as an antecedent to or anecdote in someone else's story: the region figures prominently in the histories of the pre-Pueblo and Pueblo cultures, and in the arrival of the Spanish and their struggles to establish New World colonial settlements. Individuals involved with the Southwestern Indian slave trade, the Rocky Mountain fur trade, and the first overland trade caravans between New Mexico and California began their perilous journeys from Abiquiu's dusty plaza. And decades of Navajo, Ute, and Apache conflicts with the Spanish, Mexican, and United States governments simmered and too often boiled into bloody warfare on the Piedra Lumbre's vast llanos. "Writing about Abiquiu," historian Stanley F. Crocchiola wrote, "is like picking at a tassel. Any strand you pick ultimately proves a story."[1]

In the twentieth century, the valley became a valued desert paradise for Anglo American expatriates who, like O'Keeffe, saw in the small Pueblo village, and in its huge backyard below the angular blue mountain called Pedernal, a last frontier of unspoiled natural beauty where the myth of the untamed American West was yet found. Some of the finest artists and writers of this century were drawn to the pristine beauty of the valley's varied and often extraordinary topography. World-renowned paleontologists valued the same land for what lay beneath it—fossilized treasure that proved to include some of North America's oldest dinosaur bones. And during the second world war, the world's first nuclear scientists came to the Piedra Lumbre to bask in the glow of its magnificent sunsets while pondering the splitting of atoms and the fate of mankind.

A common theme persists through the centuries: cultural placement and displacement. The valley's first settlers, descendants of the Four Corners Anasazi ("ancient ones"), were probably forced from their villages by nomadic Indians; the domain of the nomads was challenged in turn by the Spanish colonists. In modern times, the Anglo Americans challenged and denounced the prior claims of both Native American and Hispanic New Mexicans.

This cycle of settlement, usurpation, and resettlement is not necessarily a fair or happy one. But like the drought that returns to this high-desert valley several times in every century, the various waves of immigrants and their subsequent impact on the region's cultural fabric seem to be, somehow, natural.

Part One is the story of the valley from the days of prehistory until the mid 1800s, centuries during which Abiquiu and its sister communities were perched on the edge of the known world: the Piedra Lumbre basin was La Tierra de Guerra, the land of war, a region fraught with multicultural conflicts, a difficult, marginal country for human habitation. Part Two is the story of Abiquiu and the Piedra Lumbre from the late nineteenth century into modern times, a century during which this valley became the "Good Country" for O'Keeffe and scores of other "outsiders" enamored with the region's beauty and isolation. The narrative is dominated by the arrival of Anglo American hands, money, and culture, and the subsequent loss, for better and for worse, of the region's frontier characteristics.

I have lived in this valley for more than twenty years. Because I was born and raised somewhere else, I am and will always be an outsider. I am also a newcomer even after decades of residency. Even so, newcomers and

Chama

NAVAJO
CANYON

Canjilon Creek

CANJILON
MOUNTAINS

*Mesa de los
Viejos*

Río Chama

ECHO AMPHITHEATRE

Arroyo del Yeso

CHAMA
CANYON

Ghost Ranch

Arroyo Seco

3

2

Mesa Prieta

*Mesa del
Yeso*

I

*Abiquiu
Reservoir*

84

Santa Rosa
de Lima
de Abiquiu

ABIQUIU
DAM

Silvestres

96

Barraneo

Abiquiu

Poe shú

Tierra Azul

Cañones

4

Pedernal

Abiquiu Creek

Río Puerco

SAN PEDRO
MOUNTAINS

5

Polvadera

SIERRA NACIMIENTO

JEMEZ MOUNTAINS

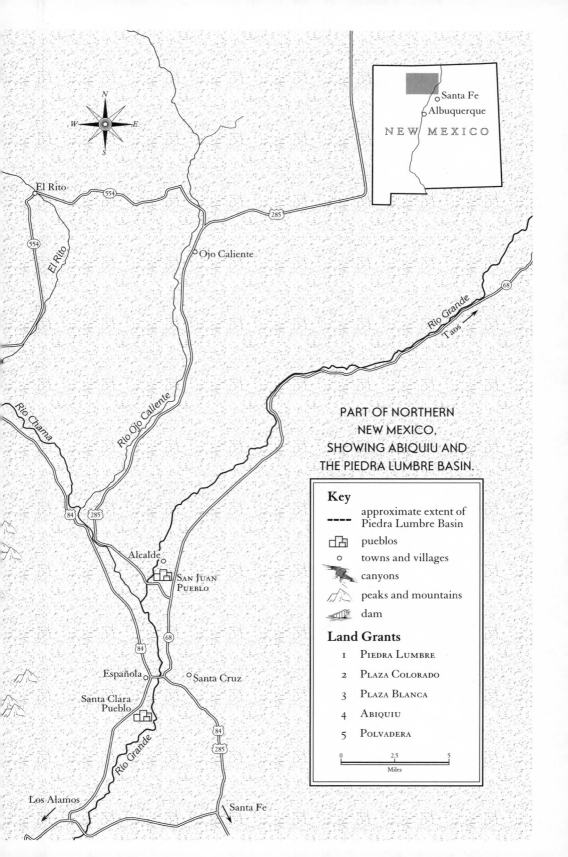

N

W E

S

El Rito

554

554

El Rito

285

Ojo Caliente

Rio Grande

Taos

68

Rio Chama

Rio Ojo Caliente

84 285

Alcalde

SAN JUAN
PUEBLO

Española

84

68

Santa Cruz

Santa Clara
Pueblo

84

285

Los Alamos

Rio Grande

Santa Fe

Santa Fe
Albuquerque

NEW MEXICO

PART OF NORTHERN
NEW MEXICO,
SHOWING ABIQUIU AND
THE PIEDRA LUMBRE BASIN.

Key

---- approximate extent of
Piedra Lumbre Basin

⌂ pueblos

○ towns and villages

canyons

peaks and mountains

dam

Land Grants

1 PIEDRA LUMBRE

2 PLAZA COLORADO

3 PLAZA BLANCA

4 ABIQUIU

5 POLVADERA

0   2.5   5
Miles

outsiders are received with reserved and usually respectful friendliness. The behavior of insiders and old-timers is rooted in their family story: historic Abiquiu and its valley community were built upon collective tolerance and independent resiliency. The pueblo was founded, after all, by Genízaro Indians—homeless, detribalized Native Americans—and from its inception, this was a community of immigrants and outsiders who shared neither language nor culture with their neighbors in the isolated Chama River Valley. "Abiquiu is a cosmic village," my friend Charles M. Carrillo told me. "Its story has always been about many kinds of people and cultures. Everyone who lives here was once an immigrant. Abiquiu is a private place, but its story belongs to the world."

Beside the old road that leads into the upper sierras above Abiquiu is an enormous pile of stones crowned by several weathered wooden crosses. Las Crucitas de las Animas ("the crosses of departed souls") is an informal shrine that marks the place where several Abiqueños died in a skirmish with nomadic warriors more than a century and a half ago. The memorial began with a few stones placed on the ground above the canyon stream; over the decades, into another century, travelers paused at this spot to set a stone on the shrine and to remember and honor those who passed this way before. These stones representing the lives of hundreds of individuals have merged into one colossal wall in the silent canyon above Abiquiu.

Just as the individual stones of the now-mammoth shrine have co-alesced into a single entity, so, too, have the individual stories of Abiquiu and the Valley of Shining Stone merged into a common narrative. Into one history. The contours and colors of the individual stories are still vital and evident, but their power has magnified as they are told in relationship to the greater story. The whole story. The history of a place is, in the truest sense, a jumbled pile of stories that finally come to settle and rest one upon another until the ending of one is indistinguishable from the beginning of another.

Part One

LA TIERRA DE GUERRA,
"THE LAND OF WAR"

AVÉSHU PIJE, "UP ABIQUIU WAY"

The Piedra Lumbre basin, located toward the southeastern end of the Chama River Valley of northwestern New Mexico, is a mountain- and cliff-ringed basin approximately ten miles wide and a little more than ten miles long. The story of this region is as old as the first stories of humankind in this part of the world. Linked in historic partnership with the lower Chama River and the Pueblo of Abiquiu, whose ancient walls are perched on a mesa five miles as the ravens fly downstream, the valley of the Piedra Lumbre has been the stage for a busy, complex, sometimes violent, always interesting multicultural human drama for several thousands of years.

An archaeological survey in the 1980s of the Abiquiu Reservoir area—that portion of the Piedra Lumbre either now permanently inundated or in danger of future inundation by the waters behind Abiquiu Dam—identified 341 archaeological sites. These sites represent human use of the basin from Paleo-Indian times until New Mexico statehood. The remains of Paleo-Indian, Archaic, Basketmaker, and Anasazi cultures litter the Piedra Lumbre's broad basin and lie in the waters of the reservoir. The evidence of these native peoples lies alongside and beneath historic Tewa, Navajo, Ute, Comanche, Jicarilla Apache, and Hispanic sites. Of these 341 archaeological sites, 278 are eligible for inclusion in the National Register of Historic Places. They will never all be excavated. Many have disappeared forever under the earth-filled dam's waters. But the variety and complexity of cultures indigenous to this valley is obvious.[1]

The junction of the Rio Chama and the Rio Puerco del Norte at the northwest corner of the Piedra Lumbre basin, twenty-three miles upstream from the first Spanish settlement of San Gabriel del Yungue, was a pivotal landmark on the sketchy New World maps of the Spanish conquistadors. The first Spanish explorers called the basin Piedra Alumbre (*piedra,* stone or rock; *alumbre,* rock alum or mineral salt), a name that referred to the mineral found in the sandstone cliffs that was used by the Pueblo people. In the first decades after Spanish occupation of northern New Mexico the name given the basin changed: El Valle de la Piedra Lumbre it came to be called, the Valley of Shining Stone, where brilliant rocks burn with fire at sundown. Beyond the Piedra Lumbre's wide, grass llanos and beautiful, multicolored cliffs was the unmapped, difficult, and dangerous province of Spain's fiercest New World enemy, El Apache del Navahu (Navahoo or Nabajoo), the Navajo.

Although the Spanish soldiers moved quickly through this region, we can imagine their military caravans slowed long enough to reflect upon the basin's dramatic topography. We can imagine that even to the youngest conquistadors marching up the Rio Chama into the dangerous Apache frontier, the beauty of the one-hundred-square-mile valley below the flat-topped mountain the natives called Tsee p'in, or Tsiping (Cerro Pedernal, "flint mountain," to the Old World newcomers), gave them pause and perhaps a momentary sense of wonder at the hostile strange country they had been thrust into.

The geologic features of the Piedra Lumbre are characteristic of the Four Corners region of the Southwest. The Chama Valley just below Abiquiu marks the end of the Rio Grande Rift and the beginning of the Colorado Plateau. The deep canyons and erosion-carved sandstone formations that become more frequent with each northwestern mile up the river valley, and that finally become the sheer walls, rugged cliffs, spires, and stone chimneys of the Piedra Lumbre, are typical of this dramatic region that boasts some of the Southwest's most inspiring landscapes: Monument Valley, Canyon de Chelly, Bryce and Zion Canyons, the Painted Desert of Arizona, the Grand Canyon.

The Piedra Lumbre is a small but blue-blood cousin to these high-desert marvels. The canyons of the Piedra Lumbre and Chama River Valley were formed exactly as were those of the Grand Canyon of the Colorado, by the constant downward erosion by the river as the earth's crust was raised one to two vertical miles over the past 20 million years. Geologists marvel at the Piedra Lumbre's exposed skeleton—the northern rim is the most dramatic, with rocks formed 90 million to 225 million years ago laid bare, one geologic layer on top of another, in laboratory-perfect cuts and cross sections.

Descent of the cliffs is a swift journey through geological time. At the top one stands upon the Piedra Lumbre's youngest rocks—the bold, vertical cliffs of hard yellow-brown conglomerate rock and sandstone. This rock, called the Dakota Formation, was made from coarse-grained sediments deposited along a beach or coastline that covered this region during the Cretaceous, 90 million to 100 million years ago.

From the yellow cliffs one steps down into the Jurassic, onto the pastel-colored shales and sandstones—red and green, lavender, pink, dusty purple, blue fading into gray—of the Morrison Formation. These eroded slopes and landslides, once lakes, swamps, and floodplains, hold the fossilized bones of Brontosaurus and other giant dinosaurs who walked this region 130 million years before us.

From the sandy Morrison one descends deeper into the Jurassic, onto the domes of dense, pure white and often transparent Todilto *yeso,* or gypsum, and dark, thinly bedded limestone, both deposited beneath a lake that covered this basin 165 million years ago. When the limestone is crumbled and broken apart, the partially decayed organic matter smells aromatic and pungent.

The seven-hundred-foot vertical cliffs of the Piedra Lumbre—the white, yellow, and dusty orange walls that gleam at sunset—are smooth Entrada Sandstone. These cliffs are the remains of an ancient desert whose sand dunes were continually swept across this part of the earth by strong, persistent winds 168 million years ago.

The scruffy hills and badlands below the cliffs, the Painted Desert of the Piedra Lumbre, are a huge sandbox of fine-grained shales and eroded siltstones that were once the floor of a lake or river channel. Here in the Chinle Formation of the Triassic are layers of pediment littered with small shells and marine fossils 200 million years old. In these hills lie the fossil rubble of prehistoric crocodile-like reptiles and the small, fossilized skeletons of the very first dinosaurs.

The sands of the Chinle spread from the cliffs several miles across the llanos to the Chama River. Here they meet the oldest geologic layer of the Piedra Lumbre, the brick maroon of the Cutler, formed more than 220 million years ago. The deep red and purplish shales of this last formation are seen along the sides of the Rio Chama's deep gorge to the east toward Abiquiu, and the dark maroon dominates canyons and tablelands from the river to the basin's southern side.

The geologic events that formed this region are well marked, their exact scientific stories preserved in the exposed rock body of the Piedra Lumbre. Even so, when the summer sun slides into the horizon and its last flames light the basin's red, gold, and purple walls, bringing the stones of millennia to life, even a geologist can see how it was really the hand of the Great Spirit that gave the Piedra Lumbre its remarkable fire.

Three life zones thrive in the llanos, mesas, and cordilleras (chain of mountains) of the Piedra Lumbre. The Chama River cuts its narrow course six thousand feet above sea level, marking the lowest elevation in the basin. Before Abiquiu Dam and its reservoir of foreign water obliterated the Chama's meandering channel, the river's northwest to southeast path across the valley was defined by sandy banks shaded by old cottonwoods, the home of hundreds of beaver, a verdant, high-desert bosque. This is the Upper Sonoran Life Zone, a haven for wildlife and humans alike.[2]

Climbing gradually off the valley floor, the mesas and flatlands offer a variety of plants that have provided food for animals and people for centuries: vigorous side-oats grama grass, needle-and-thread grass and drought-resistant galleta, blue grama and Indian ricegrass, winterfat and several varieties of sagebrush. The summer llanos are bright yellow with the flowers of the rabbitbrush, locally called chamisa. There is four-winged saltbush, whose seeds the natives used for baking powder, and snakeweed, a bushy plant that graces the mesas with clusters of yellow flowers in September and whose narrow, woody stalks became brooms in the hands of both the Indian and the Spanish occupants of the valley.

Cactus grows easily in this sandy soil: low, sprawling patches of prickly pear, an emergency food for cattle and sheep during extended drought; cane cholla, whose tree-like arms can grow nine feet tall and produce bright magenta flowers in June, followed by yellow, edible fruit in July and August. Two varieties of yucca—banana and narrowleaf— thrive on the Piedra Lumbre. The prehistoric people of the basin used the stiff leaves of the yucca for baskets and mats, rope, cloth, and sandals. The yucca's early summer flowers were food, and the roots were pounded and soaked into *amole,* shampoo.

As the land lifts away from the river onto the sandy tablelands and across these llanos to the striated sand hills and painted badlands, the grasslands meet the woodlands of piñon (or pinyon) pine and one-seed juniper (or cedar), the berries of which are gathered and hoarded by people, songbirds, coyotes, and rodents. The crimson flowers of the Indian paintbrush—called hummingbird flowers by the Navajo because of the blossom's attractiveness to those tiny birds—color the mesa sides and canyons from early summer until fall.

The llanos of the Piedra Lumbre basin have been home for jackrabbits and quail, wild turkey, prairie dogs, mule deer, antelope, coyote, and bobcat. Later the basin became valuable grazeland for sheep and cattle, and occasionally its rough soil was broken into small cultivated fields irrigated with water from the Chama River or one of its tributaries.

Where the gentle llanos and low woodlands slope up to meet the rugged talus hills at the foot of the Cliffs of Shining Stone, the Traditional Life Zone begins. Seven thousand feet above the sea, willows and oaks grow from the dry draws and across the high meadows on top of the cliffs. The meadows are edged by ponderosa pine and douglas-fir that shade a thick understory of grasses speckled with wild roses in the summer. At this altitude, cedar trees four centuries old boast trunks no man can embrace. Beaver, badger, porcupine, mountain lion, bobcat, and deer have lived here since the time before time, but the bear that once roamed the sierras above the Piedra Lumbre basin are gone.

The valley of the Piedra Lumbre is edged by some of the largest mountain ranges in northern New Mexico. The Jemez Mountains form the horizon to the south and east; to the north the cliffs back into the Canjilon Mountains and the southern lip of the San Juan Mountains that wrap the Piedra Lumbre's western flank and meet the San Pedro Mountains at its southwestern border. Peaks in each of these ranges are in the Canadian Life Zone, the realm of the clouds: Pedernal, Polvadera, Tschicoma in the Jemez, the crests of the high sierras southeast near Abiquiu and north near Canjilon—all touch the sky nine thousand to more than eleven thousand feet above sea level. Forests of spruce and balsam, fir and aspen, offer a dense and fragrant environment where the summer heat and aridity of the desert plateau shimmering below becomes a distant memory. There is deep snow in the winter, and in spring heavy runoff floods the dry streambeds that cut across the Piedra Lumbre en route to the Chama. Elk roam here, as do snowshoe rabbits, lynx, fox, and black bear.

Somewhere in time the human story of the Piedra Lumbre began with the Chama River, whose headwaters gather in the high mountains sixty miles north and west in southern Colorado. After winding southward through the mountains on the eastern slope of the Continental Divide, the river emerges from a steep, rugged canyon on the northwestern flank of the Piedra Lumbre. Before the river was dammed, its channel bisected the basin into a northern third and a southern two-thirds before exiting through a spectacular deep canyon to the southeast.

As the river flows southeasterly, the mesaland along the Chama's southern shore remains rugged and steep. But the landscape of the river's northern shore softens a few miles above the Pueblo of Abiquiu, and the Chama flows quietly past flat and fertile bottomlands. After passing El Cerrito—the distinctive rock ridge northwest of the village—and the jagged, narrow cliffs that hug the river's sides just before it passes below the mesa of Abiquiu, the valley of the Chama leaves behind the austere topography and geology of the Colorado Plateau and enters the gentler, pastoral country of the Rio Grande Rift.

Of all the tributaries of the Rio Grande from Española south, only the waters of the Chama reach the Great River 365 days of the year. It is an honor acknowledged with mixed gratitude, for the Chama is blamed for the Rio Grande's murkier qualities. The Rio Grande is clear and nearly blue before it collides with the Chama, whose many tributaries give the river's water its ever-changing hues: the white waters of the Rio Gallina ("turkey creek") enter the Chama from the west, several miles above the Piedra Lumbre; the Rio Puerco ("muddy creek"; sometimes called the Rio Coyote, and known as the Day p'ohu' u, "coyote water," or Nap'otap'o, "muddy water," by the Tewa) may be the primary culprit for the Chama's turbid waters; and the water of the Rio Nutrias ("otter river," locally called the Arroyo Seco, "dry stream," or Canjilon Creek) is clear, except after a cloudburst, when its current wrestles with the orange, red, and yellow clays and sands of the Piedra Lumbre and becomes a deep brown in the Chama's waters.[3]

The Chama River is already a cloudy current when its channel reaches Abiquiu, but its waters gain more pigmentation from the Rito Colorado ("little red river"), today called El Rito River, below Abiquiu. And if the arroyos have run from the Cañon del Cobre, the copper canyon northwest of the village, the Chama will have the color and character of shiny, liquid brown-red silt long before it gives up its name to the Rio Grande.

The river was first named P'opin p'oe ("red river") by the San Juan Tewa, whose pueblo is situated just above the confluence of the Chama and the Great River, P'osóegé, the Rio Grande. Most Spanish names given to the rivers and canyons and mountains of the region were a translation or near approximation in meaning to the native names. Rio Rojo ("red river") or Rio Puerco ("muddy river") should have been among the European names for P'opin p'oe (Poping). But the early Spanish explorers identified the river in their notes and conversations by its proximity to an old Tewa village, Tsáa máa onwíkeji ("wrestling pueblo ruin"). Tsáa máa, probably named for annual wrestling events held on the mesa beside the village, was a Tewa pueblo abandoned soon after Oñate set down the Spanish flag at San Juan Pueblo in the summer of 1598.

The mesa of the old pueblo of Tsáa máa was marked by a small, pointed mountain, Tsáa máa p'in. The Tewa may have referred to the entire region as Tsáa máa, but, for reasons not completely understood, the Spanish newcomers soon spoke of both the region and the river that flowed through it as Tsama, pronounced by the Castilian tongue as Zama, and finally Chama. And P'opin p'oe was forever after known among non-Tewa peoples as the Rio Chama ("wrestling river").

The Chama provides the valley with the water that is its lifeblood. But it is Cerro Pedernal, Tsee p'in to the Tewa (both names meaning "flint or flaking stone mountain"), that is the region's heart, and perhaps the keeper of its spirit, too.

Pedernal has been a landmark on the physical and spiritual maps of a dozen cultures spanning a thousand years. The cerro's flat, distinctively truncated head holds a familiar yet mythological posture on the New Mexican horizon for up to fifty miles in several directions. From the north or south, Pedernal appears to be shaped like a long, flat knife; from the east and west, its narrow summit is a mere knob. In reality it is both of these: Pedernal's truncated neck is long and narrow, its summit an island of chert standing three thousand feet above the floor of the Valley of Shining Stone.

Over the centuries, Pedernal has become sacred ground to several Native American tribes. Like the Piedra Lumbre and all of the region of Abiquiu, Pedernal is part of the ancestral lands of the Rio Grande Tewa, who have ceremonial sites on the cerro's sloping sides.

Navajo myth explains that Changing Woman, one of the four principal figures in the Navajo Origin Myth, was found wrapped in many colored lights on a flat-topped mesa to the east of Navajoland, somewhere in the Jemez Mountains. Diné singers do not agree upon the exact location of Changing Woman's origin, but there is speculation that the sacred ground is in the mountains west of Abiquiu, specifically, upon the peak called Pedernal.[4]

The Navajos' historic enemy, the Jicarilla Apache, also include Pedernal in their people's Emergence Story.[5] Jicarilla oral historians remember how Pedernal was the first mountain seen by Spider Woman: "When Spider Woman first came up on this earth, there was only one mountain, and that was to the east. Flint Mountain was its name. It is still there, west of Abiquiu."[6]

Pedernal is not among the highest peaks in New Mexico. From the sky, the *cuchilla* (knife) of Pedernal, 9,862 feet above sea level, vanishes into the immense mountain and canyon country surrounding it. The topography of the Jemez Mountains is dominated by a sixteen-mile-wide crater, Valle Grande, the circular scar that marks the volcano that shaped northern New Mexico when it blew its remarkably huge top and scattered ash as far away as Texas, Oklahoma, and Kansas several million years ago.

Centuries before the time of Christ, Native Americans from all corners of the Southwest walked long distances to reach and then excavate Pedernal's chert beds. Artifacts found on the slopes of Pedernal itself have been dated to 7000 B.C.; the earliest artifacts made of Pedernal's distinctive white chert were found in a Paleo-Indian cache in a valley east of the Rio Grande whose contents may have been used nine thousand years before the birth of Christ.[7]

Axes, tools, and arrow- and spearheads made of Pedernal chert are found in ruins throughout northern New Mexico and southern Colorado, at Chaco Canyon to the west, and in the ruins of the once-great pueblo of Pecos to the east. "From the scattering of archaeological evidence . . . one can guess that the chalcedony and chert of Cerro Pedernal played an important role in the economy of varied Indian cultures in New Mexico for ten thousand years or more."[8]

Although Pedernal was visited regularly by various native peoples thousands of years before the time of Christ, the basin of the Piedra Lumbre was not settled by a substantial sedentary population until the eleventh or twelfth century A.D.

A handful of the more accessible Chama River Valley pueblo ruins were located by the turn of the twentieth century, but it was not until the 1920s and '30s, when archaeologists began using airplanes—including Charles Lindbergh's—and aerial photography, that the remarkable extent of prehistoric life in the Chama Valley emerged. Dozens of remote and hitherto unknown pueblo ruins, shrines, towers, chipping sites, and garden plots were located and photographed from the sky. It was soon understood that a sizable population filled this region by the mid 1200s and that these "primitive" farmers successfully cultivated more of the valley's floodplain in the time of prehistory than their historic successors.[9]

The turn-of-the-century Tewa called the country of Abiquiu and the Piedra Lumbre *Avéshu pije*. (*Avéshu* is among the old Tewa names for the village of Abiquiu; *pije* is Tewa for toward.) Avéshu pije was the country "up Abiquiu way," the western edge of the Tewa's territory, defined by their four cardinal mountains. North and west of Avéshu pije was the land of their ancestors, the Anasazi, the faraway country of the frontier: "To be outside the sacred mountains was to be off the spiritual map of the world. It was to be, in the oldest, most meaningful sense of the word, in wilderness."[10]

The country of Abiquiu and the Piedra Lumbre would maintain this end-of-the-known-world reputation until well into the early 1800s, long after the Spanish perched their farthest New World outpost on the mesa of Abiquiu and ventured with no little trepidation across the Piedra Lumbre and into the unmapped hinterland beyond.

It is believed that in the eleventh and twelfth centuries the descendants of the Mesa Verde Anasazi built a succession of villages down the Chama River Valley from the Piedra Lumbre basin south to the Rio Grande. Prolonged drought, exhausted fields, internal or external strife, or some combination of all of these forces caused the Anasazi people of Mesa Verde and the Four Corners region to migrate into the region now called northern New Mexico, where the Spanish encountered their descendants, the historic Pueblo Indians, in the mid 1500s.

The prehistoric communities that flourished in the Chama Valley were sedentary, farming cultures that duplicated the architectural style and culture of the Anasazi: their villages were composed of multistoried structures built of stone and adobe. The pueblo apartments enclosed a large plaza, and each village had sizable kivas—circular ceremonial chambers set into the ground.

Tsiping, Pesedeuinge, Homayo, Sapawe, Howiri, Abiquiu, Poshuouinge, Tsama, Posi, Te'ewi: the Chama Valley pueblos numbered twenty and more, and each housed up to several thousand individuals. Their villages were perched on mesa tops or on protected ledges with wide views of the surrounding countryside. Their inhabitants used irrigation ditches to water fields of corn, beans, squash, cucurbits, cotton, and tobacco on the terraces and fertile floodplains along the river. They were accomplished potters, basket weavers, and tool makers. They followed the movements of the sun, moon, and stars and aligned their lives with the natural and spiritual world they understood themselves to be a part of.

Early ethnographers and anthropologists toured Avéshu pije with pueblo guides and interpreters. It was an exhausting and often unwelcomed task, prying open the cultural and spiritual wilderness of the Native Americans who once called this valley home. "The difficulties encountered have been many," Smithsonian ethnogeographer John Peabody Harrington wrote in 1910. "The Tewa are reticent and secretive with regard to religious matters, and their cosmographical ideas and much of their knowledge about place-names are hard to obtain. Their country is rugged and arid. . . . The region has never been accurately mapped. All of the maps at the writer's disposal are full of errors, many of the features shown being wrongly placed or named, while others are omitted altogether, and still others given where they do not exist."[11]

On foot, by horseback, and upon buckboard, Harrington explored the mountains, mesas, canyons, villages, and ruins of villages throughout the country of Avéshu pije. His voluminous report, *The Ethnogeography of the Tewa Indians,* was the first published text to define and denote in great and glorious detail the province of the Tewa. The finished work encompassed some six hundred pages of geographical, cosmographical, and meteorological information; Tewa legends, myths, and folk stories; and Harrington's initial study of Tewa phonetics. Harrington was known to miss major topographical landmarks, and he misidentified others, but his contribution to the history of the Tewa is hailed by Tewa scholars and historians as "one of the most comprehensive treatises ever assembled for the geographical terminology of any non-Western society."[12]

By the turn of the twentieth century, the Spanish had called northern New Mexico home for three hundred years, and their arrival had virtually banished the Tewa from Avéshu pije. Even so, Harrington found that the historic Tewa had preserved their ancestors' identity with this land: Harrington was shown Páesemp'in (the "deer horn mountains"), now the Canjilon ("deer antler" in New Mexican Spanish) Mountains; Paesemp'ohu'u ("deer horn arroyo"), renamed Rio Canjilon by the Spanish; T'ahu'u ("dry arroyo"), today called the Arroyo Seco; Tsee p'in ("flaking stone mountain"), Cerro Pedernal; Humantsihu'u, Arroyo de los Comanches, named by both the Tewa and the Spanish for the use of the streambed by this greatly feared nomadic tribe. South of Abiquiu, Harrington's Tewa guides walked him around the base of T'omajo p'in ("good piñon mountain"), renamed by the Spanish Sierra Negra ("black mountain"). East of the mountain, across the Chama's red waters, Harrington's entourage rode past the Spanish settlement of Tierra Azul ("blue earth"), Nantsánwáebu'u ("blue earth corner") to his Native American guides.

Both the Tewa and the Spanish names given to the Chama Valley's illustrious landscape are rich in myth and legend. Exactly which culture originated a particular place-name is not always clear, and one culture often adopted the myths of the other. In the country of Avéshu pije, the oral histories of the Spanish and the Tewa overlap and even merge.

For example, the mountain that forms the Piedra Lumbre's northwest boundary was called Mesa de las Viejas ("mesa of the old women") by the Spanish; the Tewa call it Kwi jó'áa á ("old woman steep slope"). Legend says the mesa was thusly named for two old women who fell into disfavor with the local witches. For punishment, the women were turned to stone, thus rendering them too heavy to travel into the spirit realm.

As another example, Cañon del Navajo ("Navajo canyon"), the lower end of Canjilon Creek near the springs called Sáve p'oe ("Athapaskan [Navajo] water") by the Tewa, may have been named by the Spanish, who, legend remembers, were ambushed here in the early 1800s by Navajo trackers. Or the canyon may have been named in the early or mid nineteenth century, when several skeletons believed to be Athapaskan were found sitting upright beside what was once a smoky fire, hair and skin still attached to their bodies, in a small cave.[13]

South of Abiquiu, below a long, rocky mesa that juts into the Chama's course on the west bank of its tributary, the Rio Ojo Caliente, is an old Spanish settlement called La Cuchilla ("the knife"). An enormous, dense grove of cottonwood trees east of this jagged promontory has been a resting ground for generations of travelers, especially during the summer heat. This part of the Chama bosque also became a favored fall gathering ground for the Jicarilla Apaches, who held an annual trade fair here throughout the 1800s. But for the historic Spanish, the cottonwood grove and the country surrounding La Cuchilla were believed to be the gathering ground for the local *brujas* and *brujos* (witches). Abiquiu lore includes many after-dark sightings of flickering and flitting lights around wagons and through trees, widely known to be the movement of witches. Chama

Valley travelers of Spanish descent avoided an overnight stop near the thick bosque beside La Cuchilla.[14]

But to the Tewa this jagged rock that cuts into the Chama River, and the country beside it, was sacred ground. It was called P'oe waa wiri ("water wind point"), and to them it was a blessed place where the Po-waha, the benevolent water-wind-air spirits that energize all of life, lived. The long, knife-like mesa to the north of the point was called P'oe waa wiripin: the Tewa told Harrington that Spanish soldiers once followed a vision of Saint Cecelia across the Rio Grande and up the Chama to this very mesa. The saint disappeared into a hole in the side of the mountain, on the far side of which the perplexed but faithful soldiers found her dropped shoe.[15]

The story of the first people of the valley perplexed early twentieth-century archaeologists and anthropologists who came from the most prestigious institutions in the world to explore the frontier of Avéshu pije. "From Abiquiu west," archaeologist Jean Jeançon wrote in 1919, "the country is still a closed book, not even a scientific reconnaissance having been made in a territory covering over a hundred miles in width, and of greater length."[16]

The success of the first archaeological studies done by Jeançon and his colleagues depended upon the cooperation of the modern Tewas who assisted them in the field. The knowledge these Native Americans carried about their ancestors, revealed around the campfire or in the field, was invaluable to archaeological understanding of the pueblos of prehistory. The spoken story was the only story; the physical remnants of the ancient cultures found in and on the land had to be pieced together, sometimes with glue, other times with the words of the valley's natives.

Abiquiu itself could not be excavated, as the old pueblo of prehistory had become the foundation for the historic pueblo in the mid 1700s. But Abiquiu's sister village, Poe shú ("calabash at the end of the ridge" village), was excavated in the summer of 1919. Situated on a mesa above the Chama River several miles southeast of Abiquiu, Poe shú was known among both the Spanish and the Tewa as the Turquoise Village, or Kwengyauinge ("blue turquoise house"), and was reputed to have had quantities of the turquoise stone scattered about its ruined walls before ranchers and farmers removed artifacts containing the precious mineral.

Within the crumbling walls of Poe shú ouinge (*ouinge* is Tewa for ruin) were many clues to the history of Avéshu pije. In the 1400s and 1500s Poe shú was a moderately large village (two- and three-story adobe dwellings surrounded two plazas, housing up to a thousand individuals) to which people from many parts of New Mexico and Arizona came to trade. The people of Poe shú were successful farmers, and modern Hispanic farmers of the land today called La Puente ("the bridge") below the old Pueblo mesa say their fields are watered by the same *acequias* (ditches) dug by the farmers of Poe shú seven hundred years ago.

The 1919 Poe shú excavation field crew included Jeançon, his professional assistant, and four Santa Clara natives. Jeançon was a skilled archaeologist, able to extricate hundreds of objects and artifacts from the old village. But Swaso, Jeançon's native foreman, and his Pueblo companions placed the excavated artifacts into context and brought the dormant story of their ancestors buried in the mesa's dust to three-dimensional life. One unusually handsome spearhead drew lengthy examination from Swaso and the Santa Clara field crew. Aside from its obvious beauty, Jeançon asked Swaso, what special value did the ancient hornblende artifact carry? Swaso took the spearhead from Jeançon and placed it inside his shirt "against his naked left breast, pressed and patted it, and repeated this performance on both his cheeks and forehead. Finally he held the point about an inch from his mouth and inhaled deeply several times. At last [Swaso] said that the so-called 'spearhead' was ceremonial and would bring the owner strength and courage in the chase and in battle."[17]

The time of the desertion of Poe shú, Abiquiu, and all of the Chama Valley and Piedra Lumbre pueblos—by the mid to late sixteenth century—coincides with the arrival of the nomadic Athapaskan tribes, the people who became known as the Apaches and the Apaches del Navahu, the Navajo, into northern New Mexico. It is assumed that the Apaches attacked the pueblos of the Piedra Lumbre and Chama River Valley with enough ferocity to warrant permanent abandonment. The exodus from Poe shú was most certainly quick: its residents took almost nothing of value with them, and even small, easily carried objects, including sacred ones, were left where they lay on that terrible day hundreds of years ago. The people of Poe shú did not return to gather up their belongings, but left everything they owned where it would be found in situ centuries later.

The people of Poe shú became absorbed into the young Tewa Pueblo communities along the Rio Grande. For the next two centuries, although visited by the Tewa—who traveled regularly up the Chama River and out onto the Piedra Lumbre where they gathered minerals from Pedernal, hunted game in the high sierras above Abiquiu, and visited sacred shrines and ancestral ceremonial grounds—Avéshu pije was an uninhabited, unfarmed, and unsettled frontier.

By the time of the Spanish arrival downstream in 1598, the story of the Tewa in the land of Avéshu pije was easily overlooked. The subsequent Spanish settlement of this valley in the next century would all but obliterate the Tewas' claims to the land of their ancestors. But the spirit of the Tewa remains, and the story of the Tewa will always be the story of the first people of the valley: "We have lived upon this land from days beyond history's records, far past any living memory, deep into the time of legend. The story of my people and the story of this place are one single story. No man can think of us without thinking of this place. We are always joined together."[18]

2

ABIQUIU AND LA TIERRA DE GUERRA

The historic village of Abiquiu was built directly upon the remains of the prehistoric pueblo of P'efu.[1] In Abiquiu, the ghosts of the long-ago past remain underfoot: cellar and fencepost-hole digging often unearths the bones and material remains of the village's first residents, and modern gardens are fertilized with the pottery sherds and flint chips from the pueblo's prehistoric potters and lithic workers.

The first village, legend remembers, was the home of the "shadowy Asa,"[2] descendants of the Anasazi who settled this mesa and farmed this valley as early as the 1200s. The Asa, or Asnyami, departed their beloved valley sometime in the sixteenth century when the devastation brought about by drought and by escalating warfare with nomadic tribes made their homeland uninhabitable. Like the people of Poe shú, the Asa walked to the Rio Grande, where some of their tribe joined relatives at San Juan and Santa Clara Pueblos. Others continued south to the Pueblo of Santo Domingo and farther south still until they turned west into the plateau and desert country of Acoma and Zuni Pueblos.

Although some of the Asa remained at each of these pueblos, legend says that most of the tribe journeyed on to First Mesa in Hopiland, where they became the tansy-mustard phratries of the Hopi, ancestors of the Oak, Chaparral Cock, Magpie, Field Mouse, Boomerang, Chakwaina, and Hunting Stick Clans who settled with the Badger Clan at the village of Awatobi. The Hopi story of the Asa, the people from the faraway village they called Kaekibi, places the Chama Valley immigrants' arrival in Hopiland just prior to Hopi first contact with the Spanish conquistadors.

In the 1600s, some of the Tewa-Hopi descendants of Kaekibi departed First Mesa and migrated to Canyon de Chelly, where they lived alongside the Navajos. Here they are credited with planting the canyon's first peach trees, a delicacy introduced by the Spaniards. In 1710, after drought forced their departure, descendants of the Navajo-Asnyami returned to the Hopi village of Suchomovi.[3]

The Hopi pueblos of Arizona were a source of great frustration to officials of the Spanish church and state. The isolation and independence of their mesa villages had allowed the Hopi people to remain unconverted and outside of Spanish control since the Pueblo Revolt in 1680. In 1742, three Franciscans (Friars Delgado, Irigoyen, and Toledo) visited the Hopi pueblos and succeeded in convincing 350 Hopi citizens to leave their homes and follow the friars to the missions established at Jemez and Isleta in present-day New Mexico.[4]

Among the Hopi converts were two dozen Tewa-Hopi-Navajo descendants of the Asa. Perhaps the oral historian among them told the Franciscans of their heritage, because by fate or by chance, the Tewa-Hopi were resettled by the friars at the old pueblo of P'efu, Abiquiu. We do not know if the Hopi people who moved onto the mesa above the Chama River called the old pueblo that lay in ruins beneath their feet Kaekibi, Avéshu, or P'efu, but we do know that the great-great-great-great-grand-children of the first people of the valley returned and became the second people of the valley.

When John Peabody Harrington's little study caravan came to Abiquiu in 1910, his San Juan guides called the village by its prehistoric Tewa name, Pefu'u or P'efubu'u (*p'e* meaning timber; *fu'u,* end; and *bu'u,* town). Only in Hopi legend was Abiquiu called Kaekibi, but Harrington found a confusing number of additional Tewa and Spanish names for the old town. "The original Abiquiu was the pueblo ruin," Harrington explained.

"When the Mexicans came to the country they mispronounced P'efu-, calling it Abiquiu. At present only the San Juan Indians preserve the old name P'efu- in their speech, the other Tewas calling the place by the Spanish name usually mispronounced so as to make it sound like Abefu'u, 'chokecherry end.'"[5]

The names Jo-so-ge and Moque, or Moqui, referred to the southern end of the Pueblo mesa where the Hopi descendants of the Asa were settled by the Franciscan friars in the 1740s. The Tewa word for "Hopi pueblo," Mokibu'u, became Moqui, the Spanish word for "Hopi." Harrington concluded that Jo-so-ge, a name given to Swiss anthropologist Adolph Bandelier by his Tewa guides when he visited Abiquiu in the 1880s, was from the grammatically incorrect Tewa name K'osoge, or Khoe só on, which loosely meant "large-legging town," or Hopi village.

San Juan informants had told Bandelier that they called the old village Fe-jui, or Fe-jyu (more correctly spelled Phé shúu ú). But the San Ildefonso Tewa told Bandelier the town was called Abi-chiu, and that this was Tewa for the screech of an owl.

The various Tewa pueblos have used different names for Abiquiu. But that the old village was and is an integral part of their story never varies: "The Tewa say that there is much Hopi blood and still more Tewa blood in the present Mexican population of Abiquiu," Harrington explained. "The Tewa state that Abiquiu was a Tewa pueblo, whose inhabitants had the same culture and customs as the people of the other Tewa villages, and spoke a dialect which was slightly different from that of any other Tewa village but no more different from the dialects of the other Tewa pueblos than the dialect of San Juan is from that of Santa Clara."[6]

Before the mesa of Abiquiu and the valley of the Chama River were resettled by historic peoples, major changes occurred in the region's population. After the prehistoric Pueblo people left the valley, the Southern Athapaskan tribes, who may have precipitated their departure, began to claim the region as their own. No one knows exactly when these people came to the Southwest from the plains: perhaps as early as the 1200s, perhaps as late as 1600. "Nomads such as the Apaches," one historian noted, "slide through the sifting screens of archaeology."[7]

Ethnically, linguistically, and physically related to the Athapaskan tribes of Canada, the Apaches had split into distinct bands in the South-west by the time of Spanish contact: the Jicarilla and Lipan Apaches settled in northeastern and eastern New Mexico; the Western Apaches—the Tonto, Mescalero, Coyotero, Aravaipa, and Chiricahua—in western New Mexico and Arizona; and the Navajos in northwestern New Mexico as far east as the Piedra Lumbre.

By the time of Spanish arrival, the Apaches had established friendly trade relations with the eastern Pueblos, but frictions between the Pueblo and nomadic cultures of the Southwest were soon heightened by the introduction of Spanish soldiers and settlers, and their horses and guns. Soon New Mexico and all of the Southwest became a battleground of raids and counterraids second to none in the world. Abiquiu and the Piedra Lumbre became center stage in the region of New Mexico that would soon be called *la tierra de guerra,* the land of war.

The first permanent Spanish settlement in the frontier of New Spain, and the second within the boundaries of the present United States, was at the village of Ohke (Okeh or Oki), at San Juan Pueblo, a mere seventeen miles downriver from the ancient villages of Avéshu and Poe shú. In early 1598, Juan de Oñate, a wealthy Mexican from Zacatecas, led a caravan of four hundred men (one hundred and thirty with families), ten friars, an unstated number of servants, and eighty-three oxcarts and wagons of household goods, food, and equipment north into New Mexico. The colonial caravan brought over seven thousand head of horses, cattle, sheep, and goats that, along with the Spanish soldiers and settlers, would forever change the life of New Mexico.

Oñate's caravan reached the Rio Grande pueblos in early July of that year. By midsummer, the Spanish colonists and soldiers had set up camp beside San Juan Pueblo at the confluence of the Chama River and the Rio Grande. The natives of San Juan Pueblo were so hospitable to Oñate and his colonists that the Spanish soon called the village San Juan de los Caballeros ("San Juan of the gentlemen"). By late summer, Oñate's settlers had moved into the friendly village and had begun taking food supplies and blankets from San Juan, as well as soliciting and accepting their hosts' "spontaneous" declarations of allegiance to the Spanish king. By early winter, the Spanish colonists had placed their own survival before that of the Tewa and were taking what they needed, even though it meant there were few foodstores or adequate shelters left for their native hosts.

By their first Christmas, the Spanish settlers had moved their community across the Rio Grande to the old Tewa village of Yunque (or Yuque) on the west side of the Rio Grande near the river's confluence with the Chama. Although this was part of the province of San Juan Pueblo, Oñate claimed the village for his colonists and renamed it San Gabriel del Yungue.

San Gabriel del Yungue remained the Spanish capital until Oñate was succeeded as governor of the colony by Pedro de Peralta in 1608. At that time, the new Spanish colony was feeling the pressure of Apache hostilities. In 1610, Peralta moved the Spanish capital to a more defensible location at the foot of the Sangre de Cristo mountains. The new capital was called Santa Fe.

In the seventeenth century, while the Tewa were occupied with the activities of their Spanish neighbors, their former homelands were being appropriated by the Navajos. Navajoland—the Largo-Gobernador region of New Mexico—was a day's journey west over the mountains from the Piedra Lumbre. The Navajos had discovered that antelope and other game was abundant in the basin below the mystical flat-topped mountain, and the nomadic tribe claimed the Valley of Shining Stone as their hunting ground.

The Navajos had also begun using the corridor of the Chama River Valley, as well as the higher, parallel routes across the Jemez Mountains, to stage raids on the Spanish and Pueblo settlements along the Rio Grande. Although the Navajos were skilled hunters and farmers, they were equally skilled warriors and raiders. The Pueblo and Spanish settlements along the Rio Grande offered irresistible riches of food, horses, and captives.

Although the Tewa no longer lived in the adobe walled villages of their ancestors on the Chama and around the rim of the Piedra Lumbre basin, they did still carry considerable emotional, spiritual, and physical ties to the region. There were sacred springs to visit, ancestral shrines to honor, and favored hunting locales in the huge sweep of mesaland surrounding the valley. Tsiping contained the highly prized chert needed for stone tools and arrowheads. And the rocks of the Piedra Lumbre were still the only location of *alumbre,* or alum, the mineral used to dye Pueblo cloth. This cloth was now an important trade commodity with the new Spanish settlers, who urged the Pueblo weavers to make greater quantities. The Pueblo people also visited sites in northern New Mexico to obtain yellow pigment, used for coloring walls, near present-day Tierra Amarilla, and red ochre, used to decorate pottery, found in the mountains near present-day Cebolla.

The obtaining of each of these necessitated Pueblo mineral-gathering expeditions that pushed deeply into the region claimed by the Navajos. The Tewa scheduled their sojourns into the Piedra Lumbre and beyond at those times of the year that the Navajos were most likely to be absent. But the Tewa presence in the basin and along the Chama River north of the Piedra Lumbre was nearly always detected by the Navajos. Because the Navajos viewed the Tewas' footprints up the valley to be those of trespassers, they often organized retaliatory attacks upon the Pueblos. But the obtaining of the minerals found in the Piedra Lumbre was deemed worthy of such harassment, and the Tewa continued to return to the land of their forefathers and mothers.

Although the Spanish and the Tewa shared a mutual enemy in the Navajos, who swooped down through the Chama River Valley to steal horses, sheep, and human captives from the Rio Grande communities in the 1600s, any comradery or alliance between the two groups ended there. The Spanish, "with their aristocratic pretensions and dislike for manual toil,"[8] brought with them the *encomienda* system, which essentially made the Pueblo people slaves to the Spanish immigrants. Throughout the colony of New Spain, forced manual labor—usually for church or village construction, and for crop irrigation and cultivation—and the seizing of whatever amounts of food and clothing the proprietor of the *encomendero* deemed necessary for his community's survival were rewarded with military protection. Until the revolt of 1680, the Tewa (long a people with adequate, and soon to be exhibited, skillful knowledge of warfare) harbored deep discontent and mounting rage toward the Spanish newcomers.

The behavior of the Spanish colonists, who came to the territory expecting to find fertile land from which would be derived a comfortable, perhaps wealthy lifestyle, was deplorable. Oñate hoped to find mineral wealth and led numerous ultimately fruitless expeditions throughout the territory in search of gold and silver, leaving the colonists to fend for themselves. As one Spanish viceroy noted upon observing the conditions of the colony of New Spain, "No one comes to the Indies to plow and sow, but only to eat and loaf."[9]

The colony expanded as settlers established haciendas and villages along the Rio Grande and its tributaries in the region south of Albuquerque north to Taos. (The Apache-favored Chama Valley would not be settled until after the Spanish reconquest of New Mexico in 1692.) The Spanish presence in New Spain was ostensibly to Christianize the "heathens" of the New World. During the 1600s, while the Spanish military was exploiting the Pueblo peoples' lands and resources, the Franciscan friars were sent to every corner of the territory to begin missions. In the first thirty-five years of Spanish rule, the friars oversaw the construction of some ninety churches, all by native labor forces.[10] Their early efforts to convert a native population that was already deeply committed to a spiritual life, rooted in traditions at least as old as Christianity, included oppressive and often violent policies against both the people and their sacred places and objects. There were localized uprisings throughout the colony of New Mexico in the 1600s prior to the unified revolt: "Full-scale revolution was a real possibility in New Mexico throughout the seventeenth century, but while the Spanish representatives of church and state were tireless in blaming each other for the colony's instability, neither side undertook to find a peaceful solution."[11]

Utes, Comanches, and Apaches were migrating into the territory with increasing numbers by the middle of the century, their raids intensifying upon the settlements of both the Pueblos and the Spanish. The Pueblo people, although perceived by the Apaches as the allies of the Spanish, were forbidden to carry arms and could not defend themselves against the nomadic raiders. By the 1670s, the ferocity of Apache attacks, combined with a drought-induced famine and a colonywide epidemic of European origin to which the Pueblo people had no natural immunity, had killed more than a tenth of the native population.

It was a difficult and tenuous time for both the Pueblo and the Spanish peoples. The lives of the Spanish colonists, even with the Pueblo workers at their disposal, were hardly comfortable and never lucrative: "The colony ran so short of food that the Spanish were reduced to roasting and eating the hides that were the principal furnishings of their simple homes."[12]

The Pueblo Revolt broke out in New Mexico on August 10, 1680. Led by a San Juan medicine man, Popé (Popay), and other Pueblo leaders, the Pueblo people of New Mexico, along with the Apaches and Navajos, formed an alliance that gathered more than six thousand warriors behind one effort to oust the Spanish from their province. Four hundred colonists and twenty-one missionaries were murdered at once. Three thousand Tewa, Tano, and Pecos warriors mounted a siege in Santa Fe that lasted nine days. Spanish women and children were barricaded in the Palace of the Governors while the rest of the capital was burned and reduced to rubble.

On the 21st of August, Governor Antonio de Otermín resolved to leave the palace, seeing that his only chance for survival was to march south to Guadalupe del Paso. The Pueblo warriors watched the Spaniards from surrounding hills, but they did not interfere with the exodus. As soon as the Spanish procession had passed, the Indians reoccupied their pueblos and homes along the Rio Grande Valley.

Following the departure of the Spanish oppressors, every Spanish village, mission, rancho, and hacienda was destroyed. Kivas were built upon the sites of the destroyed churches, Christian names and marriages were cast aside, and the use of the Spanish language was forbidden. "From a historical view, the Revolt delivered a severe blow to the prestige of the Spanish empire and stands as the most spectacular victory achieved by Indian arms within the present limits of the United States."[13]

During the twelve years before Spanish reconquest of the territory, interpueblo rivalries, disagreement among various tribal leaders, and a revival of Apache and Navajo hostilities against the Pueblos weakened the bonds that had facilitated the successful revolt. But the revival and reaffirmation of Pueblo traditional culture and religion initiated by the revolt was perhaps the real and lasting victory for New Mexico's native peoples: "During the dozen years following 1680, when the Pueblo peoples were completely free of Spanish domination, the many strands comprising

Pueblo religions and traditions were slowly gathered together again, embraced, and reaffirmed. And they have not been loosened since."[14]

Twelve years passed before the Spanish returned under Captain General Diego de Vargas. The factionalism between the various pueblos had weakened their ability to gather together into a swift resistance to Spanish reentry: "The rifts between the Pueblos were big enough for Vargas to march his army through."[15]

The small army under de Vargas, the newly appointed governor of New Mexico, marched up the Rio Grande and accepted the submission of each pueblo along the way without bloodshed. However, Pueblo resentment toward Spanish rule grew in the first year after de Vargas's arrival, and plots for revolt and small localized uprisings occurred throughout the territory. In December of 1693, the Spanish under de Vargas engaged in a fierce battle with Native American leaders in Santa Fe. In a fight that was far from bloodless, de Vargas fought long and hard with the Tano people who occupied Santa Fe. The Spanish garrison finally overcame the native warriors, and after rounding up seventy Tano rebels, executed seventy of them. The four hundred Tano who surrendered to the Spanish were distributed as slaves among the soldiers and Spanish settlers.

The Pueblo people were so outraged by this renewal of slaughter and Spanish dominion in their territory that many of them fled their villages for the mountains and the upper Chama River Valley, taking with them whatever supplies of food and arms they could carry. De Vargas knew that direct confrontation with the warriors of the Pueblo resistance hiding in the mountains and high country would result in heavy Spanish casualties, so he waged a war of starvation and economic strangulation. De Vargas's army destroyed or captured the Pueblo crop reserves, and by July of 1696, de Vargas reported to his royal superiors that those Tewa from the Rio Grande pueblos who had withdrawn to the foot of Cerro Pedernal were running short of food.

The Tewa camped in the valley of the Piedra Lumbre had to survive on their dwindling livestock herds, which they grazed out of reach of Spanish raiding parties on the llanos of the Piedra Lumbre basin, and on whatever wild foodstuffs they gathered from the nearby mountains. Their food situation became so desperate that they were forced to send expeditions northwest into Navajo country to ask their enemies for grain.

By the spring of 1697, the Tewa who had sought refuge under Pedernal had returned to their home villages and accepted Spanish dominion. Most other Pueblo refugees throughout the territory did the same, although there were many who opted to join the Western Pueblos of the Hopi, or who went to live with the Navajos or Plains Indians. There was continued unrest and disgruntlement among the Pueblos—as late as 1704, the Spanish leaders were alarmed by rumors that the San Juan and San Ildefonso Tewa were meeting with Hopi and Navajo leaders in the Piedra Lumbre valley—but no renewed hostilities occurred, at least with the Pueblos.[16]

Between 1705 and 1713, most human—and certainly all Spanish—activity in the region of the Piedra Lumbre and the Chama Valley was correlated to the ebb and flow of warfare. After the reconquest, it was no longer only the Navajos that the Spanish military confronted on the Piedra Lumbre. The Utes (called Yutas by the Spanish), whose ancestors had come south from Canada during the thirteenth century, began challenging traditional Navajo territory in the early 1600s. After the turn of the eighteenth century, the Utes were using the Piedra Lumbre basin as much as and maybe more than any other nomadic tribe, with seasonal hunting camps as far south as the mesas and bluffs beside the Chama River, within a mile of present-day Abiquiu.

During the period of Pueblo independence the Utes had coalesced into sizable bands and began bold, energetic attacks on the larger Rio Grande settlements. When the Spanish returned, the Utes continued their depredations against the Pueblos and the Navajos and were soon at war with the Spanish.

Initially, the one hundred soldiers and eight hundred settlers brought into New Mexico in the fall of 1693 were housed at the haciendas and communities of La Cañada de Santa Cruz, which was at that time called the Villa de Santa Cruz de la Cañada. The capital at Santa Fe was reserved for Spanish officials and for military and civic dignitaries who returned to New Mexico with their families.

Of the nine hundred who accompanied de Vargas's reconquest, only forty were from families who had lived in New Mexico prior to the Pueblo Revolt. A majority of the new settlers were called Españoles Mexicanos (Mexican Spaniards) because, although Spanish in culture, they were Mexican born and raised. Many of these were direct descendants of the conquistadors, often of Native American mothers who had taught them the skills of the Pueblo people.[17]

Unlike their predecessors who had come here with Oñate, the Spanish *pobladores* (pioneers) of the late 1600s were an industrious group already well-versed in the trials awaiting them on the New Mexican frontier: "These new settlers were prepared to do their own work. They knew how to grow the main crops native to the region, corn, beans, squash, and they had skills in the raising of sheep, goats and other livestock. Among their numbers were masons, weavers, leather workers, blacksmiths, carpenters, shepherds and also persons able to keep records in the absence of any official notaries. These people did not come to New Mexico expecting to achieve wealth and glory."[18]

Upon reconquest, de Vargas had assured the Pueblo leaders that the new Spanish colonists were not to be given *encomienda* privileges but were to abide by the *Recopilación de leyes de los reynos de las Indias* ("the Laws of the Indies"). These laws protected the lands used and occupied by sedentary Native Americans from outside encroachment and also abolished compulsory Christianization and all forced, unpaid Pueblo labor.

By the first years of the eighteenth century, Santa Fe and the community of La Cañada de Santa Cruz—both part of the Rio Arriba ("upriver") country of New Mexico—were crowded to capacity. At that time, and throughout the next century, the colonial government of New Mexico initiated a clearly defined procedure by which land from the royal domain was granted to families and groups of settlers. Three categories of land grants were made in New Mexico: a community grant was given to a group of settlers together; individual land grants were allocated to a family for a farm or ranch; and land was granted to the individual Indian pueblos. Titles were confirmed to Spanish settlers only after they had resided on the granted land for several years—a difficult and dangerous task in northern New Mexico, with lands frequented by Navajo, Ute, and Comanche raiding parties—and had built homes, dug an irrigation system, planted crops, and participated in the local militia.

The land of a community grant was divided up into small allotments given to individual families upon which they built their residences and raised crops. The remainder of the land, constituting most of the granted acreage, was the *ejido,* the common lands, and was used by the entire community for livestock grazing and for firewood and timber gathering.

Individual land grants did not necessarily mean only one family would develop and live upon that parcel of land; members of the extended family, and invited friends and their families, built homes and raised crops on an individual's granted land. These kin-based *plazas* (village centers) often grew into communities as large as those on lands designated for communities and villages.

The New Mexican government issued strict guidelines for colonial settlement patterns based upon a prototype town developed in the 1500s during the Roman colonization of Spain. The royal ordinance dictated that new towns be built around a single plaza, with intersecting roads laid out in a grid pattern. The Spanish colonists followed official orders when they could—most villages were laid out around a plaza—but New Mexico's topography tended to influence the size and shape of the settlements of northern New Mexico. With so little arable land, large communities were not feasible, and the settlement pattern of northern New Mexico became scattered clusters of small, basically self-sufficient hamlets.

Settlement of the Chama River from the Rio Grande to the Piedra Lumbre proceeded slowly in leapfrog fashion in the first half of the eighteenth century, with several colonial steps forward followed by many taken, often hastily, backward. The Chama River Valley was a natural, if risky, choice for settlement. For obvious reasons, most settlements were founded by military men and their families. In spite of the lethal problems posed by the nomadic tribes, the pastoral land of the Chama River and the Piedra Lumbre basin beckoned to those with vision and a hefty amount of courage and self-reliance.

By the 1720s, the Spanish government initiated formal land grants on previously unsettled lands up the Valle del Rio Chama. These small kin-based *placitas* of former soldiers and their families were the farthest frontier outposts of the Viceroyalty of Spain, which could afford them little military protection. Defense against nomadic attack was among these settlers' first concerns, and it was natural for a prominent military man to become a settlement's leader.

The first communities founded beyond the protected walls of La Cañada were on the Rio Grande several miles north of the Pueblo of San Juan, at the former colonial capital of San Gabriel; and on the Chama River a few miles upriver from La Cañada at present-day Chamita and Hernandez. All of these 1714 land grants encroached on the province of San Juan Pueblo, and each grant was given to a Spanish family whose ancestors had claimed the same land before the Pueblo Revolt.

The story of the Chama Valley in colonial times is the story of the Martín Serrano family, whose descendants founded or participated in the founding of virtually every community between La Cañada and the Piedra Lumbre. Hernán Martín Serrano and brothers Luis and Pedro, Hernán's cousins or nephews, were all prominent military leaders born in the colony of New Mexico before the Pueblo Revolt. Pedro and Luis both returned to New Mexico with de Vargas, as did their children and grand-children, who followed in the Martín Serrano tradition as colonial military men of great influence.

Blas Martín Serrano founded and settled the community of Ojo Caliente on the Chama tributary of the same name in 1735; his cousin, Miguel, son of Sebastian of Alcalde, co-founded the neighboring communities of Tierra Azul and Santa Rosa de Lima in 1734; and brothers or cousins Gerónimo and Ignacio Martín Serrano were given the San José del Barranco Grant in 1735. There were eventually so many Martín Serranos in the Chama Valley that the extended family came to be called "Los Martines"; the name eventually changed to Martínez and to the singular name Serrano. In twentieth-century Rio Arriba County, the Martín or Serrano surname is found in twenty percent of all Hispanic family trees.

There were other equally intrepid families who settled the Chama Valley in the 1720s: de Beytia (Abeyta), de Mestas, and Torres, whose enormous grazing grant encompassed land from the eastern boundary of the old pueblo of Tsama to the western border of the Piedra Lumbre hill, several miles west of present-day Abiquiu. (This immense parcel of land was later divided into the smaller land grants of El Rito, Vega de Lobato, Plaza Blanca, Plaza Colorado, Tierra Azul, La Puente, Plaza de la Ca-pilla, and San José del Barranco.) In 1735, more land was granted for settlement, including various Martín Serrano placitas near Abiquiu, the westernmost that of San José del Barranco on the mesas above the Chama River southwest of Abiquiu.

The Piedra Lumbre basin itself would not be settled until after the turn of the nineteenth century. It was, however, used for colonial livestock herds. The first ranch on the Piedra Lumbre belonged to one of the wealthiest men in colonial New Mexico, José de Riaño (or Reaño) y Tagle. Riaño, a Spaniard of considerable Old World influence who came to New Mexico from the Montañas de Santander, never lived on his ranch built several miles due west of Abiquiu on the southeastern side of the Piedra Lumbre basin. Riaño kept his family in an elegant two-story home in Santa Fe and managed his sheep empire at a safe distance from the frontier of the Piedra Lumbre.[19]

Riaño built a small ranch, known as the Vega de Riaño or Casas de Riaño, along the lower portion of Cañones Creek northeast of Cerro Pedernal. A few miles upstream from the Riaño rancho was the magnificent mesa-top ruin called Tsiping by the Tewa. In the 1200s, Tsiping, like Casas de Riaño in the 1700s, was the farthest outpost of civilization. From the lonely, beautiful tablelands below Pedernal, Riaño's shepherds, like the prehistoric inhabitants of this valley before them, went about their daily tasks with one eye constantly scanning the horizon for nomadic visitors.

While the Piedra Lumbre was a natural choice for livestock, it also offered additional business opportunities that ultimately made its lands twice as valuable to someone like Riaño: trade with the Utes. From the first, the settlers of the Chama Valley engaged in illegal trade with all nomadic tribes. The officials of Santa Cruz and Santa Fe insisted that trade with the nomads occur under their auspices at designated times and locales, but the colonists ignored these rules: they often had no choice, as peace with both the Utes and the Comanches was hinged on the nomads' securing of valued settler trade items.

Although settlements on the Chama River only a few miles downstream from Riaño's ranch were attacked by Utes in the 1730s, Riaño's shepherds were left unharmed despite the infringement of their livestock upon the Utes' winter home. The Utes valued the Piedra Lumbre's vast antelope herd, but they evidently also had come to value the relationship with Riaño's people, from whom they could obtain horses and Mexican-made utilities.

Upon Riaño's death in 1743, his widow traded the valuable lands of the Piedra Lumbre for a second house in Santa Fe. Riaño's will attested to his success as both a rancher and a trader: he left his wife and son 1,027 breeding ewes, 1,298 wethers, 74 bulls, 26 steers, 207 breeding cows, 46 heifers, 47 calves, and a herd of horses. He also left his widow 150 pesos worth of pelts—no doubt obtained from the Utes—and a mulatto slave.[20]

Upon trading their house in Santa Fe for the Piedra Lumbre ranch of the Riaños, another prominent military man, Antonio Montoya, along with his three grown professional soldier sons, moved into the Chama Valley settlements. Like the Riaños, the Montoyas did not place their families in the Casas de Riaño on the Piedra Lumbre but kept their loved ones at a safe distance from the Ute frontier.

With his wife, Antonio Montoya (a former Santa Fe councilman whose signature was among those that inaugurated the Santa Fe Fiesta of 1712) moved into a house at Santa Rosa de Lima de Abiquiu, a settlement of twenty families directly below the old pueblo of Poe shú. Santa Rosa, for whom the village was named, was the first canonized saint of the New World and was a favorite among New Mexico's colonists. A chapel for the saint had been under construction for nearly six years by the time of the Montoyas' arrival in the valley, its completion halted again and again by Indian attack. Throughout the 1740s, the villagers of Santa Rosa de Lima de Abiquiu worked tirelessly to complete their *capilla*. But by 1750, after the village was devastated in a particularly fierce Indian raid, the dream of a chapel below Poe shú was forever abandoned. Several years later, a second site for a village called Santa Rosa de Lima de Abiquiu was chosen upstream, closer to Abiquiu mesa. The second community was successful in its building of a capilla for the beloved saint.

Antonio Montoya's sons—Miguel, Juan Manuel, and Bernardo Baltazar—were granted lands on the mesa of the old Pueblo of Abiquiu. Their neighbors were the Tewa-Hopi-Navajo descendants of the Asa who had built a cluster of dwellings at La Plaza del Moqui at the southern end of the mesa. The Montoyas built the first colonial dwelling at the northern end of the mesa and from there oversaw their sheep ranch and shepherds on the Piedra Lumbre.

Although the Montoyas' operation was initially successful, it lasted only two years. In 1745, the disagreements and hostilities between the colonial government and the nomadic tribes escalated into war. The Utes raided the Chama Valley settlements, including the Vega de Riaño on the Piedra Lumbre. Brothers Miguel and Juan Manuel Montoya, and several of their sons, were out on the grasslands with their shepherds when the Utes attacked the ranch. Juan Manuel was killed, as was Miguel Montoya's son; Miguel himself received fourteen wounds before he finally fled the Piedra Lumbre with his three surviving shepherds.

In the next year, Antonio Montoya died at Santa Rosa de Lima de Abiquiu, and the following year, his third son, Baltazar, died. In 1747, Miguel Montoya, without the support of his brothers and father, gave up ranching on the Piedra Lumbre. The house on the mesa was left under the care of the Montoyas' Indian servants, and Miguel moved the remainder of the Montoya family to safer grounds in the Rio Abajo ("downriver") region near Albuquerque. In doing so, Miguel spared himself and his family possible death and certain trauma in a carefully orchestrated Ute-Comanche attack that would devastate the valley settlements before the end of the summer.[21]

All of the placitas and ranchos on the land grants of the Chama Valley from La Cuchilla to the Riaño ranch under Pedernal were referred to by the colonial authorities as the settlements of Abiquiu. By 1744, the Spanish settlers of the region totaled only twenty scattered families. Unlike the wealthy Riaños and Montoyas, the lives of the average colonists of the Abiquiu region were based on subsistence agriculture and small livestock herds. The various men, women, and children of an extended family of a rancho functioned as an autonomous agricultural and defensive unit that utilized everyone's energies. There were few comforts in their lives: having enough to eat and staying alive were the rewards these hardy *pobladores* (pioneers) hoped for.

The adobe dwellings of a plaza shared walls and were built around an inner courtyard upon which all windows and doors opened. In addition to the fortress-like structure of the homes themselves, each placita was protected by a *torreón* (defensive tower) that was in material and appearance exactly like those built by the prehistoric people whose villages lay in ruin often directly underneath the new colonial ones.

The men dug acequias that brought the water from the Chama River to their crops and newly planted orchards of apple, peach, pear, and plum trees. The women and children, accompanied by elderly family members, tended the fields where they grew corn, *frijoles* (pinto beans), squash, onions, wheat, and various grains and other vegetables. They kept goats from which they obtained milk, cheese, and meat. The livestock corrals adjoined the house walls, although only milk cows and mares with young were kept close to the dwellings. And even though the closest hilltops were considered dangerous Indian territory, the men and teenage boys, always armed and ready for ambush and conflict, ran herds of sheep and cows on the rich pastureland above the valley.[22]

The men of the family placita periodically left to hunt buffalo— there were always men left behind to defend the village—and also to trade with the Utes, without whose even semi-amicable relations colonial settlement of the Chama Valley would have been impossible. The men of the Chama Valley often resembled their adversarial Native American contemporaries on the frontier, as they wore buckskin garments and leather moccasins called *teguas,* named for the Tewa Indians of the Rio Grande who made and traded them.[23]

The first dwellings were often rough jacal (wood poles sealed and plastered with adobe mud, usually stood upright, side to side) structures, with mud floors and vigaed (beamed) and then thatched ceilings. These primitive one- and two-room homes often formed the foundation for the larger house which was later built of adobe brick—and sometimes stone and mud—as need and resources grew. Kitchens were often outside in a brush-covered ramada where an adobe beehive oven, or *horno,* was built.[24]

In the early 1700s, much to the dismay of the frontier colonists, the Utes entered into a brief but effective alliance with the Comanches. The Comanches had entered New Mexico from the mountains to the north in the beginning of the century where they infringed on the lands of the Apaches, with whom they became arch-enemies and adversaries. Numerous Spanish military campaigns against the Comanches, who moved quickly and easily through the mountainous terrain and onto the eastern plains of New Mexico by horseback, had failed to subdue that tribe's slave and horse raids on the settlements.

The main target of the Utes and Comanches in the early 1700s was the Taos area. But by the 1740s, the Ute-Comanche warpath extended west and south through the corridor of the Rio Ojo Caliente and into the Chama Valley settlements.

All of the male colonists, wealthy or poor, with or without previous military experience, were required to serve in the local militia. Because most of the Abiquiu settlements were begun by military leaders, and counted several experienced soldiers among their residents, they became accustomed to organizing their own defense and even initiated counter-raids when necessary. In 1746, when the Miguel Martín Serrano family at Santa Rosa de Lima de Abiquiu below Poe shú was raided by Comanches, the Martín Serranos and their fellow villagers did not expect or wait for presidio military support. After one Comanche raid on their plaza, Miguel Martín Serrano told the colonial authorities, "They (Comanches) carried off my entire herd of horses and I and my sons went forth with some of the residents and took it away from them and I took those belonging to the enemy away from them together with their leather jackets and saddles."[25]

Family members were occasionally lost in these raids, either killed or taken as captives, but on the whole, the colonial militias were very successful. For their services to the community, the members of the militia were allowed to keep whatever booty they obtained on these expeditions, including hides, dried meat, horses, and Indian women and children.

The pobladores of the Chama Valley managed to hold the lands of Abiquiu for Spain until 1747, at which time a Ute-Comanche raid of such intensity and force emptied every plaza, large and small, on the Chama River and its tributaries between the Vega de Riaño and La Cañada. The infamous Indian raid upon the Abiquiu settlements happened on the first day of August 1747. Numerous plazas and communities were struck at once. Even those with ample soldiers lost numerous residents: Santa Rosa de Lima, where the Miguel Martín Serranos lived, lost twenty-three women and children—all taken captive and all but one never again seen by their kin.

The village men hastily formed a retaliatory force to track the Ute-

Comanche retreat, but they were unable to catch up with the raiders. The men of Santa Rosa de Lima found only the gruesome remains of three of the captured women alongside the lifeless body of an infant.

According to reports given after the raid by the Valdez family—cofounders and leaders of the village of Santa Rosa—the Comanche presence in the Chama vicinity had been repeatedly reported to colonial military authorities in the capital. After the attack the Abiquiu settlers loudly complained that although local scouts had been tracking and reporting Comanche movements, no presidial troops had been dispatched to protect the valley. In an eloquent and angry report, Juan Lorenzo Valdez stated that the absence of military support left the defense of Santa Rosa de Lima de Abiquiu on the shoulders of "six to eight Indians and four or five residents and these so poor that to do their guard duty they had to use their little jack mules, and this was for a week only, our settlers being again left to themselves and it was our misfortune that at this time the Comanches fell upon us."[26]

Although slow to respond to Abiquiu scouting reports, the militia in Santa Fe immediately sent troops up the Chama River and into northern New Mexico to find and punish both the Utes and the Comanches. One confrontation resulted in a fierce battle between the royal troops and the Comanches and their allies a short distance beyond the town of Abiquiu "in which, according to the record, one hundred and seven Indians were slain, two hundred and six captured, with nearly one thousand horses."[27]

Over the next four years, the Spanish military waged an exhaustive campaign against all the nomadic tribes, seeking either peace or extermination, whichever seemed more attainable. The Comanches fled the territory and escaped punishment. The Utes who ranged over northern New Mexico, however, were hunted down by angry Spanish garrisons, their warriors slain and their lodges burned. Several years later it was learned that the Utes who frequented the Piedra Lumbre region were actually innocent of the 1747 Chama Valley atrocities: "The Utes were left to bear the burden of Spanish retaliation which, as was often the case, fell upon the first nomadic group which was encountered by the Spanish punitive expedition. The Utes in this instance paid for their former association with the Comanches."[28]

The tribal affiliation of the attackers mattered little to the Abiquiu valley pobladores, whose collective desire was to place as many miles as possible between themselves and the nomadic tribes. Official permission to withdraw from the Abiquiu region did not come until the summer of 1748, nearly a full year after the Comanche raid, but we can assume that most women and children left the valley months before. When word came for the legal abandonment of all ranchos in the Chama River region, remaining settlers had eight days to vacate: corn and wheat crops were left unharvested in the fields, and sheep and other livestock were left to fend for themselves on the open range.

The Abiquiu plazas remained empty for two years, after which time the new governor, Thomas Velez Cachupín, decided it was necessary to re-populate and secure the Chama Valley territory again. Even knowing of Cachupín's prowess as a negotiator, and that he had successfully struck several treaties with various nomadic tribes, those settlers who had wit-nessed the terrifying power of the Utes and Comanches in 1747 were reluctant to return to their exposed and vulnerable homes on the Abiquiu frontier.

Juan José Lobato, the *alcalde mayor* of Santa Cruz, was given the thankless task of convincing the Chama colonists that resettlement was a safe and viable choice. Alcalde Lobato had to resort to threats of house and land title forfeiture, as well as to attacks on the settlers' pride, before he could persuade even a handful to return to the abandoned plazas along the Chama River.

Although accompanied by a detachment of royal troops, Alcalde Lobato was probably not a popular man on April 16, 1750, the day he led the Chama Valley settlers out of the safety of La Cañada and back into the Abiquiu frontier. Returning with the Spanish colonists were thirteen Genízaro Indians, who were to be given the abandoned house of the Montoya family on the mesa of Abiquiu. It is not clear from the records whether these thirteen Native Americans, all of whom were identified as Moquis, or Hopis, were the same as those who had settled the Plaza del Moqui with Fray Delgado in 1745, or if they were former Hopi servants of the Montoya family previously brought to the Santa Clara mission for baptism, perhaps captured on one of the brothers' military campaigns.[29]

The term "Genízaro" and the people it is applied to is perhaps more affiliated with Abiquiu than with any other locale in New Mexico and the Southwest. Used in eighteenth- and early nineteenth-century New Mexico, Genízaro was not a racial term, but an ethnic one: "It [Genízaro] was used by the local Hispanic folk to designate North American Indians of mixed tribal derivation living among them in Spanish fashion—that is, having Spanish surnames from their former masters, Christian names through baptism in the Roman Catholic faith, and speaking a simple form of Spanish."[30]

The term has often been mistakenly used to denote people who were "half-breed," synonymous with *coyote* or *mestizo*. But the Genízaros of New Mexico were completely Native American. They were full-blooded members of non-Pueblo, Plains Indian tribes who had been abducted during intertribal raids and later ransomed to the Spanish. Because adult males were killed on the spot by warring nomadic tribes, the early Genízaros of New Mexico were always women and children. Their tribal origins included Kiowa, Pawnee, Wichita, Paiute, Navajo, Ute, Apache, and Comanche. The term was also applied to Pueblo Indians who by choice lived among the Spanish, and also to Native Americans such as the Hopi converts on Abiquiu mesa who had left their native homes and tribes for various reasons to live with the colonists.

The word "genízaro" is derived from the Turkish *yeniceri* or *yeni-cheri—yeni,* new, and *cheri,* troops. The Janissaries (or Janizaries) were an elite Turkish military auxiliary composed of Christian-born, Islam-raised and trained slaves and conscripts. In Spain, "genízaro" was used to designate Spaniards with atypical blood mixtures, including those of European derivation. Because the Turkish Janissaries were noted soldiers, many historians have assumed that all Genízaros in New Mexico were under obligation to serve and in fact served with the Spanish military. Although many Genízaros did serve (as did many Pueblo warriors) and distinguished themselves throughout the territory in eighteenth-century militias, the term was "a purely ethnic designation with no military connotations when it was first applied to the genizaros of New Mexico."[31]

Although the ransomed Genízaro women and children were placed into servitude as maids and cooks, as shepherds and woodcutters and farmers, in Spanish colonial households, they did not suffer the same crimes of slavery experienced in other parts of the Americas: "Spanish treatment of the Genízaro was at best a sort of benevolent paternalism and frequently was less than ideal; but Indian treatment of the captive was even harsher; and the options open to the Genízaro were limited. He had to learn to make the best of what was available to him. This led to the development of a flexible, pragmatic individual, who learned to survive in a dangerous and ever changing frontier."[32]

The Spanish tutelage of the ransomed Genízaros rested on pious purposes: a Genízaro child would be reared as a Christian, and although they were unpaid servants performing the most mundane daily chores, upon reaching adulthood they were free to marry and begin their own lives. Many were too poor to do more than continue as workers under the same *patrón* who had raised them, but this was not unique to Genízaros. Many colonists were poor and worked for a *rico* landowner most of their lives. But the frontier colonies of New Mexico were basically classless societies: a rich man could lose everything in a single Indian raid, while a poor man, be he a Mexican-born colonist or a Genízaro, skilled in counterraiding and frontier guerilla warfare, could make a fortune from booty taken from counterraids on the nomadic tribes.

As the Genízaros intermarried among themselves, their children were a mixed progeny who spoke neither language of their parents and did not observe their tribal customs. These children of Plains Indian captives ransomed to the Spanish were the true Genízaros: they were a new people, completely Native American yet belonging to no tribe; they were familiar with Hispanic culture yet were not Spanish.[33]

In the church records, the term "Genízaro" was used as often as it was omitted. The Franciscans of the eighteenth century often distinguished people as being either Indio (Indian) or Español (Spanish). Sometimes the complex *casticismo* (caste elitism) system of colonial New Spain was reflected in the church records and an individual would be further identified as to his or her exact ancestry: *mestizo* was a mixed Spanish-Indian ancestry; *coyote* was an individual with a European father and New Mexican mother who might or might not be Hispano. If a Genízaro married a Pueblo Indian, he or she became Pueblo in the records. If he or she married an Hispano, their children were called *coyotes, mestizos,* and *mulatos* in the church registries. When the record did include the term "Genízaro," it might also indicate that he or she was an Indio Criado, a servant, and from what tribe he or she had been taken, such as Indio Comanche.[34] But overall, the term "Genízaro" was never explicitly defined among the record keepers; the ethnic lines between the colonial settlers on the New Mexican frontier and their Native American neighbors tended to blur, especially to the educated and elite Franciscans who often lumped together all of the lower caste categories in the early frontier records: "It may be that originally the term Genízaro was no more than a convenient catchall category used by Spanish colonial bureaucrats to define a bunch of unassociated folks who did not quite fit into any of the established categories of the social system."[35]

In lieu of rigorous Spanish campaigns against nomadic tribes, Genízaro numbers multiplied at an astounding rate, and by 1776, a full third of New Mexico's population was Genízaro![36] Most of these could and did become *vecinos*—tithe-paying, law-abiding, Christianized settlers who owned land and livestock and lived on equal terms with their colonial neighbors—in the communities they were placed into. By the middle of the nineteenth century, Genízaros were rarely identified as a separate ethnic group in the records of frontier communities.

By 1750, the missionaries of the territory claimed there were 17,500 Christianized Indians in the Rio Arriba region of New Mexico.[37] Among these were hundreds of freed Genízaros who had no real home or place in colonial New Mexico although they spoke a simple form of Spanish, had Christian names, and could utilize basic farming and ranching skills taught them by Hispanic masters. It was difficult to convince the Genízaros, who were culturally nomads, to settle down and contribute to colonial community building in a fashion favored by Spanish authorities. Their renown as warriors—a skill that must have been passed on to them by mothers who kept the ways of their fathers alive in their oral histories, or by boys who before capture had learned nomadic war practices from fathers and older brothers—was quickly utilized by the Spanish military, who placed them at outpost communities that had little other military protection.

In the 1740s, '50s, and '60s there were several communities in the territory where groups of freed Genízaros were either living together or had been placed by authorities: Analco, a barrio near the San Miguel church in Santa Fe; in Trampas near Taos; Carnue in Tijeras Canyon near

Albuquerque; at San Miguel del Vado on the Pecos River; and south of Albuquerque at Tomé and Belen. Ojo Caliente had a Genízaro popula- tion in the 1740s, but that village was hardly successful in acculturating them into Hispanic life: like the Abiquiu settlements, Ojo Caliente was frequently raided by the Comanches and Utes and subsequently aban- doned over and over again. The Hispanic residents could flee to the homes of relatives in La Cañada, but the Genízaros became homeless nomads.

In Abiquiu, the colonial authorities took a bold and innovative step: instead of tucking a handful of Genízaro individuals and families into or alongside an existing Hispanic placita, Governor Cachupín, in May of 1754, awarded a community land grant for a new pueblo on Abiquiu mesa directly to thirty-four Genízaro families. Cachupín and his peers were not entirely un-self-serving in this land grant: Abiquiu was still the northernmost frontier settlement, with legions of problems yet to be solved with its hostile, nomadic neighbors. In the four years since forced resettlement of the valley colonists by Alcalde Lobato, the villages had been abandoned and resettled several times. If colonization of the Chama Valley was to be successful, a colonial military outpost—a buffer zone between the Hispanic settlers on the Chama, and the nomads who fre- quented the mountains and the Piedra Lumbre region north and west— was needed. The Genízaros seemed to provide the Spanish authorities with the perfect solution to its problems in Abiquiu: proven and tenacious fighters, in Abiquiu they would be protecting their own lands and fam- ilies, and in doing so would give the entire region a stronger military base.

But selfish Spanish colonial interests aside, the Abiquiu Pueblo Grant was an important step toward Genízaro acculturation. Abiquiu was the first pueblo for non-Pueblo people. Here the Genízaros would not be the misfit foreigners but would be the majority and the norm, owners of their own homes, overseers of their own lands, with the opportunities afforded any colonial settlers: "Abiquiu thus became the location of a social experiment that was unique in New Mexico, promoting formal cultural change for a group of persons born into hunting-gathering societies."[38]

The Pueblo of Abiquiu was built like a fortress, which was its primary function, upon the old ruins of P'efu. From its perch above the river,

The Cliffs of Shining Stone on the northern edge of the Piedra Lumbre basin, with the Puerto del Cielo chimney formation in the background. These cliffs marked the passage north and west into Navajo country—the Land of War—to the first Spanish explorers of the region that is now northern New Mexico. (© 1988 Jonathan A. Meyers)

Looking south across the Piedra Lumbre basin at Cerro Pedernal and the northern edge of the Jemez Mountains. The Chama River cuts the basin east to west, the llanos climbing gently to the woodlands that step into the mountains surrounding the basin. Polvadera peak to the left. (© 1996 Kent M. Bowser)

The Chama River just west of Abiquiu. After emerging from a steep, walled canyon, the river flows through the farm country beside the old settlements of Silvestres and Barranco before passing the mesa below the old pueblo. (© 1992 Jonathan A. Meyers)

Petroglyphs such as these on rocks above the Chama River just north of Abiquiu are found throughout the region and can be dated to the prehistoric Pueblo people who inhabited the Chama River Valley and the Piedra Lumbre basin before the Spanish arrival near Española in 1598. (© 1996 Kent M. Bowser)

Looking at the Church of Santo Tomás and the main plaza of Abiquiu Pueblo from Moqui (Moque), the plaza of the Hopi who built homes on the mesa in the 1740s. Irrigated fields are to the north below the pueblo mesa. (T. Harmon Parkhurst, ca. 1915; courtesy Museum of New Mexico, negative Nº13698)

La Villa Nueva de Santa Cruz de la Cañada, established by the Spanish in 1695. It was to this settlement east of the Rio Grande that Abiquiu's first Spanish settlers fled in times of Indian attack. (Orville Cox, 1921; collection of Martha Cox Boyle)

The ruins of the *capilla* of Santa Rosa de Lima, ca. 1920, Abiquiu's Spanish sister village founded in the 1750s on the banks of the Chama River. The village of Santa Rosa de Lima was not easily defended, and its villagers sought refuge in the more fortified Genízaro Pueblo of Abiquiu during the frequent Indian attacks against the Chama Valley settlers in the 1700s and 1800s. (Courtesy Museum of New Mexico, negative N°22844)

Padre Antonio Martínez, born in Abiquiu in 1793, was an outspoken critic of the United States entrance into and occupation of the territory of New Mexico. Padre Martínez, although today hailed as a champion of Hispanic education and religious and political rights, was villainized in Willa Cather's novel *Death Comes for the Archbishop.* (Courtesy Museum of New Mexico, negative Nº11262)

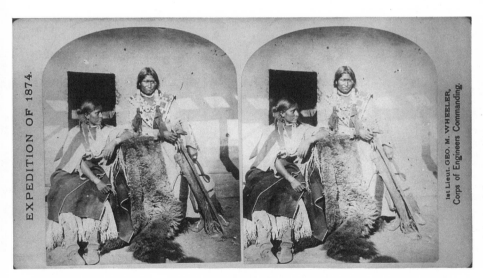

A Jicarilla Apache couple newly wedded in Abiquiu. The U.S. government opened an Indian agency at the pueblo for several tribes of the Jicarilla Apaches, as well as the Capote and Weeminuche Utes, in the early 1850s. Both tribes claimed the region as their ancestral homeland. (Stereoscopic photograph taken by Timothy H. O'Sullivan during the Wheeler Expedition's visit to Abiquiu in 1874; courtesy Museum of New Mexico, negative Nº40211)

Chief Ouray of the Utes, seated center, became a prominent and respected negotiator between his people and the United States government in the 1860s and '70s. Ouray was born in or near Abiquiu, where his Genízaro parents—his mother a semi-Christianized Tabeguache Ute, his father a Jicarilla Apache captured and raised by the Utes— were members of the old pueblo community. (William H. Jackson, 1873; courtesy Museum of New Mexico, negative №58629)

Padre José M. Gallegos was born in Abiquiu before 1820 and was raised at his father's remote Arroyo Seco ranch on the Piedra Lumbre. Like his teacher and fellow Abiqueño Padre Martínez, Gallegos was excommunicated by Bishop Lamy for his criticisms of the United States church and legal policies in New Mexico in the 1850s. Gallegos continued to be a considerable political force in New Mexico as a territorial congressman and treasurer and as superinten-dent of Indian affairs under President Andrew Jackson. (Frederick Gutekunst; courtesy Museum of New Mexico, negative №9882)

partially protected by the high sierra country on its south, west, and east flanks, the new pueblo looked north across the river into a rugged country of red and white canyonlands. The far horizon to the north and east was cut by the spine of the Rocky Mountains, called the Sangre de Cristos ("blood of Christ") by the Spanish, that marked the eastern shoulder of the Rio Grande Valley between the small frontier outpost of Taos and the presidio of Santa Fe.

The Hopi of the Plaza del Moqui were allowed to remain and become residents of the Genízaro pueblo. But all other previous claims to the mesa—which included the lands granted to the Montoyas, the Juan Trujillo family, and the heirs of Miguel Martín Serrano—were revoked by the colonial authorities.

In its early years, Abiquiu was called the Plaza of Four Nations, with four distinct tribes inhabiting the north, south, east, and west sides of the plaza. (History did not record the four tribes this name referred to.) Heavy double doors were built at each corner of the pueblo, and during times of attack, people and livestock were barricaded within the plaza. The church was designed to be the heart of the village fortress, its walls and windows constructed with the size and strength considerations given a fort, although Santo Tomás would not be finished for several decades.

Each family had a kitchen garden at the Huertas del Moque, the garden center south of the pueblo. Individual garden plots, protected from livestock by adobe walls, were a measured fourteen varas wide and forty varas long. The new Puebloans grew chiles, beans, melons, cabbage, and chickpeas. The village water supply flowed year-round from springs that bubbled from the ground at several locations above and at the foot of the mesa. Down along the Chama River the pueblo's residents dug acequias and planted fields of corn, wheat, and barley. The village livestock herds grazed the high country to the south and west of the village proper.[39]

The pueblo elected its own war captains and a village governor. The war captains were valued for their expertise and leadership of the valley militia, especially during colonial campaigns into Indian country. But the Genízaro governor had little real power. The resident friar, and the Spanish colonial authority standing behind, beside, and sometimes before him, held the real power in Pueblo life.

The mission was the vehicle by which Spain held its frontier settlements, especially those at the sites of Indian pueblos, under its control. In a pueblo like Abiquiu, the Franciscan friar was in charge of the spiritual, educational, and vocational activities of the pueblo's residents. Every aspect of mission life, from the building of the church to the weaving of cloth and the tanning of hides, was delegated and overseen by the friar. With only twenty Franciscans serving more than 18,000 converted Indians by 1776, the burden on an individual missionary was exceedingly heavy.

The Mission of Santo Tomás Apostole de Abiquiu—the name chosen by Governor Cachupín for the new pueblo's mission—was a *reducción,* a hamlet begun strictly for the acculturation and Christianization of nomadic Indians. Non-Indians could not live at a reducción, and only those Native Americans specifically assigned to the mission were allowed to be residents.[40]

Along with the tasks of homes and herds, Abiquiu's Genízaro gentry participated in formal and regimented religious instruction. Mass was celebrated every Sunday. There was a nightly rosary, and twice daily the friar held catechism for the unmarried members of the mission. The missionary also taught the new Abiqueños Spanish *alabados* (religious songs or hymns) and oversaw formal instruction, to both children and adults, of the Spanish language. Reading, however, was taught only to a selected few.[41]

The success of most New Mexico missions in the teaching of the Spanish language was not very high in the early years, and the failure of most friars to learn any of the native languages resulted in Native American congregations that understood little of what they were participating in. Abiquiu, however, was a dramatic exception, as its Indian residents quickly learned Spanish: with so many Plains Indian languages native to the tongues of the pueblo's population, it was necessary that a common language be adopted. Even so, many Abiqueños remained fluent in Ute and other nomadic languages until well into the next century, their bilingual abilities a valuable asset in the extensive trade and travel—legal and otherwise—occurring on the frontier.

The task of the Franciscans in Abiquiu—to promote Spanish culture and spiritual beliefs among the Genízaro, as well as to maintain the village as a military outpost on the edge of the frontier—would eventually be successful. But success would come slowly to this remote mission, and only after the Spanish colonial authorities confronted and subdued the beliefs and superstitions harbored in a village where the embers of so many ancient cultures glowed in the shared community fires.

Beginning in the year of its inception, when the first Franciscan friar, a Mexican named Feliz Joseph Ordoñez y Machado, was assigned to save the souls of the Genízaro population carving out a meager life on its mesa top, Abiquiu distinguished itself as a place of *maleficio* (sorcery). Although the Genízaros of Abiquiu were considered Christian converts, their lifestyles betrayed deep connections to previous cultures and spiritual practices.

When the pueblo was a mere three years old, an illness of unknown origin swept through the community. Few of the valley's Hispanic settlers were affected, but the Genízaros of Abiquiu died in wave after wave of the sickness. The symptoms of the illness included an abnormally enlarged or distended abdomen, with the victim incapable of sleep yet unable to leave his or her bed. The veins of the stricken body swelled so that the person vomited blood and bled through the nose. Few who contracted the illness lived longer than a year.

Fray Ordoñez suffered all of these symptoms during his two years at the Mission of Santo Tomás, and three months after his departure from Abiquiu, the friar died. When news of Ordoñez's death reached the valley, rumors that witchcraft and pagan rituals were responsible for the illness began to circulate.

Ordoñez was succeeded in 1756 by an experienced and respected friar, Juan José Toledo. Fray Toledo had served other Indian missions on the New Mexico frontier and was among those intrepid priests who had brought nearly four hundred Hopi, including those now settled at Abiquiu, to New Mexico from Arizona in 1745. Toledo arrived in Abiquiu to find that although the church of Santo Tomás had been under construction for several years, it was not completed. The community's crop yields were poor, and the already impoverished quality of the mission was further enhanced by the general pessimism exhibited by valley residents in regard to the plague that had taken the lives of dozens of individuals. Toledo soon learned that around Abiquiu it did not matter whether one's

God was Christian or Native American: Genízaro and Hispanic people of Abiquiu and its satellite communities along the Chama River firmly believed that they were living under the weight of a terrible curse.

Prior to Fray Toledo's own battle with the illness he wrote letters to the governor of New Mexico voicing his concerns for the spiritual welfare of the pueblo. In particular, Toledo complained to the governor about the behavior of one Genízaro, Miguel Ontíveros, a self-proclaimed sorcerer. Known locally as Miguel el Cojo ("Michael the lame"), Ontíveros, Toledo told the governor, persisted in the pagan ways of his forefathers, often conducting hunting rituals similar to those practiced at the Tewa pueblos and among tribes of the Great Plains.

El Cojo's powers were even feared by the local nomadic tribes: the Utes camped on the Piedra Lumbre believed the Genízaro sorcerer caused the death of a Ute *curandera,* or woman healer; and the Apaches of the region sent their own *curandero*—El Canoso ("the gray headed")—to aid the troubled Pueblo. El Canoso did his Athapaskan best to exorcise the illness from Abiquiu, but he, too, gave up, claiming it was El Cojo's demonic rattlesnake that rendered Apache medicine useless.

Neither church nor civic authorities in Santa Fe offered help to the plagued pueblo. By 1760, a frustrated and ill Fray Toledo began his own investigation. He hired the services of Joachin Trujillo, an Abiquiu Genízaro born to Kiowa parents, captured as a child by the Comanches, and later ransomed to the Spanish. With the aid of his brother, Juan Largo of Santa Ana Pueblo, Trujillo, as Toledo's *descrubridor* (informer and investigator) began to assemble lists of the region's pagan troublemakers. This list included various Genízaros of Abiquiu Pueblo, but it also named Genízaros living at San Juan, Nambe, Isleta, and Sandia Pueblos, and others living in the communities of Chimayo and Santa Fe.

After three years of investigations and anxious reports, the colonial authorities took fifteen Genízaros cited by Trujillo into custody. The official inquiry into Abiquiu's witchcraft problems took three years to complete: during this time five of the eleven accused Genízaros died in jail, most probably from the same illness they were believed to be the conjurers of.

Back in Avéshu pije, Fray Toledo's faithful, led by Joachin Trujillo, began a concerted and extensive search of the valley for El Cojo's pagan idols. When their crusade turned up nothing resembling the weapons of a *brujo,* Toledo had El Cojo flogged, hoping to induce the sorcerer to hand over the demonic paraphernalia believed to still curse the village. When this failed, Toledo asked the governor in Santa Fe to send the alcalde mayor of Santa Cruz to burn El Cojo at the stake. Apparently the severity of this punishment gave El Cojo's infamous determination pause, for he promptly produced the wanted idols. Miguel Ontíveros was then imprisoned in Santa Fe.

But the tribulations of the young Abiquiu mission did not immediately end: the women and young girls of the parish began suffering from *energumenas,* possession by demons. While Fray Toledo celebrated mass, women would fall to the floor, flailing their arms and legs while screaming and shrieking obscenities at everything and everyone non-Christian. Toledo soon understood that the Hispanic residents of the parish wanted all vestiges of native religion swept from their valley.

With the friar's blessing, Joachin Trujillo led a second crusade: the target of this purging was any and every Native American shrine, altar, ceremonial site, and sacred object yet found in the land of Avéshu pije. The prehistoric villages that lay in partial ruin as far west as Pedernal abounded with "pagan" paraphernalia and shrines. Each of these was found and destroyed, including a magnificent stone lion shrine once sacred to the people of Poe shú, located in the mesaland south of Abiquiu. Hopi and Tewa petroglyphs of serpents and spirals, birds and medicine men found in caves and on the rock walls of remote mesas and arroyos were either covered and surrounded by Christian crosses or were obliterated.[42]

In retrospect, the Abiquiu sorcery struggle appears to have been a wrestling match between the new Christian-promoting authorities and those natives still practicing indigenous Native American cultural expression in a community where neither tradition was entirely secure. Modern physicians have remarked that the symptoms of the Abiquiu plague mirror those commonly connected to acute infectious hepatitis culminating in cirrhosis of the liver.[43]

Ironically, in spite of the efforts of the Spanish colonial church and state to the contrary, Abiquiu would remain a superstitious village, its name and landscape linked forever with New Mexico legends of brujos and brujas.

Modern Abiqueños know that church fiestas may be attended by brujos dressed as handsome strangers with bewitching eyes; and *tecolotes,* owls, known to embody brujas, are widely regarded in the Chama River Valley to be omens of untimely death.

The "pagan" ceremonies so deeply enculturated in the first Genízaro residents of the pueblo were never completely forgotten. Even into the twentieth century, Abiquiu's annual feast days—the fiesta of Santa Rosa de Lima on August 30th, and the fiesta of Santo Tomás in late November—have continued to include Tewa dances. Until the 1930s, San Juan Pueblo singers came to Abiquiu to assist the dancers on feast days. The Na-nille (pronounced na-knee-yeh´) and O-nille (o-nee-yeh´) are still danced before the church annually by young Abiqueños wearing bright costumes with colorful ribbons, shawls, and bells on their moccasins, to a drum beat and songs that echo ceremonies at San Juan and other Tewa pueblos along the Rio Grande.[44]

Modern Abiquiu demonstrates in its Christian celebrations how the Native American roots of those first Genízaros were never severed, but grew alongside and eventually into the Christian roots of the valley's settlers. Modern Abiquiu padres, unlike their baffled predecessors in the eighteenth century, have come to accept and respect the pueblo's unique heritage, and honor the community's traditions that move easily between several once-disparate and even adversarial spiritual beliefs.

In April of 1776, the Pueblo of Abiquiu was visited by Fray Francisco Atanasio Domínguez, the Franciscan in charge of all the New Mexico missions. The church of Santo Tomás had finally been completed under the leadership of a young, energetic, Austurian friar named Sebastian Angel Fernández. The interior of the thick-walled adobe brick church at Abiquiu, which the locals insisted on calling Santa Rosa de Abiquiu, ignoring the governor's wishes that it patronize Santo Tomás, was not large. The floor was bare earth, and although there was no altarpiece or image of Santo Tomás, Domínguez wrote favorably in his record of the "five large, almost new paintings on buffalo skin" obtained and arranged on the mud wall by Fray Fernández.[45]

Fray Domínguez's report about the mission at Abiquiu had little good to say about the Genízaro pueblo. Everything about the villagers—

the way they dressed, spoke Spanish, farmed their land, or built and decorated their dwellings—was disagreeable to the Spanish friar, whose report reflected the low opinion most aristocratic Franciscans held for their Native American converts: "The houses in which the Indians live are arranged in accordance with their poverty and lack of interest," Domínguez wrote. "On the open sides the pueblo has many good farmlands, which are irrigated by the river they call Chama. . . . The lands are extremely fertile, but their owners, the Indians, are sterile in their labor and cultivation, so they do not yield what they might with attention, and as a result so little is harvested that the Indians are always dying."[46]

Domínguez had surely read the records and was privy to the events that had plagued Abiquiu in the last decade. But apparently he did not understand that those Genízaros who had survived the physical and emotional assaults of maleficio were now using a good proportion of their healthy energies to ward off the Apache, Navajo, Ute, and Comanche attacks against their community.

The official census listed forty-six families with 136 persons living in the Pueblo of Abiquiu. The non-Indian, Spanish settlement of Santa Rosa de Lima (the second settlement of this name), built around a chapel in a small plaza close to the banks of the Chama, numbered forty-nine families with 254 persons. Domínguez had more complimentary words about the physical appearance of the Hispanic settlement, although his ever-observant eye noticed how the chapel of Santa Rosa, built by the settlers themselves, had mother-of-pearl satin vestments that were so old "that even to look at it is indecorous."[47]

The colonial settlers on the New Mexican frontier spoke their own form of Spanish—a local patois of provincial, simple Castilian full of archaisms, the result of a lack of schools or contact with the rest of Spanish America. Domínguez spoke a courtly European Castilian, but the archaic language of the mostly Mexican colonists of the frontier of New Mexico was not nearly as difficult on Domínguez's educated ear as the Spanish spoken by the Abiquiu Genízaros, who, like those Genízaros in Santa Fe, were said to be "not very fluent in speaking and understanding Castilian perfectly, for however much they may talk or learn the language, they do not wholly understand it or speak it without twisting it somewhat."[48]

Domínguez's report lumped all Genízaros into one cultural mud puddle and ultimately betrayed his belief that these detribalized un-Christian folks were next to useless to the Spanish crown: "For they all come from the same source, and these were taken for this pueblo [Abiquiu]. There is nothing to say about their customs, for in view of their great weakness, it will be understood that they are examples of what happens when idleness becomes the den of evils."[49]

Homely mud and adobe den of evils and idleness or not, a few months later Domínguez was forced to return to the pueblo of the Genízaros. In July of 1776, Abiquiu's church and plaza would be the last outpost of Spanish colonial civilization that Domínguez would see before he embarked on his five-month journey into the wilderness of New Mexico, Colorado, Utah, and Arizona with Fray Silvestre Vélez de Escalante. The two friars were under colonial orders to seek a route from Santa Fe to the California Spanish presidio at Monterey. They were accompanied by eight men with thirty horses, ten mules, and twenty head of cattle to serve as meat en route. The small expedition of Domínguez and Escalante would cover two thousand miles of virgin frontier that would include the vast, unmapped land of the Yutas (the Great Basin of Utah) and a difficult but successful crossing of the Colorado River. Escalante, the expedition's twenty-four-year-old diarist, faithfully recorded their journey across the route that would later become the foundation for the Old Spanish Trail to the Pacific. Although the young friars never reached Monterey, they did peacefully meet with dozens of Native American tribes, many of whom had never before encountered Europeans.

The expedition departed Santa Fe on July 29, 1776. After an overnight at Santa Clara Pueblo, the caravan of the Franciscans rode northwest up the Chama River. The nine league trail (about twenty-seven miles) between Santa Clara and Abiquiu was "rough, tortuous and brush covered."[50] At the outpost of Abiquiu the friars were briefed on the frequency of Ute visits in the valley—friendly and not—and were also told of recent Navajo and Comanche threats. It was well known to the friars, to their men, and to the Genízaros of Abiquiu curiously observing the royal caravan from the pueblo shadows that once they departed the mesa of Abiquiu they entered *la tierra de guerra,* the land of war.

On the morning of August first, after celebrating high mass with the Genízaros of the mission of Santo Tomás, the friars and their eight companions, two of whom were young Genízaro brothers (not from Abiquiu) who would serve as the expedition's Ute interpreters, followed the Chama River northwest past the tiny settlement of Barranco and into the deep, narrow Chama canyon that finally opened onto the wide, spacious, grass- and antelope-speckled Piedra Lumbre basin. The caravan followed the river bosque across the Piedra Lumbre llanos. About halfway across the basin they departed the Chama River and cut north toward the Cliffs of Shining Stone. The daily siesta was taken near Arroyo Seco, which of-fered the travelers a steady trickle of welcomed water. Escalante must have heard some of the Tewa stories about the region, for while propped on his elbows in the shade of some juniper tree, staring off at the magnifi-cent sandstone walls which were soft pastel red and yellow under a glar-ing midday summer sun, he wrote: "They say that on some mesas to the east and northeast of this valley, alum rock and transparent gypsum are found."[51]

Two weeks into their journey, when the expedition was on the Dolores River in what is now southwestern Colorado, two Abiquiu Gení-zaros caught up with the Domínguez and Escalante caravan. It was un-clear to the friars what Felipe and Juan Domingo wanted to achieve in the wilderness, or if the Genízaros' presence was a blessing or a curse: "This afternoon we were overtaken by a coyote and a genízaro of Abiquiu," Fray Escalante wrote on August 14, "the first named Felipe and the second Juan Domingo. In order to wander among the heathen, they had fled from that pueblo without the permission of their superiors, protesting that they wished to accompany us. We did not need them, but to prevent mischief which either through ignorance or malice they might commit by traveling alone any longer among the Yutas if we tried to send them back, we accepted them as companions."[52] If the Franciscans ever viewed Juan Domingo and Felipe as assets to the journey, it was never recorded by Escalante in his journal.

During late October and early November, the friars tried repeatedly to find a way down the steep canyons and across the water of the Colorado River of northern Arizona and southern Utah. When it was learned that the Abiquiu Genízaros were good swimmers, they were chosen, again and again, to bodily test the depth, strength, and width of the Colorado. At what would one day be called Lee's Ferry, the two Genízaros "entered the river naked, carrying their clothing on their heads. It was so deep and wide [about one hundred yards] that the swimmers, in spite of their prowess, were scarcely able to reach the opposite shore, and they lost their clothing in the middle of the river, never seeing it again."[53] The campsite the expedition used that night near this attempted crossing was named Salsipuedes, "get out if you can."

On the morning of November 7, 1776, Domínguez and Escalante, with Don Pedro Cisneros, the alcalde mayor of Zuni, accompanied by Felipe and Juan Domingo, left camp to inspect a canyon and ford believed to be a river crossing used by the Paiutes. To reach the river down what would later be called Padre Canyon "it was necessary to cut steps in a rock with axes for the distance of three varas [about ten feet] or less."[54] After reaching the canyon's bottom and finally the waters of the Colorado, the five men rode downriver "about two musket shots, sometimes in the water, sometimes on the bank, until we reached the widest part of its current where the ford appeared to be. One of the men [Felipe or Juan Domingo] waded in and found it good, not having to swim at any place. . . . We waited, although in some peril, until the first wader returned from the other side to guide us and then we crossed with ease, the horses on which we crossed not having to swim at all."[55]

By sundown on November seventh, after thirteen days of frustratingly unsuccessful attempts, the friars, horses, supplies, and men of the expedition safely crossed the Colorado River. In doing so, the Franciscans became the first white men to cross the canyonlands of the Colorado. The ford was named El Vado de los Padres, The Crossing of the Fathers, but among Genízaro historians it is remembered that the skillful swimming and guiding by two Abiqueños made the crossing possible. Today, the narrow steps they cut into the stone with hand axes, the deep walls of Padre Creek Canyon, and the Crossing of the Fathers and the Genízaros are all inundated by the waters of Lake Powell.

3

PIONEERS OF THE PIEDRA LUMBRE

In February of 1766, Martín Serrano cousins Pedro and Juan Pablo stood before Governor Cachupín at the Palace of the Governors in Santa Fe. Pedro and Juan Pablo were both lieutenants in the militia of Abiquiu; Juan Pablo also served as the lieutenant alcalde of Santa Cruz de la Cañada. Governor Cachupín knew that in the Rio Arriba country the Martín Serrano name was akin to frontier royalty. Martín Serranos had marched up the Rio Grande with Oñate's caravan; the sons of the first Martín Serrano colonists later fled the province in the wake of the native revolt. And their sons returned ten years later to begin the colony again under de Vargas. There was virtually no chapter in the New Mexican colony's history that did not include a Martín Serrano story, and there was not a town or *plazuela* north of Santa Fe that did not count a Martín Serrano descendant among its residents.

Pedro's father, Blas, was given land on the Ojo Caliente River in 1735, where he was among the founders of the Comanche-harassed village of Ojo Caliente. Juan Pablo's father, Miguel Martín Serrano, was a son of the esteemed Captain Sebastian Martín Serrano of Alcalde, and was among those granted Tierra Azul south of Abiquiu in 1734. We can imagine that both Juan Pablo and Pedro Martín Serrano were eyewitnesses to, and armed defendants during, the brutal Ute-Comanche assault on the Chama Valley settlements in 1748.

The Martín Serranos had come from their Chama River Valley homes to the governor's office in the Palace of the Governors to request lands from the royal domain. Pedro asked for the Piedra Lumbre, "all the lands embraced in the same boundaries marked out to José de Riaño"[1]—the vast basin of mesas and llanos that constituted the Valley of Shining Stone formerly ranched and abandoned by Riaño and then by the Montoyas. The Piedra Lumbre was legally defined "on the north by some red bluffs; on the east by a stony hill; on the south, Pedernal Hill; and on the west, by the mesa adjoining the Cañon de la Piedra Lumbre."[2] Pedro and his wife, Margarita de Luna, had fifteen legitimate children, and the lieutenant asked the governor to bear "in mind that I have no other proper place for the subsistence of my stock, in which depends myself and large family."[3]

Governor Cachupín was certainly in favor of giving the lieutenant the Piedra Lumbre—it was to the crown's ultimate advantage that the northwestern frontier be secured, and who better than a military man to hold this farthestmost domain—but Cachupín followed official protocol and asked Pedro to disclose the size of his herds and the dimensions of the land itself. "At present time I have four hundred and eighty head of branded cattle," the lieutenant replied in a written statement, "and one hundred and sixty-four horses and mules, and twenty-seven hundred sheep."[4] He then informed the governor that the Piedra Lumbre was three leagues east to west and the same north to south.

Juan Pablo Martín Serrano requested the lands commonly called La Polvedera (a local corruption of Spanish *polvareda,* meaning cloud of dust). This triangular-shaped piece of land reached to the Piedra Lumbre's southeastern boundary and included Pedernal Mountain and the fertile lands watered by the Rito de Pedernal, Rito de Polvedera, and Rito de Chihuahueños that flowed clear and strong year-round below the prehistoric fortress of Tsiping. Juan Pablo told the governor that he had one hundred cattle, eighteen horses, and four hundred head of small stock, and that the Polvedera lands covered one and a half leagues east to west and three leagues north to south. These lands formed the northern edge of the Jemez Mountains. Juan Pablo mentioned in his signed statement that "there are a few patches of land on the tract called Polvedera fit for cultivation . . . the balance only for grazing."[5]

The next morning, February 12, 1766, Governor Cachupín granted Pedro the Piedra Lumbre, and Juan Pablo the Polvedera, and sent orders to Alcalde Manuel García Paraja of Santa Cruz to deliver the royal possessions to the new grantees. The Polvedera Grant encompassed 35,761 acres; the Piedra Lumbre 49,749 acres. Together, the Martín Serrano lands covered more than one hundred square miles of the province's most wild, beautiful, and dangerous country. But the cousins knew this region well: in 1760, Pedro had begun grazing his herds on the valley llanos that were then the property of Lieutenant Domingo de Luna of Tomé. De Luna, who probably never set eyes on the Piedra Lumbre, had acquired the grazing rights for the Piedra Lumbre basin from the Montoyas. De Luna sold these rights to Pedro Martín Serrano, whose wife, Margarita de Luna, a Rio Abajo native, was a close relative of Domingo's.

By the time of his formal request for the Piedra Lumbre, Pedro Martín Serrano had actually bought the Piedra Lumbre from de Luna. In fact, the lieutenant asked Governor Cachupín to grant him ownership of land for which he already held title, and upon which his herds had been grazing—and multiplying—for almost six years. But Pedro knew that none of the previous owners had requested or been given a settlement grant; to avoid future confusion, Pedro requested a grant de novo for the Piedra Lumbre.

Although he had a far smaller herd of livestock to boast of than his cousin, Juan Pablo was already well established in the social and political hierarchy of the Chama Valley when he was granted the Polvedera. Juan Pablo was a militia leader and a valley landowner. His family was one of those who lost title to lands on or near Abiquiu mesa when the Genízaro pueblo was established in 1754. Juan Pablo reminded the governor of this loss in his written request for the Polvedera. When Cachupín granted the lieutenant the Polvedera he did so "in view of his need, his personal merits, and his belonging to a pioneer New Mexican family."[6] However, the grant was made on the condition that possession of this land did not

"injure the rights of the Indians of the Pueblo of Abiquiu."[7] To acquire
complete title, Juan Pablo would have to successfully settle the lands
within four years.

Exactly seven days later, on February 18, 1766, Alcalde Paraja of
Santa Cruz, with Gerónimo Martín (a resident and founding father of
Barranco, alcalde of Abiquiu, and a brother or first cousin to Blas Martín
Serrano), accompanied Pedro Martín Serrano to the edge of the Piedra
Lumbre basin. "I, with Gerónimo Martín," wrote Alcalde Paraja, "took
by the hand the said lieutenant of the militia, Pedro Martín Serrano, and
walked him over the aforesaid tract, where he plucked up grass, and
threw stones and shouted 'long live the King our Lord.'"[8] It is doubtful
that Pedro Martín Serrano and his uncle Gerónimo walked with Alcalde
Paraja the entire Piedra Lumbre. They may have ridden several boundaries by horseback, and then stood on a well-positioned hill and clarified
which stony hill constituted the eastern border, which red bluffs the west.
Pedro's shepherds and herds may have been visible, perhaps along the
river bosque or out across the llanos on the tablelands below Alto del
Navajo above the Rio Puerco's muddy confluence with the Chama.

Alcalde Paraja had a busy day: that same afternoon he placed Juan
Pablo in possession of the Polvedera Grant. After receiving approval from
the Indians of the Pueblo of Abiquiu and from José Martín, the adjoining
landowner and an uncle of the lieutenant, the alcalde and Jose Martín
witnessed Juan Pablo's grass plucking and stone throwing, and his admo-
nitions of loyalty and thanks to the Spanish king beneath the blue shadow
of Cerro Pedernal, of which Juan Pablo was now owner.

Pedro and Juan Pablo set up a single rancho along their shared
border and installed Genízaro shepherds and some family members at the
Vega de Riaño. The cousins, who between them had the single largest
herd of sheep and cattle in the Chama Valley, may have lived on the lands
seasonally to satisfy settlement requirements, but like every Piedra Lumbre rancher before them, the Martín Serranos maintained their primary
family households downriver near Abiquiu.

In the 1760s, the Martín Serranos held prominent positions in the
Abiquiu valley community because they were able, through military service, to earn cash wages which enabled them to buy livestock as well as to
acquire land. Most valley settlers had little or no opportunity to earn

money, and bartered and traded for the few animals and house goods they had. Land acquisition was out of the question for most *pobladores.*

By the mid 1700s, sheep and cattle were the major item for trade and barter both within New Mexico and between the colony and Mexico. The first sheep introduced to New Mexico by the Spanish conquistadors were churros—hardy, light-fleeced sheep common to Spain, with succulent, flavorful meat. The churros were renowned for their hardiness and ability to forage even in the most arid climates.

As many as 500,000 sheep were driven from New Mexico to Chihuahua and other Mexican markets by the early 1800s.[9] These animals belonged to a handful of wealthy ranchers, called *patrones,* whose lands were divided up into *partidos* (shares), each of which was under the care of a *partidario,* or *borreguero* (shepherd). A partidario was given a share of the lamb crop produced under his care each season.

Under this share system, some Hispano settlers and Genízaros of the Abiquiu valley were able to build up their own herds and eventually increase their own landholdings and personal fortunes. But many partidarios struggled to break even each year, and many fell into debt to their patrón after difficult winters or devastating Indian raids.

Over the next century, Martín Serrano sons and sons-in-law, grandsons and grandnephews, set up individual ranchos on various parts of the Piedra Lumbre basin and up in the sierras of the Polvedera lands—at the Vega de Riaño, the Ancón de la Becerra ("the cove of the calf"), and small camps along the Rio Puerco. Each of these ranches was essentially self-sufficient with little support during Indian attacks, of which there were many. Both the Utes and the Navajos protested settlement on the Piedra Lumbre basin, and the lives of many young Genízaro and Hispanic shepherds were lost in skirmishes with the native tribes in the 1840s and '50s: "They were miserably clad in tattered blankets, armed with bows and arrows," one American soldier wrote of the New Mexican shepherds. "These and their big shepherd dogs constitute their sole defense, although they are subject to be attacked by Indians, and their flocks and herds scattered by Indians and wolves."[10]

The Abiquiu settlements at the turn of the nineteenth century numbered nine separate yet interdependent, kin-related plazas along the Chama

River beginning north and west of La Cuchilla: San Miguel on the lands called Tierra Azul; San Rafael (on the Plaza Colorado Grant), San Ignacio (on the Plaza Blanca), and the plaza of Santa Rosa at La Puente below Poe shú; north and west were the Plaza de la Capilla de Santa Rosa de Lima, the Genízaro plaza of Santo Tomás, and the Plaza del Moqui of the Hopi, both called the Pueblo of Abiquiu, the designated fortress for the valley settlers in times of attack. West of Abiquiu on the Chama's rocky bluffs was the settlement of San José del Barranco. To the south of this village, higher in the sierras and reached by a trail first blazed by the prehistoric Tewa, was the plaza of San Antonio, where Gerónimo Martín built a ranch and seven-room house. The last plaza of the Abiquiu settlements was called Guadalupe; it lay near the red mouth of the Cañon del Cobre arroyo, on the fertile farmlands today called Los Silvestres ("the wild place").

In spite of drought and Indian raid, the Chama Valley population steadily grew. By 1793, the Abiquiu settlements had 1,558 residents. Only 156 of these were designated as "Indians," indicative of the assimilation of the Genízaros into *vecino* settler ranks.[11] By 1805, the Abiquiu valley census named 607 Spanish men and 611 Spanish women, while the named Genízaros numbered 70 men and 64 women.[12] By 1808, the total population of 1,938 included only 122 Genízaros to 1,816 Hispanos.[13]

By the 1800s, the Hopi people as an ethnic group in Abiquiu were completely absorbed into the Genízaro and Hispanic families. Occasional baptismal entries indicated an infant was Moqui (or Moque), but these were most likely captives brought back to Abiquiu by the local militia after expeditions into Hopiland.

Continued Indian raids caused periodic abandonment of the Piedra Lumbre and Polvedera lands in the latter part of the eighteenth century. In 1806, because of the unending harassment of his shepherds by the nomadic tribes, Pedro Martín Serrano's grandson, Mariano Martín, requested—on behalf of himself and the Martín Serrano descendants—revalidation of his grandfather's grant. Mariano may have been concerned that the grant's legality would be challenged because of abandonment, or because of the confusion brought to its title by so many heirs holding partial ownership. The tradition of partible inheritance meant each child, and then grandchild, great-grandchild, and so forth, was given a piece of a family's estate. Among less wealthy families, partible inheritance meant the dividing of even very small plots of land. In some instances, it meant the family dwelling might be subdivided, with a single room given to each child. Where necessary, rooms were divided into allotments measured by ceiling *vigas,* or beams.

In response to Mariano Martín's request, the governor issued a decree revalidating the Piedra Lumbre Grant on the tenth of August of 1806. By time of the revalidation, the Martín Serranos had shepherds' *parajes* (encampments) on the basin and up in the sierras, and at least one substantial *puesto* at or near the Vega de Riaño on the southern border of the Piedra Lumbre. But not even the intrepid Martín Serranos had yet ventured to make a permanent ranch farther north and west than the foothills below Pedernal.

In October of the same year that the Piedra Lumbre Grant was revalidated, Mariano Martín sold a tract of previously unsettled land on the north side of the Piedra Lumbre to a young Abiqueño, Pedro Ignacio Gallego. This parcel of land was situated on the lower end of the Arroyo Seco north of its confluence with the Chama, on irrigatible lands miles across the llanos from the Martín stronghold at the Vega de Riaño. Gallego planned to build a ranch on a beautiful plateau of land below the crumbling red island mesa called Mesa Huerfano, close to where Domínguez and Escalante had paused for their afternoon siesta fifty years before.

Gallego, a single man and a captain of the militia of the Rio Arriba, paid Mariano Martín four hundred pesos for more than three thousand acres along the Arroyo Seco. The Gallego family (the name changed to Gallegos at or about the time of American occupation in the late 1840s) was to the Rio Abajo region of New Mexico what the Martín Serranos were to the Rio Arriba: *primeros pobladores* (pioneers and first settlers), with military and familial ties to Oñate and de Vargas, wealthy landowners and leaders in their communities.

Pedro Gallego married Ana María Gabaldon in Albuquerque on April 1, 1811. He brought his bride north to the Chama Valley, where they set up their first home. Gallego was a skilled militiaman and quickly proved to be an adept and ambitious young settler on the Piedra Lumbre basin. Although his wife and daughter remained in Abiquiu, in the next two decades Gallego and his three sons built the first residence on the north side of the Piedra Lumbre—a multiroom *jacal* house, stables, and corrals at the Arroyo Seco. They cleared and planted at least one hundred acres of fields irrigated by an acequia that brought water from a hand-dug reservoir. The Gallego ranch had its own gristmill turning over the stream, and *la era,* a threshing floor made of earth mixed with ox blood.

The Gallego men became the farthest outpost of Hispanic settlement. As such, they learned to handle the hostilities of the Navajo and Utes, who protested the Gallegos' use of their ancestral hunting grounds, and whose raids escalated in number and intensity with each passing year of the 1800s. The Gallego men were forced to flee to Abiquiu's fortified plazas again and again in the first four decades of the nineteenth century, but they did not abandon the Arroyo Seco ranch. Local lore says that on at least one occasion the raiding Utes were cornered, perhaps by Don Pedro's sons and shepherds, on the top of Mesa Huerfano northeast of the Arroyo Seco ranch. The Ute warriors perished on the red-and-yellow sandstone butte which had one accessible path to or from its lofty summit. The mesa was temporarily renamed Mesa Hambre ("starvation mesa") by those who knew of the demise of the trapped Ute warriors above the Gallego homestead.

Don Pedro served as alcalde of Abiquiu as early as 1819, and as an elected member of the second territorial deputation in 1826. Gallego's firstborn son, José Manuel, left the wide open spaces of the Piedra Lumbre when he was eighteen and was among the first students to graduate from the school led by another Abiqueño, the soon to be famous Padre Antonio Martínez of Taos.

José Manuel Gallegos attended seminary in Durango, Mexico, and was ordained into the priesthood in 1840. Padre Gallegos, like Padre Martínez (whose character gained infamy in Willa Cather's *Death Comes for the Archbishop*), was an outspoken critic of American occupation and policies in the 1850s. And like Padre Martínez, Padre Gallegos was one of five native priests excommunicated by the archbishop, Jean-Baptiste Lamy. Padre Gallegos had many powerful friends, including Governor David Meriwether and Colonel Manuel A. Chávez, and even after his falling out with the archbishop, José Manuel went on to become New Mexico's first congressional delegate in 1855–56. Gallegos served Congress again in 1871–73 and became territorial treasurer in 1865. President

Andrew Jackson appointed José Manuel Gallegos superintendent of Indian affairs in 1868.[14]

After Don Pedro Gallego's death in 1840, his other two sons continued to farm and ranch at the Arroyo Seco, as did several sons-in-law and their relatives. But tensions between the Navajo, Utes, and the United States army intensified in the 1850s, and raiding parties made farming and ranching at the Arroyo Seco and on the entire Piedra Lumbre basin nearly impossible.

In the year following the young Pedro Ignacio Gallego's bold purchase of the frontier lands called the Arroyo Seco, legend remembers that one Juan Bautista Valdez, an Abiquiu resident and an heir to the Polvedera lands, had an encounter with Pedro Martín Serrano III—Mariano's brother—that opened the door for the first community settlement on the Piedra Lumbre. Apparently Martín Serrano was working in his fields, possibly near the Vega de Riaño, when a band of Navajos attacked him. Martín Serrano was able to protect himself, but the Navajos managed to run off with his horses. Martín Serrano was headed toward Abiquiu on foot when he met up with Valdez. Martín Serrano asked Valdez to give him horses upon which to return home. Valdez, recognizing Martín Serrano's predicament, and how "he was not only inconvenienced but ashamed,"[15] agreed, but only if he was given a piece of land in exchange for the horses.

Martín Serrano accepted these terms, and in 1807 Valdez and his family, plus seven other settlers, were granted a small wedge of land in the moist and fertile Cañones Canyon tucked between the mesas below the northeast flank of Cerro Pedernal. They called their village, which was linked to the Abiquiu settlements through kin and tradition, Cañones.

4

THE FEARING TIME

The relatively peaceful trade relationship with the Utes in the late
1700s led the Hispanic settlers of the Chama Valley to view fertile valleys
north and west of the Piedra Lumbre—the traditional hunting grounds of
the Utes—with land-hungry eyes. In 1806, a group of Abiquiu ranchers
under Francisco Salazar petitioned the governor for the pasture and agricultural lands wedged between Mesa Prieta and Mesa de las Viejas in the
narrow canyon of the Rio Chama west of the Piedra Lumbre. Two years
later, thirty-one settlers were given this grant, called the Cañon del Rio
de Chama. They planned to build a new town, San Joaquin, but this
community never materialized and the entire grant would eventually
be abandoned due to Indian raids in the next few decades. The Utes
wanted to trade with the settlers but did not want to give any more land to
them.

Although trade between individual settlers and Native American
tribes was illegal, there were trade fairs licensed by the Spanish authorities. Taos held the largest fairs, but Abiquiu's soon became substantial
affairs because the pueblo was the closest outpost for the Utes, whose
primary interest was the obtaining of horses from herds such as that of the

Martín Serranos. The Taos and Abiquiu trade fairs were overseen by the governor's officials from Santa Fe and Santa Cruz.

Plains Indians were invited to both fairs and brought buffalo hides, pelts, chamois, meat, slat, suet, tallow, deer and antelope skins, and plunder—including prisoners, both Native American and Spanish—for trade and ransom. The Utes traded much dried deer and buffalo meat but were renowned for their skill in the tanning of hides. Their finely dressed hides and buffalo robes were greatly favored in the settlements, and one hide could be traded for a good horse or for two hunting knives on the Abiquiu plaza.[1]

The Indians sought the settlers' cotton blankets, pottery, maize, stones (including turquoise), metal tools and objects, and the ransom of their own kinsman held by the Spanish. The Comanches favored the Taos fair, while the Utes favored the annual event held in Abiquiu. Father Domínguez witnessed the Abiquiu fair in 1776:

> Every year, between the end of October and the beginning of November, many heathens of the Ute nation come to the vicinity of this pueblo. They come very well laden with good deerskins, and they celebrate their fair with them. This is held for the sole purpose of buying horses. If one is much to the taste and satisfaction of an Indian (the trial is a good race), he gives fifteen to twenty good deerskins for the horse; and if not, there is no purchase. They also sell deer or buffalo meat for maize or corn flour. Sometimes there are little captive heathen Indians (male or female) as with the Comanches, whom they resemble in the manner of selling them. They usually sell deerskins for belduques [knives] only, and they are given two of the latter for one of the former. With the exception of firearms and vessels, the Utes sell everything else as described with regard to the Comanches, but they are not so fond of trading as has been said of the latter.[2]

If all of the invited nomadic tribes came at the same time to these fairs, there was considerable tension that often led to bloodshed. And the relationship between the settlers and the various nomadic tribes was suspicious at best: "At these meetings, real and fancied insults stirred the

Indian's desire for revenge. The settlers frequently cheated the Indians in trading, stole their horses, and unjustly accused them of sharp practices. So flagrant was such double dealing on the part of the settlers that the governors were forced to attend the fairs personally and even maintain a guard over the horse herd of the Indians to prevent theft."[3]

Although a needed and wanted part of colonial life—the tanned hides and robes obtained through trade with the Indians provided New Mexican settlers with their only source of commerce with Mexico—there were considerable risks to life and limb at these New Mexican trade fairs. By the close of the annual fall event emotions among the frontier's people were running high and unchecked: "Trading, then, could be a very risky business for an unscrupulous Spaniard, as well as for anyone standing too close to an aggrieved Comanche."[4]

After the trade fairs ended each fall, and the governor's men returned to the capital, a brisk and illegal Ute-colonist trade continued through the winter, spring, and summer beyond reach of official control, at remote rendezvous like the Piedra Lumbre. Frustrated at the disregard communities like Abiquiu had for colonial laws, authorities in Santa Cruz or Santa Fe offered a reward to any informant who disclosed the names of unlicensed traders. The established punishment for illegal traders was ten lashes if he was an Indian or Genízaro, and a ten peso fine if a Spaniard.[5]

The Spanish laws forbidding unlicensed trade were an attempt to keep the peace between the colony and the nomadic tribes. But, in fact, the illegal trade may have itself promoted better colonial-nomad relations, as it was extremely lucrative for both parties. The trade provided the New Mexico colony with trade goods valued in Mexico, and the Indians acquired horses, European tools, and weapons. The trade was so profitable that Spanish alcaldes and military leaders, especially at outposts like Abiquiu, flagrantly violated the decrees and built their fortunes from this commerce.[6]

From the time of first settlement, individual ranchos along the Chama River had opened their doors to individual Ute trade partners. A tentative trust developed between the colonists and the Ute traders over years of contact, perhaps lasting several generations. Settlers like the Martín Serrano cousins traded with the same Utes year after year. The family had a healthy and substantial fear of the Utes, having witnessed the tribe's sudden change of loyalty to the Montoya and Riaño families. But with so many experienced soldiers in their immediate ranks, the Martín Serranos had an equally healthy confidence in their ability to manage a trading relationship with the tribe.

The Utes were already very much at home in the Piedra Lumbre basin. The area's large antelope herds, and abundant water and grass reserves, had made the Piedra Lumbre a winter home for several bands of Utes—mostly Sabuaganas (White River) and Capotes, whose summer homes were the San Juan region of northern New Mexico and the San Luis Valley of southern Colorado. By the Martín Serranos' time, there was a stream east of Pedernal known as Sabuaganas Creek, named for the band of Utes who set up their winter tipis along its banks. Later changed to Rito de Chihuahueños, both names are indicative of the ancient affiliation the Utes have with the Piedra Lumbre basin, and their apparently peaceful relations in the mid to late 1700s with the Martín Serrano family and their herdsmen who also used this region.

Early contact between Abiquiu's *pobladores* and the Utes is not well documented. Abiqueños were hesitant, even when directly asked by Spanish military commanders, to share their knowledge of the trails and country of the northwestern frontier. Royal decree forbade travel into Ute country, and fear of punitive consequences kept Abiqueños silent as to the extent of their frontier expertise. But as witnessed by friars Domínguez and Escalante, numerous Abiquiu Genízaros spoke fluent Ute and were familiar with the trails into and through Ute country as far north as Utah Lake.

The settler-Indian trade was absolutely essential to colonial New Mexico's economic survival. Still, it has been described as a "small scale, individual, and rather shabby affair."[7] Abiqueño traders, both Genízaro and Hispanic, took long expeditions into Ute country with mules and horses often carrying an insignificant amount of goods. The profit realized by most of these traders was small, and the risks disproportionately large. Historians can only guess how often or how many settlers engaged in private trade, as the Spanish archives lack details of those ventures not legally sanctioned. We know of only those traders who were caught and punished.

Members of the Martín Serrano clan show up as both defendants and prosecutors in the court records pertaining to illegal trade in the Chama Valley settlements. In 1783, the alcalde of Abiquiu, Santiago Martín, Pedro Martín Serrano's second son, was informed by Fray Diego Muñoz de Jurado that ten Spaniards—one of whom was his own brother—and two Genízaros of Abiquiu Pueblo had recently departed for Ute country. Santiago Martín had no choice but to pursue his brother's party into the frontier north and west of the Piedra Lumbre. The reluctant alcalde overtook the trading party, but the record shows that only eight men were arrested and his brother was not among them. These eight were brought to trial at Abiquiu Pueblo, where Alcalde Martín confiscated their illegally obtained goods. However, no one was whipped or fined, or spent any time in prison.[8]

The Spanish authorities in Santa Fe were not ignorant of the familial connections that pervaded Abiquiu politics. In 1797, twenty-two men accused of illegally trading with the Utes were taken downriver to trial in Santa Cruz instead of Abiquiu. Their profits were small: most of the men carried only a *fanega* (about two and one-half bushels) of corn or flour to trade. Even so, the colonial authorities decided to make an example of them, and the two dozen traders, all but two of whom were illiterate, received fines and short prison sentences in La Cañada de Santa Cruz: "Apparently the change of venue was due to the notorious record of leniency by the alcaldes of Abiquiu in proceedings against their neighbors on such charges."[9]

What is omitted from the official record, even downstream in authority-minded Santa Cruz, is perhaps more important to the story than what is included. The leniency of the Abiquiu alcaldes toward those on trial was due in part to the deference given family members, but also reflected their own participation in the unlicensed trade that contributed as much to the valley's economy as its vast sheep herds, if not more. In addition, the pathetic profits reported by the convicted Abiquiu traders of the 1790s, although indicative of a real desperation for trade goods on the part of the colonial settlers, suggests there was additional booty the court chose not to record: Indian captives.

The Spanish had been unofficially, but very actively, engaged in the

Indian slave trade for almost two centuries. In 1778, and again in 1812, Spanish *bandos* prohibited Indian slavery, but the bans were widely ignored. The trade in Indian captives continued briskly and profitably through the Mexican and then the American occupations of New Mexico until after the Civil War. Although the practice was frowned upon publicly, and complained about by church officials, the Spanish territorial administrators (like the Mexican and U.S. officials who would follow them) did little or nothing to discourage the Southwestern Indian slave trade.

The trafficking of slaves in Spanish New Mexico began in the early 1600s with the discovery of rich silver deposits in places like Zacatecas, Mexico. When the native Mexican Indian population failed to provide enough workers for their mines, the Spanish turned their sights upon the nomadic, un-Christianized (that is, uncivilized) nomads to the north in New Mexico. Great warriors and horsemen like the Utes and Comanches were quick to see the profits to be had by supplying the Spanish with the slaves they needed. The slave trade of the 1700s and 1800s was also very lucrative for Hispanics who ventured into Indian country as traders or as raiders.

Abiquiu, situated as it was on the edge of the frontier, became a busy slave trade outpost. We can only guess at the numbers of unrecorded captives who passed through Abiquiu on their way to Santa Fe and the rest of the Spanish province. Many Indian captives were bought on the plaza by local *ricos* and placed into servitude in a Chama Valley household. Others were bought in Santa Cruz or Santa Fe, where they remained as household servants. As with the Genízaros of New Mexico, these servants were baptized and given the family name and received their freedom upon reaching adulthood. However, those captives not bought by a New Mexican in Abiquiu, Santa Cruz, or Santa Fe were sent south to face a less hopeful fate in the silver mines of Chihuahua.

Everyone participated, rich and poor settler alike. Until 1824, the Genízaros of Abiquiu, like the Pueblo Indians of the territory, could not sell their land. The fortune to be found in the sale of captives provided an attractive alternative to the small profits realized from subsistence agriculture or sheepherding. Fluent in Ute and other native languages, and familiar with Indian territory, the Genízaros of Abiquiu were natural scouts, guides, translators, and primary participants in the slave trade.

Among the Native Americans themselves, the weaker, less sophisticated tribes were preyed upon by the stronger. The Utes, Comanches, and Apaches, equipped with horses and advanced firearms, kept tribes like the Paiutes of Utah in perpetual terror and subjugation. The situation pushed the Paiutes, who lived in earth dens and had no farming skills, further into destitution—some tribes even began to sell their own children—while the Utes and Comanches strengthened with each season's profits.

But even the Utes and Comanches lost children to slave raiders. The Spanish traders cared little what tribal affiliation the captives represented, only that they were young and strong.

While providing Mexican mining towns with a steady slave labor force, the Spanish sanctioning of the New Mexican slave market also kept the various tribes of the Southwestern frontier hostile to one another and less able to pose a united front to the Spanish military. In their constant raids upon one another's offspring, the Utes, Comanches, and Apaches sapped the strength of the enemy tribe, indirectly aiding the Spanish in their quest to control the territory.

Fray Domínguez gives only passing mention of the appalling condition and handling of the "little captive heathen Indians" brought into the New Mexican trade fairs at Taos and Abiquiu. But later historians would offer more detail and shed a darker light on the early Spanish slave markets: "The brutality of these trade fairs—which were the private ventures of the governing men of New Mexico—made the rendezvous of the grizzled mountain man seem tame. These 'carnivals' would match the horrors of any slave market during the height of the Roman Empire, or indeed, any of those which made the Near East famous for its trade in chattel."[10]

As military leaders of the Rio Arriba, the Martín Serranos would have had more opportunity than most to trade horses for slaves, or to take captives themselves while on military expeditions on the New Mexican frontier. Church records indicate that Abiquiu alcaldes Santiago and Jose Martín each have numerous baptismal entries of Indian captives who became servants in their households and eventually adult members of the Chama Valley community. Between 1754 and the 1840s, members of the extended Martín Serrano clan from the various Abiquiu-area plazas baptized into their families more than two hundred Indian children listed in the church records as Ute, Comanche, Genízaro, or simply "Indian of unknown parentage." These captives were as young as eighteen months, and as old as twenty-six years, with the majority between four and seven years of age.[11]

Many colonists claimed they were forced to trade Indian captives for horses and firearms. In March of 1813, seven Abiquiu traders led by Mauricio Arze and Largos García made their way into Ute country, eventually reaching Utah Lake, where they began to barter with the Timpanogos Utes. The Utes only wanted to trade slaves for the goods Arze and García's caravan carried. When Arze and García refused the captives, the Utes slaughtered eight of their horses and one mule. The Timpanogos chief finally intervened, and the traders hastily departed the lake area. After several more hostile exchanges with various tribes in Utah, the Arze and García caravan reluctantly accepted twelve slaves and 109 pelts for their goods at the village of Ute Chief Wasatch.

The Navajos, largely absent from the Piedra Lumbre and Chama River Valley in the mid to late 1700s, reappeared with renewed hostility and vigor in the first decades of the 1800s in raids such as the one witnessed by Pedro Martín Serrano on his fields below Cerro Pedernal in 1806. Some historians believe that the escalation of Navajo raids on New Mexican settlements such as those in the Chama Valley were initiated by, and in retaliation for, the Hispanic slave raids on their camps.[12]

In 1818, the Navajos, in partnership with the Utes who were now beginning to resent the encroachment of Hispanic settlers and ranchers onto their traditional hunting grounds in northern New Mexico, raided the Piedra Lumbre basin and the Chama Valley. They took herds of sheep, goats, and other animals, and forced the abandonment of the newly settled Cañon de Chama. The Piedra Lumbre shepherds hastily retreated to Abiquiu, as did the Gallego family on the north side of the basin. Subsequent Navajo and Ute raids throughout the 1820s made colonial use of the Piedra Lumbre grasslands intermittent and dangerous.

New Mexico was now a territory of Mexico, and the Mexican army quickly proved to be as weak and ill equipped to handle native hostilities as the Spanish had been. With only one hundred Mexican soldiers in the permanent garrison in Santa Fe until 1836,[13] the pobladores of Abiquiu and all other frontier outposts could expect no military help beyond what their community could itself muster.

Militia service had many risks, and settlements like Abiquiu listed an often disproportionate number of widows and single women among their residents.[14] The nomadic Indians were better equipped than the Mexican army or the militias: the territorial Mexican army had chronic shortages of clothing, guns, ammunition, and horses. Militia men often defended themselves with little more than bows and arrows. Even so, the Abiquiu volunteer militia did not simply stand guard over their homes and farmlands, but struck out into the frontier after Indian raiders. Although there are many reports of successful volunteer campaigns into Navajoland—as early as 1818, the men of Abiquiu's militia, on a campaign into Navajoland, killed seven Navajos, took two captives, and drove back 93 horses and 2,300 sheep—these expeditions often resulted in the loss of many human lives.[15]

Fifty men might compose a militia from a community like Abiquiu. The militia rode on horseback into the frontier in search of Indian settlements, where they would strike a single camp, burning fields and slaying those who resisted. The returning caravan often included six to twelve Navajo children tied to a militiaman's saddlehorn, with stolen blankets and trinkets loaded on mules and other horses. Back home in Abiquiu, the militia members were free to keep or dispose of this war booty as they chose. After Mexican independence from Spain in 1821, cash was introduced onto the New Mexican frontier. Militiamen could now exchange Indian captives for silver. A single Navajo child was worth between 75 and 150 pesos, and pesos could buy a Hispanic or Genízaro *vecino* land, livestock, and upward mobility.

Shaky peace treaties were enacted in the late 1830s and early 1840s between the Mexican government and the Navajos, but the settlers placed little faith in any territorial government's attempts to placate the Navajos. When Governor Manuel Armijo refused to return captured Navajos to their own people, even in exchange for New Mexican captives taken during Navajo raids on Abiquiu and other towns, it must have seemed to the settlers that the Mexican authorities placed more importance in the obtaining of slaves than in the ending of the frontier skirmishes. The two-way murder and mayhem continued and was at a fierce pitch at the time of American entry into the territory.

By 1846 and the U.S. army's arrival in New Mexico, the Native American slave trade touched every community—Native American, Hispanic, and Anglo—in the Southwest, from Santa Fe to Los Angeles, from Utah Lake to Chihuahua. Bought and sold, captured or obtained through barter, the nomadic tribes and Hispanic traders shuttled individuals between the native camps and the settlements. The Americans found the New Mexican militias to be as proficient at raiding as the nomadic tribes they lived in constant fear of. One 1851 visitor wrote: "The Mexicans were as fully established and systematic in this trade as ever were the slavers on the seas and to them it was a very lucrative business."[16]

The currency on the frontier changed from pesos to dollars, with a subsequent escalation in the value of Indian captives. In 1851, an Indian boy could fetch $100 from a trader, a girl between $150 and $200. Young Navajo women were especially valued in New Mexican communities for their weaving skills.

The U.S. government piously denounced the slave trade but, like their predecessors, did little to stop it. Indian Agent James S. Calhoun wrote the commissioner of Indian affairs in Washington of the "exceedingly pernicious"[17] quality of this commerce, adding that "the constant and unrestrained intercourse of traders with the Indians of this territory is, perhaps, the greatest curse upon it."[18] Calhoun proposed licensing all New Mexican traders, but even the subsequent restrictions placed on the trade did not stop the trafficking of slaves. Those with the required licenses simply used them as passports into the frontier, where they continued to trade horses for humans.

One such licensed trader was the influential and later greatly decorated José María Chávez of Abiquiu. Chávez was granted a license by Calhoun to trade in the Utah territory in September of 1850. Chávez's license made no specific mention of, or restriction against, slave trading, although Calhoun (and everyone else in Santa Fe and Abiquiu) knew full well that the securing of captives was Chávez's chief interest with the

Utes.[19] Chávez's substantial home on the northeast corner of the Abiquiu plaza included a room without windows, called the Ute Room, where, oral tradition claims, Ute visitors were placed overnight. There was a lock on the outside of this room's door, and we can imagine that many of those Native Americans who spent the night under Chávez's roof were not merely house guests, but were captives awaiting their fate in Santa Fe. (This room was later renamed the Indian Room when the house became the property of painter Georgia O'Keeffe.)

The prejudice and ill-feelings among Hispanic New Mexicans for the nomadic tribes, predominantly the Navajos, was widespread by the time of American occupation. Without investigating the causes of the hostilities between the settlers and the various Indian tribes of New Mexico and the Southwest—specifically, the slave raids on native camps—the Americans assumed the prevailing prejudice and, in conjunction with the booty-paid volunteer militias, continued the decades-old raids on Navajo camps. These attacks on the Navajos in the 1860s were so fierce the Diné called those years Nahondzod, the Fearing Time.

Nahondzod lasted eight years and ended with the Navajos' removal to the Bosque Redondo. At that time, the Indian slave trade in New Mexico ended. For the first time in one hundred and fifty years, Abiquiu settlers, like those in many other outpost communities in the territory, were able to tend their fields and follow their herds without fear of Indian ambush.

The decades of the slave trade added dozens of Navajos to the Abiquiu valley's already multicultural population. Navajos, and all of the Native American captives brought into Abiquiu, like the Genízaros before them, were freed upon reaching adulthood. The Navajo people of the valley soon intermarried with the Hispanic and Genízaro settlers and became full-fledged members of the unique cultural group called Abiqueños.

The personal stories of modern Abiquiu families give names and faces to the greater history of the territory. The great-grandfather of Joe I. Salazar, a Cañones native and lifetime rancher of the Piedra Lumbre, was a Ute taken from his tribe by the Spanish militia as a boy. The story of that Ute child has been handed down through generations of Salazar ancestors in Abiquiu and Cañones, as told by Joe I. Salazar:

In those early days, the Spaniards were fighting Indians. I guess the Spaniards went up north and they stole a little Indian. He must have been about, according to hand down legend, eight or ten years old.

There was a rich man in Abiquiu by the name of Miguel Salazar. He used to own the Plaza Blanca and the Plaza Colorado . . . and Salazar went to Abiquiu, to a store, and he seen that little Indian that was stolen. And he approached the man and asked him about the little Indian. And he said they had got the little Indian from up north someplace, Ute tribe. Miguel Salazar took a liking to the little Indian. He said, "I'd like to have him. I want to buy him." He bought the little Indian from the man and took him back to Plaza Blanca . . . sort of adopted him. And he named him Miguel Salazar after his own name.

. . . and this Miguel Salazar had a son Juan Antonio, who was the father of my father, Daniel Salazar.

Another family story handed down in oral history illustrates the scenario in reverse, with another great-grandfather captured by the Apaches and taken away from Abiquiu and into the Indian frontier as a child. In the 1840s, Jesús Archuleta was sent with another boy to find the family burros. Jesús' father, wary of Indians who frequented the sierras above their home near the plaza of Abiquiu, told the boys not to cross the rito, even if the burros had wandered across the creek and into the mesa country on the other side. The boys found the burro tracks and followed them to the creek, where the animals had crossed, and their tracks continued up the hill the other side. The burro tracks were fresh, and the two boys decided they could easily and quickly find the animals. Ignoring their elders' warnings, they crossed the rito into the mesa country. Before they found the stray animals, Apache warriors ambushed them. The older boy was able to escape, but twelve-year-old Jesús was captured and carried out of the valley by the Apaches.

Jesús was taken west, where he became a slave to the Apache who had caught him. Benjamín Archuleta, Jesús' great-grandson, told the story many times to his nephew, Dexter Trujillo, who retells the story.

"This Indian that had him [Jesús] as a slave used to work him real hard. And then Jesús got sick, with a blister on his kneecap." The Apache who captured young Jesús moved frequently from hunting camp to hunting camp. When Jesús could no longer keep up, he was left behind on the trail: "And then another Indian who was on his way going somewhere found Jesús on the trail. He was a Ute. He took some flint and slit open Jesús' wound and cleaned it out and then took Jesús home with him, up to the Ute country." Jesús lived with the Utes for more than a decade.

After American occupation, Jesús was noticed by a U.S. soldier: "The Utes used to send Jesús to get the [tribe's] rations. The American soldiers noticed that this guy who went to pick up supplies didn't look like the other Indians. One soldier asked him where he was from." The soldier learned that Jesús had been captured by Indians as a child, and that he was from Abiquiu: "The soldier told Jesús that if he wanted to come back with him the Indians couldn't hurt him in the soldier camp. But apparently Jesús was too scared, and returned to the Utes." After several conversations over a period of many months, the U.S. soldiers convinced Jesús he could safely return with them to Abiquiu. After nearly twelve years, Jesús returned home to his family.

5

THE OLD SPANISH TRAIL

exican Independence from Spain, and that country's subsequent acquisition of the Territory of New Mexico in 1821, caused few ripples of
change in the colony. News of the political rearrangements in Mexico City
took months to reach Santa Fe and then were met with passive acceptance. The presidial system and military regulations of the Spanish were
kept basically intact under Mexican rule, and the laws of Spain "to the
extent that they are not contrary to the particular conditions of the country" remained in effect.[1] The Mexicans had few resources—military or
financial—to offer the territory, and New Mexican citizens were left, as
they had always been, to get by as best they could on their own.

The status of New Mexico's Genízaros, however, did change under
Mexican law. Full citizenship was granted to sedentary Christian Indians
under the Mexican Constitution. The Puebloans continued to manage
their own civil and social affairs, for which they had ample experience. But
the Genízaros of the Pueblo of Abiquiu had to deal with opportunities and
problems completely new to them without the benefits of the community
cohesiveness and internal social structure the Rio Grande Pueblos had
developed and relied upon for centuries. The most perplexing issue to

Abiqueños was that of private land ownership. With formal citizen status, each Genízaro resident of the village of Abiquiu was given an individual allotment of the pueblo's lands and the legal right to dispose of that land as he or she pleased.

In 1825, Abiquiu's inhabitants petitioned the Mexican government for distribution of the individual farm tracts already used by the pueblo's citizens. This partitioning of the Genízaro lands proved to be a difficult task: Abiquiu's lands were hilly and of an uneven quality, and the exact boundaries of the pueblo lands were difficult to establish. The Rio Chama to the north of the pueblo had changed its course in the seventy-five years since the land was granted. The southern boundary was defined by the "road of the Teguas which goes to Navajo": because there were several trails in the sierras south of Abiquiu, there was a heated dispute between Abiquiu's residents and those of the Vallecito de San Antonio Grant— Gerónimo Martín's lands—as to which trail marked the southern boundary. There was some initial distribution of Genízaro lands in 1825, but the final partitioning was not legally settled until 1841.

Beginning in 1825, there were numerous land sales between the Genízaros and the valley's non-Pueblo residents. Most of these sales involved the agricultural lands along the Rio Chama to the north of the village mesa. Land was sold for *pesos fuertes*—"strong pesos" or cash—as well as for various amounts of corn, wheat, beans, and other crops. Land was also traded for "pesos of the earth" (livestock), including cows, calves, jack mules, sheep, burros, and horses, and for buckskins, buffalo hides, pelts, ponchos, and different kinds of cloth, including cotton and linen. The lands involved rarely included a house or a dwelling—indicative of their use solely as farm- and ranchlands over the previous decades.[2]

By the time of Mexican occupation, adobe homes, whether in the larger population centers like Santa Fe and Albuquerque or in the outpost settlements like Abiquiu and its satellite plazas, were still the dwelling of favor. Even the wealthier families lived in utilitarian homes of three or four rooms, with few furnishings. Floors were packed mud, windows were made of mica, and doors were more often than not covered with simple hides. Most of the cooking was done out of doors in hornos. Blankets rolled against the walls of the rooms served as chairs during the day and were unrolled on the floor for beds during the night. Abiquiu's houses, like most in New Mexico, were still designed and constructed with defense, not aesthetics, as the builder's primary concern.

The single greatest change brought to Abiquiu and all of New Mexico during the Mexican occupation was the loosening of trade restrictions between the territory and the United States. The first decade of Mexican rule saw a flood of commercial activity between Santa Fe and eager American traders from the east. The Santa Fe Trail opened a mere two months after New Mexico swore allegiance to Mexico, with Governor Facundo Melgares warmly receiving William Becknell and his caravan of merchants into his offices at the Palace of the Governors in November of 1821.

The merchandise and trade goods long absent in the New Mexican colony now poured into the territory in the wagons and across the pack animals of the Missouri traders: "Mostly they carried cloth and clothing, ranging from plain cotton handkerchiefs to imported silk shawls, but their loads also included tools, kitchen utensils, and household goods from pins to pens and from wallpaper to window glass."[3] Wealthier New Mexico homes now saw the addition of bedframes, chairs, and glass windows, and even the homes of the lower classes might have plank floors and wooden doors made by local craftsmen who now had access to iron and steel tools.

Although by far the most trade between New Mexico and the outside world passed over the Santa Fe Trail between Santa Fe and Independence, Missouri, a substantial profit could be had by merchants who had the foresight to turn their eyes westward to California. The old trails west and northwest of Abiquiu now became the means to establish a trade relationship with the faraway settlements on the West Coast of North America.

The Old Spanish Trail was not actually Spanish in origin. Although the Spanish administrators of the late 1700s had envisioned such a trail that would connect New Mexico with the colony of Monterey, the route's ancient ruts were blazed by the Tewa, Navajos, Utes, Apaches, and Paiutes, and it could easily have been called the Old Indian Trail, after those who had been using parts of the trail for centuries. The Domínguez and Escalante Expedition used what became the eastern end of the trail in 1776, and illegal Spanish traders along with numerous American, French,

Canadian, and Spanish fur trappers were also familiar with and frequented sections of the trail long before its official opening in 1829.

The twelve-hundred-mile trail that linked Santa Fe and Los Angeles actually departed civilization at the old outpost of Abiquiu. Unlike
the Santa Fe Trail, the Old Spanish Trail was never used by wagons, as
much of the terrain it crossed was impassable except by horse or by mule.
Even a surefooted pack animal was challenged by sections of the trail, and
riders became accustomed to dismounting their horses and walking over
many miles of the trail: "The Old Spanish Trail was the longest, crooked-
est, most arduous pack mule route in the history of America."[4]

There was no direct route: the Grand Canyon and the Colorado
River, plus several tribes less friendly to white traders than the Utes,
blocked a straight trail between New Mexico and the Pacific. Several
variations of the trail existed in the 1820s and '30s, with some caravans
taking a more southerly route, while others wound farther north. But the
route specifically called the Old Spanish Trail departed Abiquiu, crossed
the Piedra Lumbre, and exited the basin through Navajo Canyon, where
it climbed onto the Colorado Plateau and wound to Tierra Amarilla,
turning northwest to cross the Continental Divide near present-day Mon-
ero. It then continued across southwestern Colorado near Durango and
angled more north than west into Utah, where it crossed the Colorado
River at Moab, and the Green River at Green River, Utah. The trail finally
turned southwest near Castle Dale and reached the southwestern corner
of Utah near present-day St. George. It angled southwest across Nevada
to Cottonwood Springs and after passing numerous springs necessary for
human and animal survival on the Mohave Desert reached the settlements
of Barstow, San Bernardino, and finally San Gabriel Mission near Los
Angeles.

Early use of the eastern end of the trail included several parties of fur
trappers. American and French trappers had been furtively exploring and
trapping the streams of the Rocky Mountains before Mexican Independence and were acquainted with much of the Southwestern frontier long
before their presence in the territory was officially welcomed. After 1821,
the fur trade in New Mexico burgeoned, and Abiquiu became a bustling
outfitter where pack animals were bought and trail guides were hired, and
where pack trains returned from the frontier laden with pelts. The dusty

plaza of the old pueblo on the mesa above the Rio Chama was soon a gathering ground for the famous and infamous of the American fur business—Sylvestre S. Pratte (son of one of the owners of the American Fur Company), his partner Ceran St. Vrain, the infamous Tom "Peg-Leg" Smith, traders William Wolfskill of Kentucky and George C. Yount of North Carolina, among many others—and the valley population swelled to more than three thousand people.[5]

In 1832, the company of Bent and St. Vrain, headquartered at Taos, established a trading post in Abiquiu under the management of Jacob Leese, a young man from Ohio. Leese stayed only one year before heading to homes in Los Angeles and then San Francisco, but he surely qualifies as among the first Anglo-Americans to set up residence in the pueblo of the Genízaros.[6]

It was not only the large American fur companies that profited from the Mexican-American trade agreements. In 1827, Abiquiu fur traders headed northwest to Utah Lake. Although a tiny affair in comparison to the French and American party before them, the Abiquiu party of two Martíns, one Chacón, one León, and a young servant of Arroyo Seco rancher Pedro Gallego traded with the Utes and returned home with thirty-one beaver pelts and an untold number of captives.

William Wolfskill and George C. Yount are credited with the first successful crossing of the entire trail in 1830–31, but an Abiqueño merchant caravan is recognized as the first successful commercial venture between New Mexico and California. A full year before Wolfskill, and using a more southerly route that forded the Colorado River at the Crossing of the Fathers, Antonio Armijo and as many as sixty men departed Abiquiu with mules carrying bundles of serapes, blankets, and other woolen goods common to New Mexico. Armijo's caravan reached the Colorado River on December sixth, an event later publicized in Mexico City newspapers: "They forded without difficulty, despite its [Colorado River] being about 2,000 varas wide, and on the banks of the said river, which are of smooth stone, there are some inscriptions which they inferred to be made by the missionary fathers, who had long ago attempted and failed to discover this route."[7]

Armijo's men, like travelers across this desert before and after them, had to eat many of their horses and mules to survive. When they finally reached San Gabriel Mission, exhausted and disheveled, eighty-six days had passed since their departure from Abiquiu. But their efforts were well compensated: Californians were eager to trade their handsome horses and large mules for the rare and beautiful New Mexican woolens.

Thus began the annual trade caravans that departed Abiquiu in late fall and arrived in California two months later. It was a greatly anticipated event in the Chama Valley, the departure of these annual mule trains in November, and then the return caravan in which hundreds of animals were driven down Navajo Canyon and out across the open llanos of the Piedra Lumbre, the last lap of their twelve-hundred-mile journey. Many caravans spent their last night out on the grasslands rimmed by the Cliffs of Shining Stone. We can imagine that a few frisky stallions and their mares stole away from the herd that last night along the cottonwood bosque of the Rio Chama and galloped away from the tired herders out under the stars glimmering over the Piedra Lumbre. By the turn of the twentieth century there was a substantial and often unruly herd of wild horses roaming the Piedra Lumbre basin and Chama Valley. Surely there was much California blood in their equine stock.

6

DISENCHANTMENT AND DISINHERITANCE

J ust as the nomadic tribes had pressured the Pueblo people to depart the Piedra Lumbre and Chama Valley, so now were the Hispanic "newcomers" slowly forcing the Navajos and Utes out of the same region. But the native tribes would not give up their traditional lands until decades of fighting had transpired, and many lives would be lost before the Piedra Lumbre and all of northern New Mexico could be considered Hispanic domain.

The opening to settlement of the region between the Piedra Lumbre and the lands of the Tierra Amarilla in the 1830s and '40s had brought Hispanic settlers deep into Ute territory. This threat to their native province so enraged the Utes that by 1844 they were engaged in a full-scale war against the Hispanic colonists and the Mexican government that sanctioned their presence in Ute country.

In the 1840s the Utes, like their enemies the Navajos, focused their hostilities upon the Abiquiu settlements, ambushing ranchers and farmers in the Chama River Valley and raiding *puestos* and sheep camps in the Piedra Lumbre basin. Unlike the Navajos, the reason behind the Utes' anger was territorial, not retaliatory.

On September first of 1844, New Mexican governor Mariano Martínez in Santa Fe was informed that more than one thousand Utes had
made camp on the Piedra Lumbre at the recently abandoned Vega de
Riaño settlement of the Martín family. Ute chieftain Ponicillo had been
escorted into Abiquiu by Captain José Vigil and Lieutenant José María
Chávez, where the Ute leader complained to Colonel Juan Andrés Archuleta about various grievances against several Rio Arriba citizens. The
chief told the Abiquiu officials that on two separate occasions during the
previous winter a company of Hispanic volunteers had, while en route to
Navajo country, attacked Ute camps. During one such attack, seven Utes
had been killed and members of their families, as well as their possessions,
had been carried off by the militia. For compensation—and to avoid war—
Ponicillo asked for ten horses, ten serapes, ten bridles, and the return of
"two small children and two boys," sons of the Utes, presently held by
Mexican citizens.[1]

The details of this meeting and the growing dissatisfaction among
the Utes toward the Mexican government were sent to the governor in
Santa Fe. Unfortunately, Governor Martínez and his staff at the Palace of
the Governors were up to their elbows in committee and council meetings
for the upcoming October festivities planned around Mexican Independence Day. The anxious dispatches from Rio Arriba military commanders
concerning the "ugly mood" of the Utes camping in the mountains and
mesas near the Abiquiu settlements could not have come at a more inconvenient time.

Governor Martínez sent a message to Abiquiu instructing Archuleta, Chávez, and Vigil to hold off the Utes. But the Abiquiu military
commanders promptly informed the governor that this was an impossible
task given that the Ute warriors had already infiltrated the valley and had
managed to halt the fall harvest with their lurking presence near the
settlers' fields. An Abiquiu messenger came into the capital and informed
the governor that the problem could not be solved at Abiquiu and that,
inconvenient as it may be, Chief Panasiyave and his Utes were planning to
march into the capital the very next day.

According to the account left by Governor Martínez, six Ute chiefs
and 108 warriors, all mounted and well armed, arrived in Santa Fe on the
afternoon of September 5. The governor's men gave the Utes a camp

outside of town in which to spend the night. Although they were guarded by Mexican troops, the Ute chiefs and their warriors caused a good deal of uneasiness in the celebration-minded city. The next morning, the Ute delegation entered the plaza and after refusing food and gifts, demanded to see the governor himself.

Inside the Palace of the Governors angry negotiations commenced between the six chiefs, led by Panasiyave, and the governor and his staff. According to the governor, the discussion disintegrated into a verbal attack on himself by Panasiyave and soon after broke out into a physical attack in which the chief struck Governor Martínez on the chest. Pandemonium ensued: "In these moments, I saw myself attacked by all the chieftains, taking up their weapons as had the said Panasiyave, who turned on me with an axe in his hand; fortunately, I was able to hit him with the chair in which I had been seated and with which I knocked him to the floor, at the same time two of my orderlies and other officials, who had arrived by accident, restrained not only the remaining five Indians but also other large numbers who started through the window of the room . . . ending in eight deaths, in spite of everything I could do to stop this tragedy."[2]

The Ute warriors who had accompanied the now slain chiefs into Santa Fe escaped the soldiers on the plaza and rode into the surrounding hills. Their route back to the Ute encampment on the Piedra Lumbre followed the Chama River and took them past settlements whose residents had no idea of the hostilities that had just transpired in Santa Fe. Before a warning could reach Abiquiu officials, the retreating Utes plundered the plaza of Tierra Azul and killed three members of the Vigil family. The plaza of Los Silvestres was also attacked.

When news of the Santa Fe massacre reached the Chama settlements, Miguel F. Quintana, a former alcalde of Abiquiu, with his brother Juan Cristóbal, decided to attempt private peace talks with the Utes. The Quintana brothers had enjoyed a long trade association with various Utes and felt confident that they could negotiate with the tribe. But times had swiftly and irrevocably changed, and the well-wishing brothers, upon reaching the Vega de Riaño camp of the Utes, were both slain.[3]

War with the Utes was now unavoidable. The governor sent men and arms north to Abiquiu, Ojo Caliente, and El Rito on the northwestern frontier, and to Taos and Las Vegas to the north and northeast. Abiquiu, where as many as three thousand Utes were gathering on the Piedra Lumbre, was deemed the most vulnerable and therefore granted the most troops and the services of a cannon which, like most of the Mexican firearms, was "mostly useless, requiring the constant attention of a gunsmith."[4]

We can imagine that Mexican Independence Day came and went with few demonstrations of patriotic feeling in the communities of Abiquiu, where the Ute raids continued sporadically throughout the winter of 1844–45. Lieutenant José María Chávez and a militia of volunteers began their own campaign against the Utes. The lieutenant told the governor his men would track the tribe throughout northern New Mexico and, if necessary, follow the Utes into the Arkansas River region in Colorado, territory claimed by the United States.[5]

During the years that Mexico claimed New Mexico, many Abiqueños, tired of the Indian-settler battles, began looking for homelands with calmer pastures. In or about the year of 1830, Julián and Mariano Chávez, younger brothers to José María, departed for California. The Chávez brothers became among the first individuals to reach California using what was called the southern Gila River route.

While their brother José María rose to prominence as an Indian fighter in northern New Mexico, and later as a brevet general in the Union Army during the Civil War, the younger Chávez brothers acquired land along the Los Angeles River and built prosperous ranches. Soon after, Julián entered Los Angeles politics: he was interim mayor of Los Angeles in 1838, was later elected to the city council, served as Los Angeles water commissioner in 1846, and was a member of the first Los Angeles county board of supervisors. The lands upon which Julián Chávez settled became known in modern times as Chavez Ravine, and the prosperous rancho once home to the Chávez family from the faraway frontier village of Abiquiu became the site upon which Dodger Stadium was built.

The ceaseless Ute raids of the 1840s broke the resolve of even the hardiest, time-tested *pobladores*. Although there continued to be seasonal use of the Piedra Lumbre llanos, those who dared place herds beyond the help of the militia at Abiquiu were playing dangerous odds. Martín Serrano descendants continued to keep sheep, goats, and horses on the Piedra Lumbre pastures until 1849, but in the spring of that year, the Utes "committed depredations there and they killed six or seven men and drove off all the stock."[6]

Two great-grandsons of Pedro Martín Serrano witnessed this Ute ambush that at least temporarily ended their family's use of the Piedra Lumbre. Aniceto Martínez, fifteen, and his nine-year-old brother, Juan, were tending their family's herds near the Rio Puerco, six or seven miles across the basin from their father's ranch, when the Utes struck their camp. The boys watched as eight herders were killed, including two young neighbors, the Moya boys. Miraculously, the Martínez brothers escaped both death and capture: "I do not remember the year," an elderly Aniceto recalled in 1893, "I left with my blanket on my shoulder and went home."[7]

In the 1840s, Aniceto's uncle, Santiago Martín, and many other New Mexicans, including more Martíns from the Piedra Lumbre, left the New Mexican frontier for California's sunshine and fertile valleys, and for that territory's distance from the Utes and Navajos. Ironically, Californians welcomed immigrants like the Chávezes and the Martíns because of their reputations as Indian fighters. Although California seemed a friendlier place than northern New Mexico, the territory of California was still striving to solve its own Indian problems and looked to New Mexican immigrants for military leadership.

Some of these California-bound immigrant caravans were led by Anglo Americans who departed the territory when troubles began with Mexican authorities, especially in view of Mexico's growing problems with Americans in Texas. One such 1841 settler party, led by William Workman and John Rowland, departed Santa Fe for Abiquiu, where its members purchased one hundred and fifty head of sheep and also hired native *borregueros* to drive the herds across the mountains and the desert to California.

Genízaro Manuel Lorenzo Trujillo, a Comanche and resident of Abiquiu Pueblo, wanted to take his family to a better life in California. Isaac L. Given, an engineer on the Workman-Rowland caravan, agreed to hire Trujillo: "I remember contracting with an able-bodied and active man, some forty years of age, agreeing to pay him all he asked—an advance of two dollars and giving him, after reaching California, a hat, a shirt and a pair of shoes; the negociation [sic], which was closed on the spot, occupied less time than the writing of this paragraph."[8]

Trujillo and his wife, Maria Dolores Archuleta, with their seven children walked many miles each day in their moccasined feet in order to spare the animals. Engineer Given developed a great respect and fondness for the Genízaro and his family from Abiquiu: "I learned, from a conversation with him, that he had been a soldier in Santa Anna's Army, in the invasion of Texas, and had been taken prisoner in the battle of San Jacinto, and taken to New Orleans from whence he had worked his way up the Mississippi and crossed the country to Santa Fe. He proved faithful and trustworthy, and upon reaching California, we parted with mutual regrets."[9]

Upon reaching Los Angeles in early November, the group disbanded, most to look for suitable lands to build homes, and to raise herds and crops. Trujillo liked what he found in California and wanted other Abiquiu friends to share this beautiful, fertile land. Many other Chama Valley folks, some led by Trujillo himself, crossed the desert Southwest in the next decade, including, in 1850, members of the Moya family who had lost young sons in the Ute raid on the Martíns' Piedra Lumbre camp the year before.[10]

In 1846, Trujillo and other former Abiqueños moved up the Santa Ana river and founded two more communities, Agua Mansa ("gentle water") and San Salvador, on opposite banks of the river near present-day Riverside. Trujillo and other Abiqueños lent their seasoned services to the local militia that defended the community against marauding Indians. On one occasion, Trujillo saved the life of Benjamin Wilson, a fellow settler and neighbor: when Wilson was shot with a poisoned arrow Trujillo sucked the venom from the wound, a skill he may have learned as a child among his first people, the Comanches.[11]

The citizens of New Mexico, always a step behind the events of the world beyond their territory's borders, did not learn that Mexico had gone to war with the United States until reports reached Santa Fe in the summer of 1846 that U.S. troops were marching their direction and would soon be upon the colony. New Mexicans knew that relations between the two countries had ended with the U.S. annexation of Texas in March of 1845. But they did not know that a minor skirmish on the Rio Grande in April of 1846 had finally escalated into full-fledged war between Mexico and its ever-encroaching, Manifest Destiny–pressing neighbor, the United States. War was declared in May, but General Stephen Watts Kearny and his Army of the West were upon New Mexico, and the U.S. flag raised and fluttering over the Palace of the Governors in Santa Fe, before New Mexicans could effectively rally any defenses.

The relatively effortless U.S. entrance into New Mexico was partially due to Mexico's inability over the last two and a half decades to protect New Mexicans from the incursions of the nomadic tribes. Long before the Americans' arrival, the instability of the Mexican government, along with its failure to integrate or boost New Mexico's economy, caused territorial politicians to discuss the creation of an independent New Mexico.

In the early 1840s, in an effort to attract colonists and investors, Governor Armijo had opened unprecedented amounts of New Mexico's land to private development. Among those allowed to obtain new land grants were naturalized Mexican citizens such as traders Ceran St. Vrain and Charles Beaubien of Taos. Although Armijo was careful to give land grants only to known and "trusted" foreigners, most of whom had New Mexican business partners, he could not control their subsequent resale of land. Although some of these land grants were disputed and even revoked by Mexico, the door to American influence in and infiltration of New Mexico had been opened.

One of those alarmed by the increasing Anglo American power and land ownership in New Mexico was former Abiqueño Padre Antonio José Martínez of Taos. Padre Martínez was an opinionated and magnetic leader, highly educated and greatly concerned with the health and happiness of New Mexico and its people, both Hispanic and Indian. Although Padre Martínez served as priest at Abiquiu only from May until September of 1826, his interest in the isolated, often uneducated settlers like those in his native Chama Valley directed much of his life's work.[12]

In the mid 1800s, the rapid infiltration of Anglo American politics and ideas in northern New Mexico sparked the already independent-minded, isolated villages to consciously seek ways to preserve their cultural identity and heritage. Although Padre Martinez's exact involvement with the lay religious organization the Cofradía de Nuestro Padre Jesús Nazareno (Confraternity of Our Father, Jesus the Nazarene)—commonly called Los Penitentes ("the penitent ones")—of New Mexico is not known, it is generally believed that the influential and outspoken priest was supportive of the Cofradía, which was well established in Abiquiu and other remote villages by the 1820s. Abiquiu was already a Penitente community, but American occupation intensified the leadership of the Hermanos ("brothers") in the community.

Since the late 1700s, when rural New Mexico had only a handful of Franciscan friars attempting to serve missions scattered far and wide on the frontier, isolated villages like Abiquiu had witnessed the beginnings of a folk religion. Abiquiu's first Penitente *morada* (meeting place), Morada del Alto, was built on a hill to the east of the pueblo by 1820; a morada was also erected of red adobes at Los Silvestres on the Chama River northwest of the pueblo sometime before the mid 1800s; and a third morada, Morada del Moque (or Moqui), was built before 1900 south of the Abiquiu plaza in the section of the pueblo built by the village's first Hopi residents.[13]

Although most accounts of the Penitentes have centered on the self-flagellation, cross-bearing, bloodletting, and other extreme rituals practiced by some of the Hermanos during Lent, the Penitentes of Abiquiu and other frontier communities were primarily a group of Hispanic men whose purpose was to strengthen and assist their neighbors and communities: physically, spiritually, and eventually politically. The Penitentes' duties and services included *rosarios* (rosary services), visits to the sick and infirmed of their communities, help to a neighbor in time of a family death or illness, the singing of funereal chants or *alabados,* and grave digging and even outright financial aid. During Lent, they observed the Passion and death of Jesus, and during Holy Week the Hermanos had numerous prayer meetings.

Church officials in New Mexico condemned the practices of the Penitentes as early as 1817, at which time most Penitentes organizations withdrew into secrecy. Padre Martínez wrote a defense of the Penitentes in the 1830s (some three hundred Hermanos attended the priest's Taos funeral in 1867), and by 1856, Bishop Lamy had recognized and signed an official rule book for the Hermanos. During the decades of extreme isola-tion of the late Spanish colonial and Mexican periods, and throughout the turbulent first years of American occupation, in secret and in public, the Penitentes of New Mexico fought to preserve and promote traditional Hispanic village beliefs.[14]

In spite of such opposition to foreign landowners by Padre Martínez and other native leaders, there was a steadily growing sense of familiarity and even comradery between the American traders and trappers and their New Mexican neighbors and business partners. Traders like Ceran St. Vrain, with offices and trading posts in remote towns like Abiquiu, be-came part of the communities they lived and did their business in, often marrying daughters of their adopted Hispanic communities. This physi-cal, emotional, and cultural infiltration of New Mexico by American frontiersmen made the region extremely vulnerable to American occupa-tion: "To what extent the presence of American traders and trappers in New Mexico for the past quarter century facilitated the Americans' ini-tially 'bloodless conquest' of the area may never be determined. Their contribution, however, as a cultural advance guard for American manifest destiny should not be overlooked."[15]

Although Mexican forces in California attempted to resist the United States, in New Mexico Governor Manuel Armijo, deeming the situation hopeless, abandoned all plans for a defense. Armijo's choice enabled U.S. troops to occupy New Mexico without bloodshed. But like Oñate and de Vargas, who also accomplished "bloodless conquests" of the same land, the U.S. army soon encountered resistance and bloody confrontation with the local populace following Kearny's uncontested raising of the U.S. flag, first over Las Vegas, New Mexico, and again in Santa Fe at the Palace of the Governors.

Ironically, it was in the Taos valley, where the largest concentration of American traders and trappers had married local women and set up homes, that the bloodiest rebellion against the American occupation oc-curred. On January 19, several hours before sunrise, Governor Charles Bent was scalped and killed by Hispanos and their Taos Pueblo allies. American sympathizers led by St. Vrain rode from Santa Fe to avenge the deaths of Bent and other Anglo foreigners killed that same day. The subsequent siege on Taos Pueblo, in which the insurgents later took refuge, did not end until 150 Indians had died at the pueblo, and the old adobe walls of the church and the pueblo had been greatly battered.

Most New Mexicans were not in a position to gather behind a revolution against the United States. Pobladores like those in the Abiquiu settlements struggled daily to simply stay alive in the face of Navajo and Ute hostilities. And among the New Mexican settlers there was even a small hope that the Americans would give them the military protection they had always needed. This hope quickly died, however, as the U.S. military proved to be as baffled by Native American raid and fade tactics on the frontier as every other occupying army before them.

In the first decade of American occupation, Abiquiu and the Piedra Lumbre were frequently the designated locales for U.S. treaties, negotiations, and confrontations with three nomadic tribes who still held various claims to the region of Shining Stone: the Navajos, the Utes, and the most recent native claimants, the Jicarilla Apaches. Abiquiu played the same role for the U.S. military as it had for the Spanish and Mexican—as a key strategic outpost from which to stage operations into Indian country.

Kearny's campaign against the Navajos began just one month after his arrival in Santa Fe. Major William Gilpin marched 185 men up the Chama River to Abiquiu. Gilpin, who later became governor of Colorado, would be only the first of many U.S. military tacticians, officers, Indian agents, governors, and other territorial dignitaries who would ride up the Chama River to the old Pueblo of Abiquiu as part of the American attempt to solve New Mexico's "Indian problem."

In 1846, the population of the Abiquiu settlements totaled 1,565.[16] By 1850, the Abiquiu village population included a resident U.S. garrison, D Company of the 2nd Regiment of Dragoons, under Captain and Brevet Major L. P. Graham. Forty-eight men and thirty-six horses lived in quarters rented from the pueblo for $280 per month.[17]

The Abiquiu Hispanic volunteer militia, bolstered by Pueblo auxiliaries, joined the U.S. troops' forays into Indian country. In spite of their military support, there was a nagging suspicion among the Americans that the community was not wholly behind the United States' cause.

Abiquiu in the 1850s was not a typical New Mexican settlement, and Anglo Americans did not completely understand its complex Hispanic–Native American heritage and the pueblo residents' trade relationships with the Utes. One American observer wrote: "It [Abiquiu] stands next to Taos in point of magnitude and importance in the matter of townships in the north of New Mexico. The scenery about this settlement is very attractive, and, as it lies on the border of the Utah Indian country, it is frequently visited by these Indians. The neighbors of the Utahs, the Navajoes, occasionally make their appearance in the town. The Mexicans of Abiquiu, from their continued intercourse with bands of the Utah Indians, are more or less linked in with them; and, in time of war, the Americans can place but little confidence in the inhabitants of Abiquiu on this account."[18]

American soldiers claimed that New Mexican militiamen, in a manner mirroring Native American warriors, often took scalps from fallen foes.[19] Whether they did or not, it is obvious that the early Anglo Americans saw northern New Mexicans as a breed apart, uncertain if the people of a village like Abiquiu were Native American or Mexican American in allegiance and custom. The Americans' mistake was their insistence on definitive boundaries: Abiquiu straddled frontiers, with only a vague and often indecipherable borderline between "us" and "them."

Although the boundary between Abiqueños and Native Americans appeared vague to the Anglo American military, the line was firmly and clearly drawn between the two groups themselves. The volunteer militia of the Abiquiu valley enthusiastically joined U.S. soldiers in raids upon Navajo camps in the 1850s and '60s. This brought the Navajos' wrathful revenge onto the Abiquiu settlements, which in turn furthered the valley's need for armed protection. Even the permanent garrison of U.S. soldiers did not deter Navajo attack nor dampen the tribe's boldness. Ranching on the Piedra Lumbre and up in the sierras of the Polvedera in the 1840s and '50s was for the most part completely halted by Indian raids.

Indian agent James S. Calhoun, later New Mexico Territory's first civil governor, had the thankless, basically futile task of "governing" forty thousand Native Americans. The Pueblos were perceived by the United States to be an industrious, peace-loving people and were granted full citizenship under Mexican and hence U.S. law. But the Apaches, Navajos, and Utes were considered "wild" robbers and murderers who had to be chastised and contained if the United States was to ever "civilize" the territory.

In December of 1849, Calhoun signed the first peace treaty between the United States and the Ute tribe in Abiquiu. At that time, the United States estimated there were between four and five thousand Utes living in northwestern New Mexico. The United States planned to govern the Utes and other nomadic tribes from frontier Indian agencies and eventually to coerce them onto reservations.

In 1850, the U.S. government opened an agency for the Utes at Taos. This agency was placed under Christopher "Kit" Carson in 1853. It was widely understood that the Ute tribe still considered Abiquiu to be part of their ancestral territory, and a second Ute agency was established at Abiquiu in 1854. Abiquiu served Capote and some Weeminuche Utes until 1877. There were additional U.S. Indian agencies established at Tierra Amarilla and at Cimarron on the east side of the mountains from Taos. But Abiquiu remained the favored locale for those Southern Utes who resisted the U.S. government's efforts to move their camps out of the Piedra Lumbre basin.

In spite of the presence of U.S. soldiers, illegal trade with the Utes continued in the Chama Valley. The U.S. authorities suspected Abiquiu merchants were supplying the Utes with ammunition and guns but were unable to stop the trade.[20] The Utes who made camp in one hundred lodges on the Piedra Lumbre in the 1850s were at peace with the Hispanics and even Anglo Americans residing in the Abiquiu settlements, although they did go to war against other nomadic tribes, and there was regular but petty pilfering of the valley livestock herds.

The cultural balance of the valley was temporarily tilted in the 1850s with the arrival on the Piedra Lumbre of the Jicarilla Apaches. The Jicarillas (named the *apaches de la xicarilla*—little basketmakers—by the Spanish) were historically connected to the country east of the Rio Grande. Their sacred ground encompassed the region bordered by the Arkansas River in southeastern Colorado, the northeastern plains drained by the tributaries of the Canadian River, the flatlands of the Pecos River Valley, and the lands northwest of the Rio Grande in the Chama River Valley. This country, deemed to be "near the center of the earth," included Flint Mountain, Cerro Pedernal, whose angular profile figured in their Creation Myth.

The Jicarilla Apaches were divided into two distinct branches: the Olleros, the mountain people, and the Llaneros, the plains people. The Olleros began hunting and camping in the Ute territory of the San Juan Mountains in the late 1840s. By 1850, there were bands of Jicarillas led by Chief Francisco Chacón encamped throughout the Chama Valley as far south as the Piedra Lumbre basin.

The Utes and the Jicarillas were allied against the Comanches in the mid 1700s, and in 1852, in an alliance with the Navajos, the two tribes went to war against the Kiowas and the Arapahos on the Great Plains. But this did not make the Utes comfortable with the Jicarillas' use of their ancestral territory. While the Hispanos periodically grumbled about the Utes' continued use of the Piedra Lumbre, the Utes verbally protested the Jicarillas' new camps along the Rio Puerco on the southern end of the Piedra Lumbre basin near present-day Coyote.

General Kearny met with leaders of the Jicarilla Apaches at Abiquiu Pueblo in the early fall of 1846. Kearny urged them to become farmers and to remain peaceful with the United States. In 1851, after skirmishes between the United States and the Jicarillas in various parts of New Mexico, a peace treaty was signed by Governor Calhoun and Colonel John M. Munroe for the United States and by chiefs Chacón, Lobo Blanco, Huero Mundo, and Josecito Largo for the Jicarillas. The Jicarillas agreed to submit to the United States and to cease all depredations, to cultivate the soil within confined territorial limits, and to relinquish all captives. In return, the U.S. government promised annuities, farm equipment, and other gratuities.[21]

In 1853, on lands along the Rio Puerco on the southern end of the Piedra Lumbre basin, Jicarillas under Chief Chacón irrigated and planted one hundred and thirty acres of corn and wheat. Although the lands they were farming were beyond the granted lands of the Piedra Lumbre, the Hispanic settlers, nervous about the Apache presence on the Piedra Lumbre, openly objected to the Jicarillas' sanctioned use of the basin. And even though this land had been used for centuries by the Utes, New Mexicans stubbornly considered all lands surrounding the Piedra Lumbre Grant to be Hispanic domain.

The first Jicarilla grain harvest in the fall of 1853 was a failure because of drought. The Abiquiu Indian agent, Edmund A. Graves, told Governor William Carr Lane that the Piedra Lumbre Jicarillas would remain peaceful if they received food and supplies from the government. But when the distribution of supplies to the tribe was suspended by a new budget-trimming administration in Santa Fe, the Jicarillas, without crops to harvest and now without adequate time to hunt and gather food supplies for the upcoming winter, began raiding Chama Valley ranches.

War against Huero Mundo's and Francisco Chacón's tribes broke out in the early spring of 1854, when the Rio Puerco Jicarillas, accused of livestock theft in the Chama Valley, abandoned their Piedra Lumbre camp and eluded U.S. troops in the snow-packed Canjilon Mountains north of the basin. At this same time, Kit Carson guided Lieutenant Colonel Philip St. George Cooke and two hundred men into the wild and largely un-known northern mountains in pursuit of the Apaches believed to have been involved in recent battles at Red River and at Embudo Mountain. Although Carson aided Cooke's locating and punishing of the Jicarillas, he later confessed sympathy for their plight, stating that the Jicarillas were driven to desperate means by the actions of the U.S. troops. Carson also believed that Chacón of the Piedra Lumbre, chief of the largest number of Ollero lodges, sincerely wanted a lasting peace with the United States, and that this chief encouraged his people to remain neutral in the war waged by other Apache tribes against the Americans in New Mexico.

Carson and Cooke tracked the Jicarillas through the difficult, snow-covered canyon and mountain country west of Taos. They crossed the Rio Grande gorge and followed tracks southwest to the Rio Caliente, the tributary of the Chama northeast of Abiquiu, where the soldiers found Chacón's Apache camp in a steep ravine. Although Chacón and his people were never actually connected with the problems near Fort Union, Cooke and his troops attacked their camp anyway. Later, Kit Carson was told by the Utes that four or five Jicarillas had been killed before Chacón's band escaped Cooke's soldiers, and that seventeen Apache women and children were missing. Some were taken captive, but many perished in the deep mountain snow. One Jicarilla woman tried to escape through the Rio Caliente but drowned in the freezing waters. Before she died, she handed her infant baby to one of the American soldiers, who gave the child to a family in Taos.[22]

By the end of summer, 1854, after months of hiding in the San Juan Mountains, Chacón and his band of exhausted, hungry Jicarillas asked for peace in Santa Fe. A truce with the United States was established with the tribe, and by the fall they had returned to their lodges, of which there were about one hundred along the Rio Puerco on the Piedra Lumbre.

Abiquiu Indian agent Lorenzo Labadie wrote his superiors of the demoralized state of the Jicarillas. Their ancestral lands were all but taken, wild game was diminishing, and they had had little success in farming. Kit Carson found the same demoralization among the Utes and Jicarillas at Taos. Both tribes were becoming increasingly dependent upon the bimonthly rations of food and the semiannual government annuities of clothing, blankets, shoes, and household and farming items. Labadie in Abiquiu and Carson in Taos knew that the Utes and the Jicarilla Apaches needed permanent homes and mutually agreeable treaties with the U.S. government in Washington.

Such a treaty was attempted on the Piedra Lumbre in the late summer of 1855. Governor David Meriwether asked Kit Carson to attend a meeting with both the Jicarilla Apaches and the Moache Utes "at the forks of the Chama River" above Abiquiu on the 10th of September.[23] This location would place the Carson-Meriwether-Jicarilla-Ute conference on the southwest section of the Piedra Lumbre where the Rio Puerco collides with the Chama.

The meeting is significant because Meriwether signed a treaty (never ratified by Congress) that could have been a valuable step toward resolution of the Jicarilla and Ute situation in New Mexico. But the meeting is also significant because during their two days together on the Piedra Lumbre, Carson managed to insult and disobey the governor to such a degree that he was placed under armed guard in the American camp and served with written charges that included insubordination and cowardice. Carson was also privy to an elaborate trick played on both the U.S. soldiers and the Ute and Apache warriors, during which they believed they were about to be attacked by Kiowas.

Upon his return to Santa Fe, Meriwether pressed charges against Carson that included disobedience of orders, insubordination, disrespectful conduct toward a superior officer, and cowardice. But before the affidavits were sent to Washington, Judge Joab Houghton, a friend and admirer of Kit's, and an influential man in Santa Fe, visited Meriwether and convinced him that Carson was fully aware of his wrongdoing and had expressed deep remorse for his behavior on the Piedra Lumbre.[24]

The treaty signed by Meriwether and the Ute and Jicarilla chiefs on the Piedra Lumbre on September 10, 1855, promised regular subsidies and a reservation for each tribe. The reasons behind this treaty's non-ratification by Congress included extreme opposition by local Hispanic landowners and ranchers who did not want lands near Abiquiu or Coyote, or north and west alongside the Piedra Lumbre, given to the Jicarillas or to the Utes.

In the following decades, both the Utes and the Jicarillas, while waiting for the United States to decide on lands for their tribes, became almost wholly dependent on government subsidies for survival. In 1867, Abiquiu Indian agent William Arny was feeding over one thousand Utes and Jicarillas from his pueblo plaza office. While the Jicarillas lived a semi-sedentary existence and cultivated corn and wheat on rented lands along the Rio del Oso and on Ojo Caliente Creek,[25] the Utes continued to roam northern New Mexico and southern Colorado. The Jicarillas also made efforts to support themselves with wage labor at the surrounding settlements, and by making and selling their baskets and micaceous pottery.

Various government attempts to move the Jicarillas always failed, with large numbers of the tribe wandering back to Abiquiu from the new agency established in 1861 at Cimarron, New Mexico, and from the Mescalero Apache Reservation in southern New Mexico to which they were forcibly marched in 1883. By the late 1800s, the only home most Jicarillas had ever known was the Abiquiu–Ojo Caliente valley, the southern Piedra Lumbre basin, and the mountain lands that reached north to Tierra Amarilla. In 1879, agent James H. Roberts wrote: "They [the Jicarillas] do not want to go any great distance from where the agency is now located, having been born here, having buried their dead here. Knowing the country as they do, they most decidedly object to being moved away from this country."[26]

The Utes were moved out of New Mexico to a reservation in Colorado in 1878. The Jicarillas did not receive a permanent home until 1886 when the United States established the Jicarilla reservation west over the mountains from the Piedra Lumbre on lands that stretched north to Dulce, New Mexico. Thus ended the historic if not the emotional affiliation of two more tribes of native peoples with Abiquiu and the valley of the Piedra Lumbre.

Negotiations between the Jicarilla Apache and the Southern Ute tribes and the U.S. government in the 1860s and '70s were greatly facilitated by two tribal leaders: Ouray (or U-ray, "arrow"), chief of the Uncompaghre Utes; and Huero Mundo, who succeeded his father-in-law, Francisco Chacón, as leader of the Olleros band of the Jicarillas. Ouray and Mundo are important and prominent figures in the history of their people. They are also important, if not recognized, figures in the story of the Chama Valley and the Piedra Lumbre, as they were half brothers whose ancestry reflected the complex cultural bloodlines of the Abiquiu region in the mid 1800s: their father, Guera Murah, was a Jicarilla Apache who was captured by the Utes as a child. Huero Mundo never lived in Abiquiu, but Ouray's mother was a semi-Christianized Tabeguache Ute Genízaro[27] who lived part of her life in the Pueblo of Abiquiu, where Ouray was most likely born in November of 1833.

J. M. Manzanares, an Abiqueño interviewed in the 1930s, remembered when Ouray and his Genízaro brother, Quenche, hunted deer and game, herded sheep, and hauled piñon wood throughout the Chama River Valley. According to Manzanares, Ouray's parents "didn't like to fight the Mexicans, so stayed with them"[28] and became respected and well-known members of the pueblo. "Ouray worked for my grandfather and Martínez at Abiquiu," Manzanares remembered. "He hoed and also planted grain. As a young man Ouray dressed like the Mexicans. He could speak Spanish, Ute, Apache, and later learned English."[29]

While Ouray was still a young boy, his mother died. With their father, Ouray and Quenche left the pueblo and went to live among the Ute tribe, where they learned their father's adopted people's ways and language. Ouray became a familiar face around Taos, where he worked at a local hacienda and may have received some schooling at a Catholic mission.

Ouray's role as chief negotiator for the Utes officially began in 1863. His father, Guera Murah, upon returning to the Utes, became a chief; Ouray surely stood beside his father at the treaty signed between the United States and the Utes at Abiquiu in December of 1849.[30] Upon Guera Murah's death, Ouray became chief.

Ouray's skills as an ambassador for the Southern Utes were strengthened by his multicultural upbringing. The first of Ouray's many trips east was to Washington in 1868, where, with Kit Carson, he signed a Ute-U.S. treaty. Ouray was often accompanied on these cross-country trips by his half-brother, Chief Huero Mundo of the Jicarillas. "Ouray had become a very unique Ute with a keen awareness and understanding of the Spanish, Ute and Anglo cultures which were all merging during his lifetime in the Southwest. . . . He was already armed to do verbal battle with the whites. His grasp of the political, social and military situations of the time was far greater than those of his fellow Indian."[31]

In the 1870s, in recognition for his years of negotiations that resulted in a cessation of hostilities between the Utes and the Americans, the U.S. government gave Ouray a one thousand dollar a year annuity and a house and farm in Colorado. Ouray died in Colorado of Brights disease in 1880 and was buried south of Ignacio, Colorado, where there is a memorial in his honor. A second memorial to Ouray was erected in Montrose, at Ouray Memorial Park. The Abiquiu-born Genízaro/Ute chief is also honored by the Colorado community that took his name, the mountain resort of Ouray.

Part Two

THE GOOD COUNTRY

7

A LAND OF BEAUTY AND EVIL

Geneneral Kearny and the Army of the West's invasion of New Mexico Territory in 1846 was followed by a less defined although equally impacting invasion of the territory by American land and resource speculators in the latter half of the nineteenth century. The arrival of the railroad in the 1870s ended forever New Mexico's centuries-old isolation. The sheep and timber industries boomed, and cash-carrying, Manifest Destiny–promoting, Anglo opportunists poured into hitherto isolated villages of New Mexico seeking to exploit the region's land and mineral rights.

The United States' attempts to validate individual and community land grant claims in New Mexico instigated a collision of legal systems and cultural values: an enormous chasm existed between the Anglo and Hispano views of land that was to ultimately prove uncrossable, especially since the U.S. government did little or nothing to bridge that gulf when it threatened to derail Anglo American capitalistic dreams in New Mexico. Land in the Anglo world was a commodity bought and sold like timber or livestock. Anglo American property laws packaged land into parcels plotted on paper in rigid, precise, mathematically divided and surveyed portions. In the Spanish and later Mexican occupation of New Mexico, land was legally described by physical landmarks and characteristics.

Spanish and Mexican grant boundaries were relational at best: borders were defined by the end of a neighbor's land, or the beginning of a mesa or a cliff face, such as the "red stony hills" and the boundary of the lands of Gerónimo Martín Serrano that marked the east and south borders of the Piedra Lumbre. The boundaries of a New Mexican land grant could be as meandering as the "trail to Navajo" which marked the Abiquiu Grant's southern border, and as fluid and changeable as the course of the Chama River that marked the pueblo's northern boundary. The most precise land boundaries under Spanish and later Mexican law were pastures and woodlands measured by metes and bounds. Some boundaries were measured by a *cordel* (a measuring cord of 9.15 yards) or in varas (thirty-three-inch cords used primarily to allocate cultivated lands and agricultural plots).

Under the Treaty of Guadalupe Hidalgo, by which Mexico ceded its northern territories to the United States in 1848, the United States agreed to recognize and respect all property belonging to former Mexican citizens in the Territory of New Mexico. This included all valid titles to both Spanish and Mexican land grants. To sort the valid from the invalid grants, Congress established the Surveyor General's Office of the Territory of New Mexico in 1854 to ascertain "the origin, nature, character, and extent of all claims to lands under the laws, usages, and customs of Spain and Mexico."[1] The process established by Congress dictated that each land claim would be examined by the Surveyor General's Office, which would then submit recommendations either for confirmation or for rejection to Congress. Confirmed claims would be surveyed out of the public domain and given a patent.

It sounded reasonable enough on American legal paper, and Congress expected the establishing of clear titles in New Mexico to proceed in an orderly and civilized manner. But there were flaws in the system from the outset: the surveyor general's primary task was to separate the public domain from the private before surveying—essentially to determine what lands in New Mexico belonged to the U.S. government. Validation of individual and community land grants was a secondary concern. Furthermore, the underfunded and understaffed Surveyor General's Office never had clear legal guidelines that would ensure New Mexico's smooth transition from the Spanish/Mexican to the U.S. legal system. The government in Washington seemed unaware that New Mexicans had been living under Spanish political and social traditions for hundreds of years. The U.S. legal system was as foreign to most New Mexicans as the English language. And there was appalling disinterest among territorial authorities to explain the U.S. legal system, and its implications to New Mexicans, in English or Spanish.

Sorting private lands from the public domain was further aggravated by the United States' assumption that the common lands, the *ejido*, where New Mexico's villagers had cut wood, grazed livestock, hunted, and gathered food and building materials—held and shared by members of a community for generations in towns such as Abiquiu—were, in fact, unclaimed public domain. In the latter years of the nineteenth century, millions of acres of the territory's common lands were seized by the United States.

The responsibility of obtaining legal title to private lands rested with native landowners. Those New Mexicans who understood that their grants needed to be validated under U.S. law, and who set about obtaining clear title to their lands, were soon confronted with court costs and filing fees far beyond their economic means. Much-needed legal counsel was obtained only after a landowner agreed to give up a third or more of the very lands he hoped to keep. While there was a shortage of helpful public officials in the Surveyor General's Office, there was no shortage of American lawyers anxious to give legal counsel to those New Mexicans seeking grant confirmation: much of the best land in New Mexico was held in Spanish and Mexican grants. Securing confirmation of these lands' title, and then receiving at least a portion of these lands in exchange for services rendered, made New Mexico's land problems a very profitable business for land speculators who worked closely with the unscrupulous Anglo lawyers who carried the "double-edged sword of duplicity"[2] in and out of New Mexican courts and communities. New Mexico land speculators in 1887 "hovered over the territory like a pestilence. To a fearful extent they have dominated governors, judges, district attorneys, legislatures, surveyors-general, and the controlling business interests of the people. They have confounded political distinctions and subordinated everything to the greed for land."[3]

Not only were the Spanish-Mexican grant boundaries imprecise and questionable under U.S. law, there was a profound lack of documentation for most New Mexican land transactions. It was not uncommon for New Mexican property to be exchanged in verbal contracts, and even those who did record a change of ownership on paper rarely filed it with anyone resembling an official: "The permissable degree of informality in land transfers was very large compared to the Anglo-American system."[4]

Information regarding Hispanic land usage and ownership was most often handed down with the oral history of a family and a community. Everyone in the community knew of and abided by these oral and familial land transactions. Children understood their family story as much by the land they lived, farmed, or grazed their animals upon as by the names of those who had come and gone across the same land before them. That Pedro Gallego had bought the Arroyo Seco, and then built a house and ranch upon it, which was then passed on to his children, who passed it to their children, was as unquestioned a chapter in the Hispanic story of the Piedra Lumbre as the four seasons that annually passed across the valley.

Foremost in the land speculation-alienation game in New Mexico were the members of the Santa Fe Ring, a group of "ambitious, unscrupulous Anglo lawyers who regarded the confused legal status of the land grants as an ideal opportunity for adding money and land to their personal assets."[5] Aligned personally and professionally with the Surveyor General's Office, their ranks included some of the territory's most influential Anglo politicians: congressional delegates Stephen B. Elkins and Antonio Joseph, and governors Samuel Axtell and L. Bradford Prince. Perhaps the most notorious ring member was Thomas B. Catron, a wealthy and successful Missouri-born lawyer who, by the 1890s, was among the largest individual landowners in the United States, with some two million acres held in his personal estate.

Catron and the Santa Fe Ring were able to secure lands through various "legal" maneuvers: ring lawyers transferred land into their legal possession through manipulation of the already confused title laws. They received partial titles as payment for services rendered in defense of the same land for its native heirs; and Santa Fe Ring members encouraged the territorial government's imposition of new land taxes that forced many cash-poor New Mexicans to sell their ancestral lands. When all else failed, ring lawyers were known to trick grant owners out of their land by telling those who could not read English that their signature or sign on the bottom of a document either assured continued ownership or entitled them to some amount of cash.

The few U.S. laws that New Mexicans might have used to obtain legal title to their lands, such as the Homestead Act of 1862 in which five years' residence on a piece of land or six months' residence and the payment of $1.25 per acre secured ownership, were often not revealed or explained to those who could have benefitted from them.

It was an appalling travesty of justice instigated and perpetuated by sophisticated, well-connected, land-and-money-hungry Anglo lawyers and businessmen. The success of the Santa Fe Ring, however, was further augmented by equally shrewd Hispanic *politicos* and *ricos* who saw which way the financial winds were going to blow across their beloved corners of New Mexico. Rather than be left out of the economic and political profits promised in territorial land and resource speculation, they used their local power and intimate knowledge of land possession and usage to sweep land titles out from under their own people.

By 1891, only 22 of 212 claims had been patented by the Surveyor General's Office, leaving thirty-five million acres of New Mexico's land legally unclaimed.[6] Hoping to move the confirmation process along, Congress dissolved the Surveyor General's Office and established the Court of Private Land Claims in the spring of 1891.

The Town of Abiquiu ultimately secured confirmation of its entire 16,708.16 acres. However, the claims of neighboring villages such as Barranco to the west of the pueblo and the Plaza Blanca and Plaza Colorado north across the Chama River were either outright rejected (Barranco) or reduced in size by the Court of Private Land Claims. That Abiquiu had first been a pueblo for Genízaros and had then undergone several formal, officially sanctioned and recorded resettlements, and that the village had often been used as a military outpost, helped the village establish its grant's authenticity to the Court of Private Land Claims when other legal documentation was absent.

In January of 1883, the son of José María Chávez, José M. C. Cháves, on behalf of himself and the other claimants of the Pueblo of Abiquiu Grant, petitioned the Surveyor General's Office requesting confirmation of their village and common lands. It would take Surveyor General George W. Julian two years to make a recommendation for validation of the grant to Congress. For reasons clear only to those in Washington, Congress did not confirm or patent the Pueblo of Abiquiu Grant. Seven years passed, and in 1892, José M. C. Cháves and Reyes Gonzales, on behalf of the residents of the Pueblo of Abiquiu Grant, filed suit against the United States. The United States had no dispute with the petitioners, and in April of 1894 the grant was confirmed.

Although the 16,547.20 acres surveyed met with villagers' approval, a dispute arose over the exact location of the northern boundary: the government surveyor showed the boundary to be the south bank of the Chama River. But the villagers protested, saying the boundary should be located along the south bank of the Chama River as it ran in 1754. After fifteen years of argument and testimony as to where the Rio Chama's waters actually ran in 1754, the United States overruled the protest of the villagers, approved the survey of 1894, and issued a patent for the Pueblo of Abiquiu in 1909.[7]

The Piedra Lumbre, like other large, undivided, and unsettled stretches of New Mexico's lands, was of great value to territorial land speculators. Although the Piedra Lumbre was not rich in timber or mineral resources and was too arid to ever become an agricultural enterprise, its arid rock and cliff-rimmed basin cut by the picturesque green ribbon of the Rio Chama, with access to northern and western New Mexico, was too large a property for land-hungry businessmen to ignore. In the next decades, and into the twentieth century, although some landowners would be Hispanic, the Piedra Lumbre as a communally shared property would be lost forever.

The first petition filed with the Surveyor General's Office for confirmation of the Piedra Lumbre was made in March of 1872 by Don Pedro's second son (and Padre Gallegos's younger brother), José Pablo Gallegos.[8]

Gallegos, on behalf of himself and the other claimants of the Piedra Lumbre, of which there were many, presented Surveyor General James K. Proudfit with the original *testimonio* of 1766, the official grant documents given to their ancestor Pedro Martín Serrano. Proudfit ruled that the Piedra Lumbre was a valid grant and, in 1877, ordered a preliminary survey. The grant, totaling 48,336.12 acres, was recommended for congressional confirmation. Congress, however, did not accept Proudfit's recommendation, and the Piedra Lumbre Grant was unpatented in 1891 when the Court of Private Land Claims took over the work of the Surveyor General's Office.

A second petition was filed in 1892. This time, the sixteen individuals named as heirs and claimants of the Piedra Lumbre were represented by an attorney, George Hill Howard. Where twenty-five years ago the claimants to the Piedra Lumbre had met no legal opposition concerning their claims to the land of their forefathers, by 1892, a coalition of Anglo and Hispanic businessmen seeking to commercially exploit the Piedra Lumbre had concocted a plan by which they could claim at least a portion of the basin as their own.

Thomas B. Catron, in an alliance with Abiqueños General José María Chávez and Ramon Salazar, a former priest who had given up the church to become a sheep rancher and land baron, had begun buying up the Piedra Lumbre from four individuals they would later allege to be the sole heirs to the grant. Catron and his conspirators simplified the Martín Serrano family tree, pruning its numerous branches to four living relatives. Catron's ring, largely through General Chávez, had then gone about purchasing those four heirs' (who included those Martíns who had left the valley for California in the mid 1800s) interests in the Piedra Lumbre. Catron argued to the Court of Private Land Claims that through these transactions he and his partners had become the sole owners of the entire grant. That the Piedra Lumbre had been used by numerous individuals who, through partible inheritance, were entitled at the very least to graze livestock on the grant, and that the grant's ownership was subsequently shared among them, was completely ignored.

The various and conflicting claims on the Piedra Lumbre were heard by the Court of Private Land Claims in August of 1893. Thomas Catron skillfully denied and devalued the claims made by the resident petitioners represented by Attorney Howard. At that time, although the court did not rule as to who the legal claimants were, it did rule that the Piedra Lumbre Grant was valid. This decision was followed by a suit in the District Court of Rio Arriba County to determine the exact rights of all the claimants of the Piedra Lumbre. It is unlikely that most of the resident claimants of the Piedra Lumbre—ranchers from the villages of Abiquiu, Coyote, and Cañones who had inherited use rights to the grant —knew their rights to the land were under scrutiny. If they did, they were certainly not represented by legal counsel on a political par with, or functioning independently from, Thomas Catron.

The suit commenced on the second day of June in 1894 and ended when the District Court of Rio Arriba gave the northern third of the Piedra Lumbre to those represented by George Hill Howard, which included the descendants of Mariano Martín, Pedro Martín Serrano's grandson; the southern two-thirds of the Piedra Lumbre was handed over to Catron's ring of Anglo and Hispanic businessmen.

The Piedra Lumbre's fifty corners[9] were surveyed in 1897, with a patent issued in July of 1902. Even before it was legally patented, Catron and his associates set about planning the Piedra Lumbre's commercial future. The Chama Improvement Company was organized by Catron, Chávez, and Salazar to guide the Piedra Lumbre's development. Catron was associated with Howard, who owned a substantial amount of the northern third in lieu of his legal representation of various grant claimants, and soon the Chama Improvement Company became the agent for the entire Piedra Lumbre. As early as 1896, a full year before the completed survey, Catron was negotiating with a firm in San Francisco interested in purchasing the grant. This sale fell through, however, and over the next few decades, the Piedra Lumbre was to change hands on a smaller, less devastating scale.

That Catron was able to put the entire grant up for sale was the result of previous court decisions in the territory that permitted one owner of a grant to force the sale of the entire grant. Because it was practically impossible to determine what or which piece of a land might constitute one heir's claim—which might be 37/54ths, or 26/60ths—the courts ruled that sale of an entire grant, and distribution of cash to each legal claimant, was the only viable answer. Even if the other owners did not wish to sell, an individual claimant could force the sale of his fellow claimants' land out from under them.[10]

By the beginning of the twentieth century, Abiquiu and the valley of the Piedra Lumbre looked very much as they had always looked, but the winds of change brought in with the Anglo Americans had begun eroding away many of the valley's oldest internal characteristics. The Arroyo Seco Ranch of the Gallegos family had fallen into Anglo hands in the 1890s, although at least the southern portion of the old ranch was resold to a Gallegos descendant in 1905. The big schemes of Catron's Chama Improvement Company never materialized, and only small-time sheep and cattle ranchers, and the spirits of those who had come and gone before, used the Piedra Lumbre basin.

In 1892, in a narrow canyon wedged between stony hills and the walls of red and yellow cliffs just beyond the Piedra Lumbre's northeast boundary, two brothers built a homestead. The canyon of the Archuleta brothers was already tainted by whispered stories about murder and *brujos:* in the 1860s and '70s, Miguel Gonzales, owner of the valley's largest sheep-ranching enterprise, placed a sheep camp near the canyon's entrance. His shepherds, however, would not stay long in the canyon, saying they heard ghosts quarreling. Apparently, in years past, sheep and cattle ranchers had fought over the canyon's grazing lands and several men had been killed: "Thereafter the canyon became infested with ghosts, especially at night. White ghosts were seen climbing the cliffs and terrible agonizing moans were heard throughout the canyon."[11] In a region already rich in superstition—the local lore of the Piedra Lumbre included tales of a flying cow who heralded not just insanity but also imminent death, and an oft repeated legend of a giant, child-eating snake that emerged from the earth near the red cliffs at sundown—the Archuleta brothers and their homestead beneath the Cliffs of Shining Stone would earn legendary status.

The Archuleta brothers built a rough wood and mud *(jacal)* stockade-style house. There was ample water in the Rito del Yeso, but the Archuletas did not settle here to farm. They chose this hidden canyon with its singular southern entrance and sheer rock walls because of its natural characteristics as a holding and hiding pen for cattle. According to local legend, the Archuleta brothers herded stolen cattle through the mountains by day and the valleys by night to their secluded, natural rock corral in Yeso Canyon. The rustled herd remained in the isolated canyon until a buyer was found and the animals could be furtively driven to their new home.

Around the valley, stories soon abounded of out-of-towners who stopped the night for what they thought was friendly and welcomed lodging at the little homestead in the Rito del Yeso canyon. The trusting visitors never emerged in the morning, and their horses and personal effects were suddenly counted among the Archuletas' tack and livestock.

Joe I. Salazar remembers, "There was a man who had a silver saddle and a real pretty white horse. He got to the homestead real late and they lodged him up for the night. But he never went back out. There were a lot of other people who happened to come here and never got back out: three men, cattle buyers, wanted to buy cattle from the brothers. They stayed the night and never left." A disgruntled ranch manager was rumored to have been beheaded by the brothers in front of witnesses when he expressed his disapproval of their business practices.[12]

The corpses of the Archuleta victims were believed to be at the bottom of the homestead well, or to be scattered, dismembered, under the Cliffs of Shining Stone and in the red sand hills below them. The unholy commotion, real and imagined, at the Rito del Yeso homestead was heard out across the llanos of the Piedra Lumbre and down the Chama River in Abiquiu. The fear of Ute, Navajo, or Comanche attack was long gone, but even seasoned shepherds and ranchers were known to flee their campfires on the Piedra Lumbre without their saddles, gear, even livestock, preferring to leave all they owned behind to the spirits of the basin rather than remain and become one of the same.

The Rito del Yeso homestead was soon given a new name: "They called it Rancho de los Brujos," Joe I. Salazar remembers. "Witch Ranch . . . Ghost Ranch. They say the spirits of the people murdered and buried by the Archuletas never died."

The Archuletas' story was one that could end only in tragedy and self-destruction. And so it did after the younger brother brought home an *olla* (pot) of gold that was payment for cattle he had sold to a Santa Fean.

The younger brother buried the gold near the canyon house, perhaps to hide it from his brother, perhaps simply to keep the damning evidence from law-abiding eyes. But burial of the gold was a fatal mistake: when the older brother, Juan Ignacio, "Nacho," learned of the riches hidden from him and could not secure its location, he killed the younger brother with an ax.

Nacho then threatened to kill his dead brother's wife and promised to feed her child to the hideous rattlesnake Vivarón, when he emerged at sunset, if she did not show him where her dead husband's gold had been buried. Apparently the brother gave his sister-in-law one night to ponder her choices, for she was able to flee the canyon in the dark with her small daughter. The two rode by burro across the dark, spirit-ridden Piedra Lumbre and then down the Chama Valley past Abiquiu to San Juan Pueblo, where they sought refuge with relatives.

The mother and the daughter eventually moved to Utah. Decades passed before the daughter smuggled out under the stars on burro-back returned to search for her father's treasure. The Archuleta daughter was able to find the hill where her father was buried, but years had faded her memory, and the landscape itself was no longer familiar, and she never found the disputed olla. To this day the fabled pot of rustler gold remains, like the bones of the Archuletas' unsuspecting overnight guests, buried without a clue or a marker in the sand of the Ranch of the Witches.[13]

The bewitched llanos of the Piedra Lumbre were bought and sold by various Hispanic and Anglo ranchers in the late 1800s and early 1900s. Sheep camps dotted the basin and mountains, and, excepting the nefarious practices of the Archuleta brothers on the northern rim of the Piedra Lumbre, life was peaceful, if not necessarily very profitable, for the ranchers of the valley.

The *patrones* (owners, bosses) of the northern third of the Piedra Lumbre in the late 1800s and early 1900s were rico Anglos and other outsiders who lived in Santa Fe or Española, and who settled in haciendas along the Chama River north to Abiquiu. However, the southern grasslands of the Piedra Lumbre were purchased at the turn of the twentieth century by a successful sheep rancher, Manuel Salazar, whose family had

come to the Rio Arriba country of New Mexico from Portugal in the
1700s. By the 1920s, Salazar, who lived with his family in an adobe rancho
near Cañones, owned some 30,000 acres of the Piedra Lumbre, upon
which he grazed thousands of sheep.[14]

Anglo cash and capitalism brought a new kind of community *jefe* to the
rural farm and ranch communities of northern New Mexico: the merchant trader. Often backed by money made from large sheep-ranching
operations in the region, most of the first merchants in Abiquiu, Española,
and north in the Tierra Amarilla area were industrious east-of-the-
Mississippi-born Anglos who understood how to use the railroad to im-
port goods not found in New Mexico. The merchants often became community bankers or lenders, as they had the capital to extend credit to local
farmers and ranchers, who paid off their debts after harvest or shearing
time. In bad years, a family's debt at the mercantile might be paid off in
land. Consequently, those with the most successful mercantiles in the
Chama River Valley were soon among the region's largest landowners.

The early mercantile stores of northern New Mexico became the
social and political hub of rural communities. One eastern visitor described the village stores as "a nine days' wonder to me. A happy family of
Mexicans, Indians, Pikes, French Canadians, railroad men, hunters and
prospectors jostled one another always in its hospitable doorway. It was
the club and social reunion of all the environs."[15]

In 1884, Abiquiu was served by three general stores belonging to
three different merchants: Alexander Douglas was a cattle and sheep
breeder, and his store doubled as the village post office for the triweekly
mail delivery; Samuel Eldot of the Eldot family, who had established
several trading posts and general stores in various northern New Mexico
communities, briefly had a store in Abiquiu; and a third general store
belonged to Manuel García. Although Abiquiu's population swelled during the brief gold and silver prospecting flurry of the 1870s, by the 1880s it
had dwindled to only three hundred occupants. The success of several
valley sheep and cattle breeders, including General José María Chávez
and his son, and the Gonzales ranch on the north side of the Chama, must
have assured the village's three merchants of enough business to warrant
their presence in the community.[16]

A Missourian named Henry Grant settled in the Chama River Valley in the 1870s and opened mercantiles in the villages of Abiquiu and El Rito, and at Tres Piedras, a stop on the Chili Line—the Denver and Rio Grande Railroad—in the mountains north of Española. Grant's largest store was the long, portal-shaded adobe building on the ancient Abiquiu plaza. In the late 1800s, the main road up the Chama Valley wound up the northeast corner of Abiquiu mesa and crossed the plaza near the church. Grant's Mercantile became a much anticipated stop for travelers and locals alike, whose horses and mules, wagons and gear-laden burros crowded about the hitching posts in front of the store.[17]

The new cash-demanding society brought to New Mexico by the Anglo Americans meant that many village men in the late 1800s and early 1900s had to leave their homes to find cash-paying jobs. In Abiquiu and the Chama Valley nearly every family lost at least one male, and often several, to the mines and lumber camps of Nevada and Utah, or to the sheep ranches or potato and sugar-beet fields of Colorado. Heads of households were away from home for six months and more each year. Young boys might begin accompanying their fathers and uncles to wage jobs as early as twelve years of age.

Those who remained at home in Abiquiu and its satellite plazas were mostly women, young children, and elderly parents. Together they tended small fields of wheat, beans, chiles, and corn and continued to graze a few head of sheep, cattle, goats, and horses on the pueblo's communal lands. In rural New Mexico, necessity meant the village women were often the master builders. While the men were away, the women of the village maintained the family home, physically and emotionally, building on rooms as the family grew, fixing roofs, and mud plastering the walls and floors every few years. When Anglos began moving into the region and sought skilled laborers to build traditional adobe homes, the women of the villages were as valued for their skills as the men.

In the Abiquiu valley there were several sheep operations that employed local men. The largest of these was begun by Reyes Gonzales, who had come to Abiquiu from Bernalillo in 1853. Before setting up sheep camps in the Chama River Valley near Abiquiu, Gonzales had been a very successful freighter, whose ox-drawn carts carried goods from Denver and Dodge City to the mining camps of Colorado. By the 1890s, Gonzales and his four sons owned extensive parcels of land on both sides of the Chama River below Abiquiu and claimed most of the Plaza Colorado Grant. While their neighbors might own several dozen sheep, the Gonzales family counted 150,000 sheep in fifteen sheep camps by 1900.

Two of Gonzales's sons, Tomas and Miguel, continued their father's sheep operation, and by the late 1920s, Miguel owned sixty percent of the valley's agricultural lands.[18] Villagers leased small agricultural plots from the Gonzales family, but the floodplain below the old pueblo would never return to pueblo ownership again.[19]

The only society that approached Anglo ideals of elegance and sophistication in rural New Mexican villages in the 1890s was found within the homes of the Hispanic and Anglo merchants and in the ranchos of the successful sheep ranchers. Many of the wealthy families in northern New Mexico were related, and an event such as a wedding brought together the Hispanic and Anglo ricos of the region. One such Abiquiu wedding was attended by young Cleofas Martínez, a Martín Serrano descendant, great-granddaughter of José Manuel Martínez of Abiquiu, whose family was granted the Tierra Amarilla Grant in 1832. Cleofas came to Abiquiu in August of 1892 to attend the wedding of her mother's cousin, one of the Gonzales family of Abiquiu.

After their buggy crossed the high waters of the Rio Chama the family arrived at the home of Cleofas's father's cousin, General José María Chávez: "The front saguan was closed by one of those rare, double high doors that had a small door cut out in one of the leaves of the larger one. These doors were built for safety against attacks of the Indians. The large door was kept closed and only the small one used. Although there was no such danger now, the custom was still adhered to for privacy."[20] In the cobblestoned courtyard was an old well from which the servants drew cold water from underground streams. The general's gardens and numerous fruit and nut trees were watered, like all of the gardens in the pueblo, by the spring-fed irrigation ditches that trickled throughout the village.

Brigadier General Chávez was nearly ninety-one years of age and was the reigning patriarch of the old pueblo he had served and protected for nearly a century. To the young Cleofas, the house of elderly José María

Chávez, built in the first decades of the nineteenth century—like the general himself, born in 1801—was the epitome of Territorial New Mexico charm.

When the old bell of the Church of Santo Tomás began to ring, young Cleofas and her family walked the short distance between the general's house and the church to the Gonzales wedding. Although many of the original adobe bricks were reused, this was actually the second church built in the old pueblo, the first having partially burned in the 1880s. We can imagine that Cleofas Martínez sat in the wedding mass and reflected upon her ancestors' struggles behind and beside these same walls: remembering Martín Serranos, Jaramillos, Montoyas, all those *primeros pobladores* who again and again held the village and the valley against the tide of violence brought upon them by Utes, Comanches, Navajos, and Kiowas in the not so long ago past. The old general, and certainly several other elderly men attending the wedding mass that day, had participated in the most turbulent events of nineteenth-century New Mexico. Still, the changes brought to New Mexico at the end of the century did not always sit well with Abiquiu's elder statesman: "Look at these five-foot thick walls and lofty, carved ceiling," Chávez instructed his young cousins when they stood beside the church doors. "These are a monument to our forefathers who built them. I am opposed to having them torn down."[21]

José María Chávez must have heard talk around the pueblo of the need for a new church. The new Santo Tomás would not become a reality until 1934, decades after the general's death in 1902. But the passing of the old church, like that of her cousin, represented to Cleofas Martínez de Jaramillo the end of a great and precious story: "As soon as Don José María passed away, this great monument, which had patiently stood the storms of centuries, blending its contour so well with the landscape around it—like a page torn out of the book of the past—was replaced by a new church."[22]

A relative of Abiquiu padres Martínez and Gallegos, Cleofas blamed the French clergy who had excommunicated her kin for the eventual demise of the old church: "This shows how little the new French priests appreciated the great faith [of] our ancestors who labored to build these great shrines to the honor of God."[23] The French clergy were no longer in power—a German priest served Abiquiu at the time of the pueblo's decision to build a new church—but Cleofas Martínez de Jaramillo correctly recognized how the departure of such a pivotal character as General José María Chávez in the valley's story marked the end of a sometimes glorious, sometimes tragic era that would never return to this ancient pueblo.

8

LAND OF BEGINNINGS AND ENDINGS

In the years preceding and then following World War I a longing developed among Anglo Americans for the simpler times of preindustrial America: "The nation had, some held, grown too fast, had lost something in that process; and now there was a yearning to return to that fast-disappearing life on the soil."[1]

The ancient cultures of the Native American and Hispanic peoples yet thriving on the lands of the twentieth-century Southwest, where "tradition and rootedness were life's primary treasures,"[2] seemed to offer a sanctuary to Anglo American pilgrims who sought a lifestyle beyond the rigid grasp of industrialized, urbanized America. In the first decades of this century, Anglo expatriates from Boston, New York, and Chicago flocked to New Mexico not to conquer or reform, not to "tame" the indigenous cultures and native traditions, but through observation and exposure, to reinvent their own. After centuries as the destination of conquerors, New Mexico became the destination for those who felt they had been conquered by their own societies.

The territory's transition in Anglo eyes from a backward frontier, where only meager remnants of civilization were found, to a pastoral paradise of cultural and personal renewal was a slow one. In the last quarter of the nineteenth century, New Mexico was considered too primitive to warrant statehood, let alone admiration or visitation: "If any geographical division of this country were to be selected for the final jumping off place for the American citizen, it would surely be New Mexico. A man could pass into the mysteries and doubts of his future existence in that region with perfect equanimity. The change could hardly be for the worse. It comprises the tag end of all that is objectionable in an imperfect civilization. The scum and dregs of the American, Spanish, Mexican, and Indian people are there concentrated."[3]

The national press vocally opposed the territory's admission to the union because of the "Romish priesthood"[4] they claimed dominated the territory's government, and they resented New Mexico's Spanish-speaking populace "who haven't troubled to learn English."[5] New Mexicans watched as other, more Anglo, western states were granted statehood—North and South Dakota, Nevada, Montana, Washington, Idaho, Wyoming, Colorado, and Utah were all admitted before 1900. Even the Indian Territory of Oklahoma was granted statehood in 1908, but the territories of Arizona and New Mexico remained outside of the "civilized" fold until 1912.

The current of public opinion in regards to its Southwestern outback took a dramatic change in direction at the turn of the twentieth century. This was due in great measure to a new image New Mexico and all of the Southwest received from those interested in promoting the region to tourists, travelers, and Anglo American and European businessmen. Prominent among these promoters in New Mexico and all of the West was the Santa Fe Railway, whose tracks crossed into New Mexico via Raton Pass in 1879.

New Mexico's isolation had proven a hindrance to development, and its lands were a huge disappointment to timber and mining speculators. But the Santa Fe Railway approached New Mexico's "untamed" natural qualities as an asset and early on realized the tourist potential of those aspects of New Mexico and Arizona that were distinctly non-Anglo: the indigenous peoples and their traditions and cultures. The railroad, with its business partner the Fred Harvey Company, set about creating a traveling environment in which American and European travelers felt cared for and yet sufficiently removed from their everyday existence on the exotic Southwestern frontier.

In conjunction with their promotion of the Southwest as a place, the Harvey Company and the Santa Fe Railway also promoted appreciation for the arts and crafts of the Native American and Hispano peoples. Beginning in 1902, sales shops of indigenous arts and crafts, complete with working Indian and Hispanic craftsmen and women, opened alongside the Santa Fe tracks at depot resorts such as the Alvarado in Albuquerque.

The promotion of Anglo America's appreciation of the Southwest was not simply the cause of the tourist vendors. Immigrant westerners like Charles Lummis, editor of California's *Out West* magazine, chastised Americans for their ignorance of their country's greatest gift—the lands and cultures of the American West. Lummis's writings celebrated Indian and Hispanic cultures in the 1890s, and he coined the phrase "See America First" just as the Santa Fe Railway's seductive posters and literature expounded in full-color illustration and rapturous text the romance and charm of the Southwest.

The aspects of northern New Mexico that discouraged commercial developers—its isolation and inaccessibility, and its peoples' persistence in traditions and lifestyles centuries old and not in the least bit modernistic—were the very aspects of the region that made it into a premier arts colony. In the years immediately before and after World War I, Taos and Santa Fe became colonies for artist, writer, and photographer expatriates who found New Mexico's communities and their "aura of innocence"[6] a haven in which they could pursue their artistic visions far from the noise, chaos, and corruption of the greater world.

The story of Taos and Santa Fe, indeed all of northern New Mexico, was one of centuries of multicultural interaction and tolerance. Artists, writers, and effete intellectuals seeking refuge from the conservatism of the urban East Coast of the United States moved into New Mexico's Hispanic and Native American communities with little effort. The Santa Fe and Taos art colonies included some of the world's finest twentieth-century painters and writers.[7] Interested in pursuing their muse, living alone or in partnership in and out of marriage, in hetero- or homosexual relationships, New Mexico's modern immigrants found a native society they could merge with, or at least live peacefully alongside.

The Museum of New Mexico was founded in 1907 partially to support the arts of the region and partially to support the burgeoning archaeological and anthropological work occurring at prehistoric sites and ruins throughout the Southwest. The museum's headquarters was the old Palace of the Governors on the plaza of Santa Fe, where Ute chiefs and Mexican troops had once clashed in a bloody fight over the governor's desk, and where almost a century before them, the Martín Serranos had asked the Spanish governor to grant them the dangerous lands of the Valley of Shining Stone.

The museum's founders, Edgar Lee Hewett and Frank Springer, were interested in the recovery, preservation, and restoration of the region's multicultural past. Swiss writer-anthropologist Adolph Bandelier, an early nonnative witness of Abiquiu's Fiesta de Santo Tomás, had begun exploring New Mexico's Paleo-Indian past in the 1880s. But very few Southwestern archaeological surveys had been completed by the early 1900s. Before World War I, American archaeological efforts were directed toward European, Mediterranean, and Asian sites. Southwestern archaeology was in its infancy, the richness of New Mexico's prehistory only just glimpsed and imagined by Bandelier and a handful of contemporaries. The American public knew little or nothing about New Mexico's long history.

The same year as he co-founded the Museum of New Mexico, Hewett founded the School of American Archaeology, later renamed the School of American Research. The School of American Research, in conjunction with institutions such as the University of New Mexico, began to conduct archaeological field schools in northern New Mexico. These included the first excavations of prehistoric sites like Poe shú in the Chama Valley. Thus, in the years before and immediately following World War I, anthropologists and archaeologists began discovering and uncovering the rich history of the region of Avéshu pije.

Nationally promoted by the railroad, embellished by artists on canvas and by writers on paper, the real cultural, archaeological, and physical wonders of the Southwest began to merge with the mythic wonders in the minds of the American public. Simultaneously with a new romanticized

Southwest came mythical heroes associated with the region: all things western, real and imagined, took center stage in the American imagination. Foremost among these were the image of the American Indian and the imagined Anglo counterpart, the American cowboy.

In the early 1900s, writers such as Owen Wister, whose novel *The Virginian* sat at the top of the 1902 bestseller list for six months, had begun to publish stories and novels that set the stage for the Mythic American West. This literature perpetuated an image of the West as the last frontier, where moral and physical rejuvenation were yet found. The main character of the Mythic West, the cowboy, provided Americans with the hero they lacked: the romantic rescuer, the rugged individualist, the self-reliant, multitalented man who did not need or seek industrialized, urbanized, overcivilized America.

The unspoiled landscape and the cultural environment American expatriates found in the Southwest offered women as much opportunity as men. Where once only soldiers and militia men, ranchers, trappers, traders, and miners dared venture to put down roots, the New Mexico of the twentieth century offered safe but looser social grounds for women seeking lives beyond the grasp of the stifling American female status quo. Many of the women who came to Santa Fe and Taos, notably Mabel Dodge Luhan and Mary Austin, became community action leaders and self-appointed champions of New Mexico's indigenous cultures and people, and were vocal political advocates for Hispanic and Native American arts, crafts, and religious traditions.

Simultaneously with the twentieth-century appreciation among Anglo Americans for Southwestern art and culture came a public awareness of, and urgency to protect, the land of the American Southwest. Where Americans had for generations been proponents for the conquest of frontiers and wilderness, now they recognized how the frontier and all it stood for was finite. And the very aspect of the West that Americans loved most—its mysterious, even dangerous wilderness, and its resistance to conquest—was slipping away. Twentieth-century Americans wanted the West to be wild.

John Muir, founder of the Sierra Club in 1892, had begun appealing for a national conservation program as early as the 1890s. Under western advocate and outdoorsman President Theodore Roosevelt, 150 million acres of public domain were placed into national forests by 1907. Aldo Leopold joined the U.S. Forest Service in 1909 and through scientific expertise and powerful prose admonished Americans for their historic abuses of land and wilderness. Muir, Leopold, and other early conservationists echoed the beliefs and attitudes of Native Americans, who viewed life as a delicate balance between man and nature, who believed man and nature were inextricably woven and interconnected. This view was in direct opposition to the historic Anglo American view in which man conquered nature in order that he might survive and even profit.

The male conservationists found an empathetic and energetic league of supporters among the Anglo American women writers and artists of New Mexico who had already embraced the Native American belief that land was sacred: the land of the Southwest was not something to be possessed, but was something to be cherished and honored, a place whose energy and wisdom had to be earned. Santa Fe poet Alice Corbin Henderson wrote:

> This valley is not ours, nor these mountains,
> Nor the names we give them—they belong,
> They, and this sweep of sun-washed air,
> Desert and hill and crumbling earth,
> To those who have lain here long years
> And felt the soak of the sun . . ."[8]

In the Southwest of the early twentieth century, where men and women alike found an atmosphere that was culturally and emotionally liberating, it is not, in retrospect, surprising that the first Anglo American to own part of, and then move onto, the Piedra Lumbre was a woman. Unlike previous Anglo owners—Thomas Catron, George Hill Howard, A. B. Renehan, et al.—Carol Bishop Stanley was not an absentee landlord of the Piedra Lumbre, but a hands-on *pobladora* who brought all she owned and all she hoped for to the adobe casa built by the infamous Archuleta brothers beneath the Cliffs of Shining Stone.

Carol Bishop Stanley, born on Nahant Island, Massachusetts, in 1879, was related to Joseph Hodges Choate, the distinguished diplomatist who represented the United States at the International Peace Conference at The Hague in 1907, and who served as U.S. ambassador to Great Britain, 1899–1905. Stanley was trained as a concert pianist and performed with the Boston Symphony and with other orchestras in New York and Chicago, where she briefly made homes, taught music, and enjoyed the company of friends in celebrated music circles.

The reasons for Carol Stanley's first journey to the Southwest are inferred by legend and substantiated by fact. The legend claims that when Stanley was a young woman she fell in love with a violinist of the Boston Symphony. Upon her announcement that she intended to marry, the Stanleys, deeming the match beneath their daughter's social position, promptly sent her West where they hoped she would forget the young musician.

Stanley's first visit to the Southwest, sometime before 1910, took her to the home and trading post of John and Louisa Wetherill on the Navajo Reservation at Kayenta, Arizona. John Wetherill was one of the five Wetherill brothers of Mancos, Colorado, who, led by Richard, discovered Mesa Verde in the mid 1880s while running cattle across the plateau country of the Utes. John Wetherill discovered the cave ruins of Betatakin in 1912 and was the first white man to stand under the Rock Rainbow (Rainbow Bridge) in 1909.

John and Louisa Wetherill's house and trading post at Kayenta, like Richard Wetherill's at Pueblo Bonito in Chaco Canyon, New Mexico, was a gathering place for the world's most celebrated anthropologists and archaeologists who came to explore the recently found ruins of Navajo-land. Theodore Roosevelt visited the Wetherills at Kayenta in 1913, and his published account of his journey to see Rainbow Bridge with John Wetherill instigated similar visits by his friends and contemporaries, at least one of whom, Natalie Curtis, was a close friend and colleague of Carol Stanley's.

Stanley left no personal diaries or journals, but the unpublished autobiography of Stanley's Boston friend, Mary Cabot Wheelwright, describes a desert journey made by Stanley and Louisa Wetherill on horseback. Wheelwright wrote: "The federal government wanted to find a certain Ute indian to try him for some crime. To Mrs. Wetherell [sic] an appeal was made to interview him and try to persuade him to give himself up. She took Carol Pfaffle [Pfaeffle, Stanley's later married name] with her and, traveling with horses for days they found the Indian at a Ute ceremony. Mrs. Wetherell persuaded him to come back to Kayenta with her. In telling me about it, Carol Pfaffle gave me an idea of the excitement she had felt in this adventure into the untouched wilderness, where she had met untamed Indians."[9]

The visit to the Wetherills changed Stanley's life. Although she returned to Boston, she never married the violinist. After several more visits to the Southwest, Stanley came to New Mexico to stay.

In April of 1916, Stanley came to Santa Fe with her friend Natalie Curtis. Curtis, a native New Yorker, was already a seasoned visitor to the Southwest, having traveled to Arizona in the 1890s. In 1900, after years of studying Native American music, Curtis began the self-appointed task of recording native songs, two hundred of which were published in *The Indian's Book* in 1907. Curtis found Anglo American attitudes toward Native American culture unconscionable and used her family's personal ties to President Theodore Roosevelt to persuade him to remove the assimilationists' ban that prohibited the singing of native songs.[10]

Stanley and Curtis passed the summer of 1916 at the newly opened Ramón Vigil Ranch of Ashley Pond. From this ranch, located on the Pajarito Plateau on the northeast edge of the Jemez Mountains, the two friends visited the Rio Grande Pueblos for various ceremonies and feasts and frequently returned to Santa Fe and its pleasant social community.

Curtis left New Mexico by August of 1916. Stanley remained in Santa Fe, where she was joined that fall at the De Vargas Hotel by another friend, Dorothy Kent, of Tarrytown, New York. In September of 1916, the two women departed Santa Fe on horseback for the Indian country of New Mexico and Arizona. Their journey was planned under the auspices of the newly formed Rocky Mountain Camp Company, an automobile and horse expedition outfitter with headquarters on the plaza of Santa Fe.

Their guide was Richard Leroy Pfaeffle, a thirty-four-year-old, Iowa-born cowboy who had worked for the Forest Service in the Jemez Mountains and at the Ramón Vigil Ranch prior to becoming assistant manager of the Rocky Mountain Camp Company. The Rocky Mountain Camp Company under Edward J. Ward, in a style soon to be imitated by Fred Harvey's Southwestern Indian Detours, took travelers by car or by horseback on guided tours of local pueblos and Spanish villages and out across the desert to prehistoric ruins and natural wonders. The company also provided tent cities where visitors could "rough-it" in relative comfort for a few days or a week outside of Santa Fe or Taos while enjoying the local sites.

At the time, it was customary for parties journeying on horseback into the Four Corners country to depart from Gallup or Thoreau, New Mexico. Stanley's journey with Pfaeffle and the new outfitter made news headlines upon their return from Chaco Canyon, Cañon del Muerto, and Cañon de Chelly, and surrounding country, as the first successful cross-country venture via horseback from Santa Fe to these remote destinations. The trip also made headlines because during the three-week journey, Stanley and Pfaeffle fell in love and quietly married.

Carol Stanley and Richard Pfaeffle embodied the East-West marriage romanticized and glorified in the western pulp fiction of their time: she was the wealthy spinster who came West, the "dudette" who fell in love first with the country and then with a man of the country. He was the experienced but penniless "dude wrangler" with little but his spurs, chaps, Stetson, horse, and years in the saddle to call his own. Western literature capitalized on such real and imagined romantic pairings, with numerous stories ending with the upper-class eastern lady riding off into the sunset with the adventurous, hitherto independent cowboy.

The term "dude" had various definitions: it referred to a tenderfoot or greenhorn, but also to someone sporting outlandish western clothing. A dude on the Santa Fe plaza was a vacationing out-of-towner dressed in shined boots and clean jeans, with a pressed bandana and silver bolero, and proudly sporting a dust-free Stetson. Conversely, a true-blue cowboy ambling down Fifth Avenue in his everyday, broken-in ranchwear was a dude to New Yorkers. The less derogatory use of the word "dude" (women dudes were called dudettes or dudines) used by the guest and dude ranchers of the West simply distinguished someone who came into the region from somewhere else and paid for food, lodging, riding, and guiding services.[11]

Those cowboys who became dude wranglers handled people and horses with equal skill and excelled in all the finer aspects of what was now legendary western hospitality. Not just any cowboy could become a successful guide and dude wrangler. The ideal was "a man of charm, warmth, and agility. He had to be a man's man, a ladies' man, a prince of a good fellow, and an authority on women, weather, wildlife, game, fish, horses, cows, dogs, sheep, and wildflowers. He also had to be an entertaining conversationalist, a convincing correspondent, a diplomat, a pal of the village banker and town marshal, and a cordial check cashier."[12] With such a prince among frontier men at her beck and call, it was not uncommon for eastern dudettes to fall in love with both the gorgeous untamed wilderness and the skilled cowboy leading her into it.

Nearly all of the early dude and guest ranches in the West shared the same foundation: they were underwritten by a wealthy owner, usually from the urban East, who had access to a long list of affluent friends who became prospective guests. These owners often went into the guest ranch business with several seasoned cowboys and guides who knew the lay of the land, both culturally and topographically, and could handle horses and people with equal patience and enthusiasm.

Richard Pfaeffle must have had plenty of that western cowboy charm to have wooed and married thirty-six-year-old Carol Stanley in just under a month on the Southwestern desert. The son of a railroader, handsome and wiry, comfortable in a saddle and around the campfire, Pfaeffle was ready to settle down and run his own guest business. Stanley was hardly the greenhorn: although she spoke with a distinctive Boston accent she could as easily discuss the preservation of indigenous cultures as she could speculate about the hitch in a certain trail horse's gait.

After his marriage to Stanley, Pfaeffle quit his job with the Rocky Mountain Camp Company to become manager of a new guest ranch operation at the old house and grounds of Bishop Lamy. Although his management of Bishop's Lodge was short lived, Pfaeffle was instrumental in the owners' (two New York families) initial decision to make the old residence into a guest ranch. Pfaeffle would be fired as manager of Bishop's Lodge within the next year, but his brief affiliation with the ranch afforded him with at least one connection that would benefit him and Stanley during the next ten years: his acquaintance with Jack Lambert.

Jack Lambert would become northern New Mexico's most celebrated cowboy over the next decades. A widely respected guide and horseman, Lambert was the epitome of the Renaissance cowboy to the hundreds of dudes, famous and anonymous, he packed into the Southwestern outback. And Lambert's handsome face, Tom Mix–style hat, leather chaps, and silver-spurred profile would grace dozens of 1920s and '30s Santa Fe Railway and New Mexico tourist advertising brochures.

In the summer of 1917, nineteen-year-old, Oklahoma-born Jack Lambert struck up a conversation with Richard Pfaeffle about horses and dudes on the curb of the old plaza in Santa Fe. Lambert was employed by a local taxi company and had already worked as a horse wrangler in Cody, Wyoming, a wild-horse tamer in Ruby Valley, Nevada, and a bridge builder in Moab, Utah. Lambert and Pfaeffle became fast friends, and Pfaeffle hired Lambert that very day. Together they began the restoration of the old Bishop Lamy's residence and grounds in Tesuque: "We took the boards off the windows, put the place in shape and had ten or twelve dudes right away. It was very successful, but it was too close to town for me."[13]

Within the first year, Lambert quit work at the too-close-to-town Bishop's Lodge and Richard Pfaeffle was fired as manager. Stanley and Pfaeffle, accompanied by Stanley's English maid, Alice Pring, moved to Española and, with Lambert as a partner, began to look for a suitable property for their own guest ranch. By the end of 1918, with Stanley's family money, the three had purchased broken-down buildings alongside the Rio Grande at Alcalde, north of Española. They named their new enterprise the San Gabriel Ranch after the old Spanish capital built more than three hundred years before near this same spot.

Pfaeffle and Lambert renovated old buildings and assembled a staff of horse and dude wranglers, automobile drivers, mechanics, cooks, and guides, many of whom were Pfaeffle's previous colleagues from the Rocky Mountain Camp Company. This corps of people who made San Gabriel into a premier guest ranch by the 1920s would all, with the exception of Jack Lambert, relocate to El Rancho de los Brujos, Ghost Ranch, on the Piedra Lumbre at the end of the decade.

Although San Gabriel was primarily a horse and overland pack outfitter, extended automobile trips into Indian country in Lincoln and Packard touring cars were gaining popularity among Southwestern travelers. Along with cowboys, the Pfaeffles hired Orville Cox, an experienced automobile guide and master mechanic, to oversee the ranch's fleet of touring vehicles.

Orville Cox would become to automobile guiding what Jack Lambert became to horse guiding in the Southwest. Fluent in several languages, knowledgeable in Pueblo, Navajo, Hopi, and Spanish culture and history, regional anthropology, and archaeology, Cox became the Southwest's most famous unknown face when he drove Ansel Adams and Georgia O'Keeffe, Godfrey Rockefeller and David McAlpin from Ghost Ranch to Canyon de Chelly in the 1930s. Among Adams's more reproduced photographs from that expedition is one of O'Keeffe and Cox, each grinning beneath a favorite black hat, with jacket collars pulled to their necks against a cold October wind.

Alcalde was served by the narrow-gauge Chili Line of the Denver and Rio Grande Railway, but most of San Gabriel's guests—who most often learned about the ranch from other guests, almost all of whom were friends of Carol Stanley's—came to New Mexico on the Santa Fe Railway, disembarking at Lamy where Cox and one of the San Gabriel Ranch Lincolns, thunderbird insignia painted boldly on its side, picked them and their trunks up trackside.

The drive across the dirt roads that led north and west from Santa Fe to Española and on up the Rio Grande Valley to San Gabriel was at best a bumpy, scenically beautiful, three-hour drive. But northern New Mexico is famous for its temperamental summer weather. A cloudless morning could turn into a dark, stormy afternoon in a few blinks of an eye. The trip from Lamy to San Gabriel could be a grueling adventure for drivers and passengers alike; drivers like Cox were valued for their ability to improvise in the face of unpredictable weather, road-challenged vehicles, and nervous dudes and dudettes. Edward Bennett, Jr., of Chicago remembers one of Cox's methods of bad-weather driving: "Orville would deflate one tire, inflate another, put a stone in his mouth and go right through the bad places."[14]

As frightening and inconvenient as these trips could become, even a rigorous automobile journey to San Gabriel was considered an attractive introduction to the Western Adventure guests had come thousands of miles to participate in: "They almost seemed to enjoy the difficult," Mary Wheelwright wrote. "Roads were practically non-existent then and the tracks were often washed out. I was amazed to find elderly people talking of breakdowns and sticking in the mud as though it were fun. They seemed disappointed when things went too smoothly."[15]

San Gabriel Ranch was midway between Taos and Santa Fe, and it soon became a popular lunch stop for Mabel Dodge Luhan's guests motoring up and down the Rio Grande Valley between the two towns. San Gabriel also began to play host to Luhan's friends who wanted to visit northern New Mexico away from the Taos–Santa Fe social scene: Willa Cather found San Gabriel courtyard's soothing ambience conducive to work and relaxation both, and she corrected the proofs to her book *The Professor's House,* which included a character based on Richard Wetherill and the discovery of Mesa Verde, in the reclusive garden in the summer of 1925.[16]

San Gabriel guests with a larger sense of adventure could participate in extended cross-country trips into the Four Corners region of New Mexico and trips to the Grand Canyon. Lambert led these two- and three-week-long expeditions by horseback, while Cox was in charge of those by automobile. By pack train or by Lincoln touring car, San Gabriel guests were comfortably taken into the middle of the most remote, authentic frontier still found in North America: "I took from two to five dudes on pack trips along with the horse wranglers I needed into country that I knew and loved," Jack Lambert remembered of his years at San Gabriel. "Sometimes I'd take whole families, or some of the Santa Fe Railway lawyers. One summer I took four four-to-six week pack trips, one of them into three states. There was no pavement and not one fence between here and Gallup or the Grand Canyon. Dick [Pfaeffle] had his hands full with the ranch, so I always did the pack trips."[17]

Cox covered the same country by automobile, with no less pride in his ability to deliver his passengers safely and on time to various remote scenic sights and events in Indian country. Cox was always in direct competition with other tours, especially those later run by the Santa Fe and the Harvey Company: "Orville loved nothing better than the snake dances, because the Fred Harvey Tour drivers would also be there. . . . After the dance, there would always be a rush to 'Cozy' McSparron's ranch at Canyon de Chelly, and during the almost certain late afternoon cloudburst Orville would deliberately mislead the Harvey parties onto some particularly treacherous short cut. While they were busy digging out of a muddy ditch, he would bring his party safely into 'Cozy's' and snag the best of the scarce accommodations."[18]

The Pfaeffles also built a small camp in the Canjilon Mountains above the Piedra Lumbre's northern boundary. The log-and-canvas cabins served as base camp for pack trips into the high mountain country above the Piedra Lumbre. Guests could choose to spend a week at the camp, taking day rides into the high timber country near the Continental Divide, or could begin three- to seven-day pack trips that followed old Indian trails through the northern New Mexico mountains. Those dudes who did not wish to spend several weeks roughing it on the desert, miles from the simplest material comforts, even with the best of cowboys and drivers, could remain a night at the camp, sleeping out under the stars and listening to the old-timers spinning the local lore around a snapping campfire.

Among Carol Stanley's many Boston friends who came for a stay at San Gabriel in 1923 was Mary Cabot Wheelwright. At that time, Stanley and her circle of New Mexico friends were involved in meetings and discussions that would eventually give birth to various Santa Fe arts and culture preservation societies.[19] With Jack Lambert, Orville Cox, and other associates knowledgeable about and interested in the indigenous arts, crafts, and customs of the Southwest, at San Gabriel Wheelwright was surrounded by those personally and directly involved with historic and cultural preservation of New Mexico and Arizona: "Their ranch was a wonderful introduction to the country, with Mr. Pfaffle [sic] giving it an atmosphere of casual adventure and Mrs. Pfaffle bringing the appreciation of a cultivated woman to the imaginative quality of the Indian and Spanish life of that region."[20]

Although she never married, Wheelwright was as enamored of the cowboy guides as her fellow eastern female immigrants, and she enjoyed the flavor of her relationships with these uniquely western individuals, who were often as curious about the Boston Brahmin women as the women were about them: "I found that being from Boston was a distinct handicap, and I was determined that one of my missions was to convince cowboys that it was possible for a person to be a good sport and also drink tea."[21]

In 1926, Stanley and Wheelwright packed by horse into Navajoland with Jack Lambert as their guide. They rode to Canyon de Chelly, where they watched the Navajo ceremony called the Tleji, the Night Chant. The next day they rode from Chinle over the Chuska Mountains to the New-comb Trading Post at Nava. Sixty miles from Gallup, they followed the main road to Shiprock, which was nothing more than a track that wound up and down the mesas and arroyos. Wheelwright recalled a peculiar incident on that ride with Carol Stanley: "As we came down the mountains I saw a thing I have never understood to this day, a solitary man on horseback, pursued by an eagle. I suppose he had robbed the eagle's nest, but I do not know."[22]

Stanley, Wheelwright, Lambert, and their pack train, now guided by an Indian friend, rode across the desert to Kimpeto, where they had been told a great medicine man, Hosteen Klah, was going to perform a Yeibichai Night Chant. Upon reaching Kimpeto, they slept on the floor of the trading post storehouse. In the middle of the night, the two women woke and walked through a fierce snowstorm: "We managed to reach the ceremony nearby where the dancers were to be seen through the whirling snow, while the fires blew out sideways.

"Out of this turmoil appeared Klah, calm and benign."[23]

From this meeting in a snowstorm on the New Mexico desert Wheelwright and Hosteen Klah began a friendship and partnership that would greatly influence the rest of their lives. Klah, a highly respected Navajo *cacique,* was aware that his people's sacred rituals would be lost to future generations unless they were preserved in written and recorded form. Over the next decade, in numerous meetings in Navajoland and in Alcalde, Klah allowed Wheelwright to record hundreds of sacred Navajo chants and myths, and he even broke the Navajo taboo that forbid replication and permanent preservation of Navajo sandpaintings. Klah's and Wheelwright's work resulted in the establishment in 1937 of the Museum of Navajo Ceremonial Art in Santa Fe.

While out horseback riding one afternoon along the Rio Grande bosque north of San Gabriel Ranch, Stanley and Wheelwright came upon the old hacienda built two hundred years before by Captain Sebastian Martín Serrano.[24] The greatly decrepit, two-story residence had once served as a military training center and outpost for Mexican troops under General José María Chávez of Abiquiu during the Mexican occupation of New Mexico. Unoccupied since the turn of the twentieth century, the old property, locally known as Nuestra Señora de la Soledad del Rio del Norte Arriba, included numerous other buildings and grounds in various states of dishevelment.

Wheelwright fell in love with the old Plaza de los Luceros, renamed for subsequent Martín Serrano descendants, and set about buying the entire ranch. Wheelwright hired Carol Stanley to work the same magic on Los Luceros' reconstruction as she had San Gabriel's. Stanley chose to renovate the house in the Spanish Colonial–Pueblo Revival style popular in Santa Fe in the 1920s. Mary Wheelwright lived at Los Luceros until her death in 1958.[25]

Although San Gabriel was a prestigious and financially sound guest ranch in the Southwest, by the mid 1920s the Pfaeffle-Stanley marriage was showing signs of strain. Friends warned Stanley that Pfaeffle was drinking to excess and spending too much money on horses and card games.

Stanley, as ranch hostess, remained at the ranch all summer, but left San Gabriel after the tourist season ended. Stanley often journeyed between the Rio Grande Valley and Arizona–New Mexico Indian country (via the Piedra Lumbre) on horseback. In 1926, with Lambert and several of her San Gabriel colleagues—exclusive of her husband—Stanley saddled up the San Gabriel horses, loaded up the pack mules, and headed for the Grand Canyon via Navajo and Hopi lands, Monument Valley, Canyon de Chelly, and Rainbow Bridge, where she signed her name in the registry kept inside a little tin box at the base of the cliffs. Wheelwright's descriptions of similar expeditions by horseback onto the New Mexico and Arizona desert give us an idea of the country which Carol Stanley knew and loved so well: "At one point the trail was so steep that I could only get up by hanging onto the tail of my horse. . . . Finally we came to the bridge and slept under the arch in full moonlight. We signed a book for visitors, and I think were among the first hundred who reached there."[26]

In the late 1920s, Arthur Newton Pack, the editor and publisher of *Nature Magazine,* the official publication of the American Nature Association (later incorporated into *Natural History Magazine,* published by the American Museum of Natural History in New York), came to San Gabriel Ranch with a group of friends and colleagues. Pack and his Princeton entourage were all in some way involved with the conservation movement in the United States. Pack, son of Charles Lathrop Pack, president of the American Forestry Association, had organized an automobile expedition into "the wild and weird land of the Navajo and Hopi Indians."

Their journey began at Alcalde in the late summer of 1929 and followed the road down the Rio Grande Valley and then northwest up the Chama River "past the Penitente village of Abiquiu": "The roads at that time were largely mere wagon tracks, accommodations were practically nil and we would have to camp all the way, with two cars carrying extra water, gasoline and food. It was safer, we heard, to travel with two cars because one could pull the other out of sand or mud."[27] They proceeded up the Chama on the narrow cliff-hugging road through the river canyon that opened onto the Piedra Lumbre basin. Their car's wheels retraced the Old Spanish Trail across the dusty basin below Pedernal, "past a variegated and spectacular array of sandstone cliffs eroded into strange formations with a continually changing kaleidoscope of color. This we were destined to know later as Ghost Ranch."[28]

The summer of Pack's first visit to northern New Mexico was to be the last golden season for San Gabriel Ranch. The stock market crash on October 29th impacted the Southwest's tourist business, although the very wealthy would continue to make their annual pilgrimages to favorite guest and dude ranches. The financial crisis experienced on the East Coast surely affected Stanley's own family's finances, and even with investors such as A. B. Renehan, a wealthy Santa Fe Ring lawyer, San Gabriel faced liquidation by the first years of the 1930s.

The ranch was facing emotional as well as financial disintegration. Jack Lambert quit the partnership in 1929 after a particularly difficult trip to the Grand Canyon during which a doctor's wife, after insisting she eat wild mushrooms, was hospitalized. "When we got back [to Alcalde] I found Dick was drinking," Lambert remembered, "so I left to spend the winter in Phoenix."[29]

Lambert met the wealthy White sisters, Elizabeth and Martha, during that visit to Arizona, and was hired to build their Santa Fe estate (which became the School of American Research in 1973), where he worked until in 1969.[30] Of Lambert's leavetaking of San Gabriel Ranch he later said: "How I loved that place! Losing it almost broke my heart."[31]

By 1931, Carol Stanley became the president of San Gabriel Ranch, Inc. which continued to advertise in Southwestern dude ranching brochures. San Gabriel Ranch still included the Canjilon Mountain Camp, but it now included a new property called Ghost Ranch, located in the cliff country ten miles northwest of Abiquiu.

In 1931, Stanley signed a contract with Hunter Clarkson, Inc., that merged San Gabriel's transportation services with the cars and drivers formerly of Fred Harvey's Southwest Indian Detours. Now an independent guiding business called the Couriercars, the San Gabriel Division was placed under Orville Cox, and the ranch's three Lincoln Touring cars—a 1928 seven passenger, a 1929 five passenger, and a 1930 seven passenger—joined the already large fleet under Clarkson's company in northern New Mexico. This arrangement would be short-lived, as the contract dissolved when Stanley moved her drivers and cars out onto the Piedra Lumbre.

Legend claims that Richard Pfaeffle, in what may have been his single most successful gambling venture, won the old homestead of El Rancho de los Brujos in a poker game. There is no official account of this card game, but if it is true, Pfaeffle would have won the homestead in the haunted canyon from a member of the Alfredo Salazar family of Abiquiu in 1929: in that year the deed for 152 acres of the Rito del Yeso homestead (formerly of the Archuleta brothers) was signed over to Carol Stanley, who was clearly staking a claim to what was left of her family's money invested in San Gabriel and in Pfaeffle's various horse breeding ventures.

Previous to the Salazars' ownership of the canyon homestead, the Archuletas had sold the property, or given the deed in lieu of debts at the Gonzales Store in Abiquiu, to sheepman Miguel Gonzales in 1921. Seven years later, Gonzales sold the homestead to the Salazars, who held the deed for just over a year before, presumably, someone in their family lost it in the fateful poker game.

Stanley began divorce proceedings in 1930, at which time she began to divide her time and energy between San Gabriel and the new property out beyond Abiquiu. The few guests that did come to Alcalde were often taken for overnights at the Piedra Lumbre ranch. The facilities at the Rito del Yeso homestead were rough and marginal compared to the luxurious accommodations at San Gabriel: there was no electricity or running water, and the homestead ranch had only the one adobe building and a corral and a few shacks used for tack and storage. But Stanley had a vision of the old ranch in Yeso Canyon becoming the San Gabriel of the Piedra Lumbre. The ranch beneath the Cliffs of Shining Stone had no real name, and for at least the first year Stanley called it San Gabriel. But after her first summer on the Piedra Lumbre, Stanley began to call the ranch by its lore-laden local name, Rancho de los Brujos, Ghost Ranch.

The final dissolution of San Gabriel Ranch, Inc., came in 1932. In the final settlement, Stanley was given 16,583.63 acres of the old Piedra Lumbre Grant held by the A. B. Renehan family of Santa Fe. (In 1929, the northern third of the Piedra Lumbre, excepting the Arroyo Seco tract owned by an Abiqueño, had been bought by A. B. Renehan, a partner and co-owner of San Gabriel Ranch, Inc.) The Stanley-Pfaeffle marriage was also dissolved by 1932. Stanley packed up all that she owned, including her baby grand piano, and with her English maid and confidante, Alice, in company with six or seven cowboys who had become her family in northern New Mexico, moved out of San Gabriel and up the Chama River to Ghost Ranch.

9

BETWEEN GREEN AND DRY

Ghost Ranch had many obstacles to overcome before it could become a successful guest ranch. Española was a half day's drive over a rough road, and no trains passed daily through the Chama River Valley. Abiquiu was still a rural Hispanic village whose native population had little interest in developing or attracting Anglo tourism. Ghost Ranch was wild and raw, an isolated outpost in a valley that lay far, maybe too far, off the beaten track. Whatever Ghost Ranch might become would take hard work and perseverance. Carol Stanley had little capital, but she was banking on the inherent value of the land itself, on the visual power of the rock and cliff country of the Piedra Lumbre, and on the region's ethereal assets—the silence of the high desert, the clarity of the sky, and the size of the horizon.

Ghost Ranch needed additional guest facilities built before Stanley could open it for even limited business. Under the supervision of Ted Peabody, Stanley's carpenter and builder from Alcalde, native laborers from neighboring villages began work on a U-shaped block of adobe rooms where the permanent ranch staff—mostly the wranglers—would be housed. To the west of the cowboy quarters that came to be called

Corral Block, a barn, a garage for the four San Gabriel Lincolns now re-painted with the initials "GR" on their doors, and various tack and storage sheds were constructed. A rambling headquarters building that housed an office, a guest lounge, and a dining and kitchen facility was placed up a small hill from the orchard. And four adobe *casitas* were built in a semi-circle behind the old Archuleta homestead, now called Ghost House, with flower and vegetable gardens planted near the old hanging tree.

After twenty years in New Mexico, Stanley spoke fluent Spanish. Old-timers remember how the stocky, middle-aged outsider Anglo was well liked by the local men and women who lived in the "Mexican Camp" across from Ghost House while they built the new facilities. Stanley still had the airs of an aristocratic woman—her English maid, Alice Pring, remained with Stanley at Ghost Ranch, and Stanley often played piano by candlelight for the staff. Friends remember that Stanley often wore stylish evening dresses, although by day she sported split riding skirts or jeans and boots. But decades under the Southwestern sun, coupled with the travails of her failed marriage and dwindling bank account, had tanned and creased her face and greatly eroded her Boston Brahmin appearance.

Stanley's only neighbors were a young forest ranger, Ed Groesbeck, who lived at the new ranger station on Canjilon Mountain, and an old Genízaro, Juan de Dios, who lived beside the Chama River at the south-ern end of the historic Arroyo Seco tract. Groesbeck often rode his horse down the Mesa Yeso trail that descended the Cliffs of Shining Stone near Box Canyon, and spent an afternoon and evening with Stanley and her cowboys at Ghost Ranch. Groesbeck remembers that "Stanley was a re-spected and liked task master" anxious to get the new ranch built and on its feet.

An early visitor to Ghost Ranch was one of Fred Harvey's grand-sons. Stanley told Groesbeck that on one occasion in the new Ghost Ranch dining room Harvey found a fork with his grandfather's company name stamped in the silver: "Harvey picked up the table fork and remarked how the silverware from the Harvey Houses was always getting stolen! Harvey laughed and razzed Carol about taking his family's silver way up there to her new ranch! Harvey came to Ghost Ranch several times, often for a week or so."

Juan de Dios Gallegos ("John of God") had lived at the River Ranch since 1905, at which time he had bought the 130-acre ranch from Anglo investors. De Dios's stone, adobe, and wood house was built before 1892, possibly in connection with the toll road of the 1870s. The place was known as El Vadito ("the little ford or crossing"), as it was positioned beside a natural river crossing near a large grove of cottonwoods and box elders on the main road between Abiquiu and Tierra Amarilla. Generations of travelers had steered their pack trains, horses, wagons, and finally automobiles across the muddy river at this shallow ford. By Stanley's time, there was a narrow bridge over the water only marginally safer than the sandy bottom of the river itself. De Dios had built an L-shaped adobe building with a kitchen and dining area, a garage for his son's Model A and Model T, a shed for tack, and several corrals for his prized steers and horses.

Stanley had probably encountered Juan de Dios during her first overland trips from Santa Fe to Indian country. De Dios's River Ranch was known by everyone—Hispanic, Native American, Anglo—who passed through the Piedra Lumbre valley between 1905 and his death in the late 1930s. De Dios, a lean, swarthy, weathered and wrinkled Genízaro, and his stories of Native American and Hispano life on the New Mexican frontier were treasured by all who heard his fireside tales. A robust rider, cattle and horse wrangler, farmer, cook, and all-around good neighbor until the last years of his life, de Dios was a living legend.

Wanden Kane, wife and fellow traveler of Pulitzer Prize–winner Oliver La Farge, was disappointed to find that old de Dios was not at home when their pack train reached the River Ranch in the early summer of 1930. Juan's son, Ignacio, cooked the La Farges a fine meal and gave them directions (they were en route to Canyon de Chelly, to the Wetherills in Navajo country, and eventually to the Grand Canyon), but Kane found it "unlucky" that old "Juan Dio" was away when they reached his much heralded river crossing beneath Pedernal.[1]

A Paiute by birth, de Dios had been taken as a small child from his parents and tribe by the Navajos. After an unknown period of time with his first captors, de Dios was taken from the Navajos by the Hispanic militia during a raid on their camp. De Dios, by this time about four or five years of age, along with at least two Navajo or Paiute girls, was brought back to Abiquiu, where he was baptized into the José de la Luz

Gallegos family in October of 1864.[2] (De Dios's Hispanic father was the grandnephew of Pedro Gallego, the 1806 founder of the Arroyo Seco Ranch.) Like all captives, de Dios was free when he reached adulthood. Although the Emancipation Proclamation granted him and his two Native American sisters and brother freedom in 1863, it appears they all remained voluntarily with their Hispanic family until they married or otherwise felt prepared to strike out on their own.

Like many other Abiqueños, de Dios's lifestyle was a combination of Hispanic and Native American traditions. The *vigas* of the River Ranch ceilings were hung with bundles of native herbs and plants used in home remedies de Dios had acquired from his multicultural ancestors. Like his Hispanic father before him, de Dios ran several hundred head of cattle in the mountains surrounding Pedernal, and he farmed fields of alfalfa and wheat alongside the Chama River.

Before the 1900s, de Dios married Marciala Chávez, who raised their four children downstream in Abiquiu after de Dios bought the River Ranch in 1905. De Dios was an avid tracker and hunter, and Anglo, Hispanic, and Native American friends sought his assistance in the pursuit of mountain lions, wild turkey, deer, bears, and coyotes. De Dios remembered the days when antelope still roamed the llanos along the Chama, and he recalled the year the last mountain sheep visited the tablelands below Pedernal. The yips of a coyote at dusk informed him of forthcoming weather, and there was never a stray cow or horse on the Piedra Lumbre whose whereabouts de Dios did not know.

By the 1920s, the Piedra Lumbre basin and the Chama River Valley were home to a large herd of wild horses, many of whom were the descendants of the California stock brought over the Old Spanish Trail. In the 1930s, the horses were led by a black stallion who was known to pester and entice the domestic mares of the Chama Valley from the Piedra Lumbre to Alcalde, and who was known to lead the herd over the Jemez Mountains as far as the Pajarito Plateau.

To the subsistence ranchers and farmers of the valley, domestic horses were an absolute necessity that few could afford to buy. Juan de Dios was a robust rider and horse wrangler until the last year of his life, and valley ranchers depended on his equestrian skills and animal smarts to orchestrate the wild horse roundups. The largest was in the late fall after the first snows had driven the herd down from the mountains sur-rounding the Piedra Lumbre. De Dios solicited help from his Navajo and Apache friends, and with the local Anglo and Hispanic cowboys, spent several days chasing, capturing, chasing, and recapturing wild horses.

There were several methods favored by de Dios and the valley cowboys: old domestic horses were set loose on the basin where they would mingle with and then lead the wild ones into a nearby corral. Another method involved riders who waited near the river where the wild herd watered; when the horses' bellies were heavy, the men moved in and caught the most valuable of the horses, usually the mares.

There were also roundups that involved several strings of riders that, in turn, stampeded the wild herd toward a designated corral in the Piedra Lumbre basin. Upon lassoing a mare or young colt, de Dios was known to use one of his prized oxen to coerce a hitherto untouched and unleadable horse back to his corral: the roped horse was tied to the mas-sive, lumbering ox, who led the horse, cooperative or not, slowly across the llanos to one of the corrals at the River Ranch.

In the last years of his life, de Dios took archaeologists to the pre-historic ruins in the valley. A lifetime spent on foot and on horseback in the basin and sierras had given de Dios intimate knowledge of the Piedra Lumbre's archaeological treasures, and the respected Genízaro's memo-ries served as a bridge between times, linking a fading yesteryear with a rapidly forgetting present.

Following an accident in a snowstorm, de Dios was taken to the hospital in Santa Fe, where he died in 1938 or 1939. Like his age, which may have been as young as seventy-eight or as old as one hundred, no one seems to agree on the year of his departure. De Dios may have been buried in the soil of the River Ranch beside the muddy Chama. If his grave was ever marked, it is of no consequence to history, as the stone and wood house, the corrals that held wild horses and tempering oxen, and the ashes of summer campfires are all lost beneath the waters of Abiquiu Reservoir.

The Pueblo of Abiquiu became the Village of Abiquiu in 1928. At that time, local historians recall, the community was given the opportunity to choose between legal designation as an Indian pueblo or as a New Mexi-can village. The villagers decided that their Native American neighbors were treated so poorly by the government that it would behoove the community to become a village, not an official Indian pueblo. A vote was taken, and Abiquiu quietly changed its status from a Native American pueblo to an Hispano village.

This decision was to have several far-reaching consequences on the town. Until 1928, the pueblo's children had attended Indian school in Santa Fe. In the years following the village vote, Abiquiu's children began to attend Rio Arriba public schools and parochial schools of the Archdiocese.

But the greatest impact of the new village designation on the old pueblo was its new tax responsibilities: after 1928, everyone was expected to pay taxes on houses and garden plots. The villagers dutifully paid their individual taxes. However, the taxes on the *ejido,* the common lands of the Abiquiu Grant which comprised most of the village's property, were collected by one individual who was to hand in the money to the state. At some time in the mid 1930s, village lore says, it was discovered that the ejido taxes had never reached official hands, and most of the Abiquiu Grant was seized by the State of New Mexico for delinquent taxes.

Upon learning of their situation the village rallied together and formed the Abiquiu Cooperative Livestock Association. With help from United States Senator Dennis Chávez, who was able to intervene on the village's behalf and convince the state tax authorities to stall the sale of the grant, and with advice from the Farm Security Administration that was helping New Mexico farmers and ranchers redeem other tax delinquent properties, the association gathered enough money to buy back their land. In 1941, more than sixteen thousand acres of the original Abiquiu Grant was returned to the village (that continued to call itself a pueblo) via the Abiquiu Cooperative Livestock Association.

The Pueblo of Abiquiu in the 1930s totalled 135 families with 563 people.[3] The village had two stores, a church, one cafe, and a two-room school attended by 43 children. Most families traveled up and down the river valley by horse and wagon, although there were twenty cars and trucks— six of which were owned by the Gonzales and Bode store—in the pueblo. The post office was in the Gonzales and Bode store, and Martin Bode, a German immigrant, was postmaster.

A hallway into the patio of the house of José María Chávez, Abiquiu. Chávez was a brigadier general in the U.S. Army during the Civil War and became a wealthy land baron through his association with the unscrupulous Anglo lawyers of the Santa Fe Ring after New Mexico became a U.S. territory. In the 1850s and '60s, this house in the old pueblo, which later became the home of Georgia O'Keeffe, often held overnight those recently captured Native Americans en route to the illegal slave markets of Santa Fe and Chihuahua. (Kenneth Chapman, ca. 1920; courtesy Museum of New Mexico, negative Nº28656)

The second church of Santo Tomás, built after the fire in the early 1880s. The old *campo santo* (cemetery) is enclosed by an adobe wall in front of the church. (Photograph ca. 1885; collection of Joseph Grant family)

Genízaro woodcutter in Abiquiu Pueblo, ca. 1885. (Collection of Joseph Grant family)

Baking in nineteenth-century northern New Mexico was usually done in outdoor ovens called *hornos*. This photograph of women and children baking in the Pueblo of Abiquiu was taken sometime before 1900. (Collection of Joseph Grant family)

The Abiquiu plaza and church, with El Cerrito in background, ca. 1885. (Collection of Robert Grant)

Abiquiu plaza was a busy trade center in the 1880s for both the Spanish and the Indian people of the Chama River Valley region. (Photograph ca. 1885; collection of Robert Grant)

Procession of Santa Rosa de Lima de Abiquiu, at the turn of the twentieth century. The residents of Abiquiu celebrate feast days for two patron saints: Saint Rose, who was the patron saint of the Spanish village of the same name built on the Chama River just below Abiquiu Pueblo in the mid 1700s; and Saint Thomas, the designated patron saint of the mission built by the Spanish government for the Genízaros of the Pueblo of Abiquiu, established in 1754. (Collection of Robert Grant)

Carol Bishop Stanley's first visit to the Southwest was to the home and trading post of John and Louisa Wetherill at Kayenta, Arizona. After moving permanently to New Mexico, Stanley made annual horse and pack trips across the desert of the Four Corners region to visit old friends. She is pictured here at Canyon de Chelly en route to the Grand Canyon with friend Jack Lambert in the summer of 1924. (Collection of Henry McKinley)

Cowboy guides set up camp, handled the horses and gear, and did most or all of the cooking for the dudes under their care. Here the White family sits at their campsite near Cañones, New Mexico, with guides Slim Jarmon (far left) and Pete Dozier (far right). (Roger H. White, ca. 1935)

Carol Bishop Stanley and Richard Pfaeffle embodied the East-West romance made famous by dime novelists in the first decades of the twentieth century: Stanley, the wealthy spinster, and Pfaeffle, the penniless cowboy, met on a horse expedition across the desert. After marrying, they began the successful San Gabriel Ranch in Alcalde, New Mexico, in 1917. Photograph of the Pfaeffles on the patio of San Gabriel Ranch. (Edward A. Kemp, 1923; courtesy Museum of New Mexico, negative N°112306)

Wrangler Jack Lambert was a popular and respected guide and cowboy who built San Gabriel Ranch with the Pfaeffles. Lambert accompanied Carol Bishop Stanley and Mary Cabot Wheelwright on their trip into Navajoland during which Wheelwright met *cacique* Hosteen Klah. Photograph of Lambert at San Gabriel Ranch, 1924. (Collection of Henry McKinley)

San Gabriel Ranch promotional brochure, ca. 1924. Richard Pfaeffle, right; Jack Lambert, left. (Courtesy Museum of New Mexico, negative N°161234)

Automobile travel was difficult across New Mexico and Arizona in the early 1920s but was considered a necessary and even pleasurable part of the Great Western Adventure. Here Orville Cox looks into the engine of one of the San Gabriel touring cars stuck in the Rio Grande near Alcalde, New Mexico, 1921. (Collection of Martha Cox Boyle)

The San Gabriel Ranch patio where Willa Cather worked on her novel *The Professor's House* in the summer of 1925. (Elizabeth B. Seals, 1932)

Pack trips into the Four Corners country from San Gabriel Ranch usually included a stop on the Pajarito Plateau above Española at the Los Alamos Ranch School of Ashley Pond's. Photograph of San Gabriel guests and wranglers at the Big House at Los Alamos. (Carol Bishop Stanley, ca. 1925; collection of Henry McKinley)

Before Orville Cox joined Jack Lambert and the Pfaeffles at San Gabriel Ranch he worked as an automobile tour guide for the Rocky Mountain Camp Company. Cox is pictured here in the company's office in what is now La Fonda Hotel on the plaza in Santa Fe, 1921. (Collection of Martha Cox Boyle)

This promotional photograph shows San Gabriel cowboys shooting craps while a woman dude and a local Native American, possibly from nearby San Juan Pueblo, look on. (Edward A. Kemp, ca. 1923; courtesy Museum of New Mexico, negative Nº151373)

The wranglers, cowboys, and guides usually ate separately from the guests at a dude ranch. Here the San Gabriel cowboys have lunch in their dining hall, 1923. (Courtesy Museum of New Mexico, negative Nº112305)

Although located on the edge of the high-desert country of northern New Mexico, San Gabriel's courtyards boasted shade trees, lush grass, and a variety of flowers irrigated with water from the Rio Grande. (Edward A. Kemp, 1923; courtesy Museum of New Mexico, negative N°53673)

Juan de Dios Gallegos at the River Ranch in 1935. De Dios, a Paiute by birth captured by the Navajos who in turn lost him to the Spanish during a raid, was raised in Abiquiu. His River Ranch, and the Chama River crossing, on the Piedra Lumbre basin below Pedernal was known and used by all travelers through this section of northern New Mexico from the late 1800s until his death in the late 1930s. (Frank C. Hibben)

Martin John Bode immigrated to New Mexico in 1914. He settled in Abiquiu by 1920, became a partner in the Gonzales and Bode store, and eventually became one of the pueblo's most respected and influential citizens. Photograph taken in 1914. (Collection of Karl Bode and Elizabeth Bode Allred)

Gonzales and Bode General Merchandise near the plaza of Abiquiu, early 1920s. Mercantiles such as this one were often the only link to the outside world for remote New Mexican villages such as Abiquiu. The post office was located inside, gasoline pumps were out front, and the village power plant—an electrical generator that served five pueblo families—was also housed in the mercantile. (Collection of Karl Bode and Elizabeth Bode Allred)

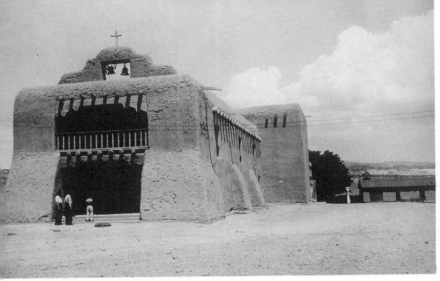

The new church of Santo Tomás, completed by 1938; the white cliffs of Plaza Blanca, O'Keeffe's White Place, are in the distance. (George Fitzpatrick; courtesy Museum of New Mexico, negative Nº55453)

Arthur Pack and his second wife, Phoebe Finley Pack, on the porch of the Ghost Ranch headquarters, 1936. The Packs bought Ghost Ranch and one-third of the Piedra Lumbre from Carol Bishop Stanley and turned her dream of a successful guest ranch at the old Ranch of the Witches into a reality in the 1930s. (T. Harmon Parkhurst; collection of the Ghost Ranch History Archive)

Stanley's crews built the three adobe cottages in the foreground and the headquarters building in the distance. The house to the upper right was built by Arthur Pack and became his home after he left Rancho de los Burros. (Roger H. White, 1935)

Stanley, and later Pack, hired local artisans and builders to construct the guest cottages at Ghost Ranch. The women of the local Hispanic communities were particularly valued for their plastering skills. Photograph of mud plastering of portion of Pack house near Ghost Ranch headquarters in 1937. (Edward H. Bennett, Jr.; collection of the Ghost Ranch History Archive)

Ghost Ranch headquarters: Carol Bishop Stanley built the first section of the adobe office, which also housed the kitchen and guest dining room, in the early 1930s. Arthur Pack's crews continued building on to the structure, which until its destruction by fire in 1983 served as headquarters for the Ghost Ranch. (T. Harmon Parkhurst, ca. 1936; collection of the Ghost Ranch History Archive)

The two-story adobe house built by Robert Wood Johnson of the Johnson and Johnson medical empire in the mid 1930s. The Johnson family came to Ghost Ranch with a bodyguard after a kidnapping attempt on their children in New Jersey: note the walled grounds and holding pond for water from El Rito del Yeso. (Collection of the Ghost Ranch History Archive)

Maggie Johnson, wife of Robert Wood Johnson, at Ghost Ranch with Sheila, the baby she adopted "instead" of buying an O'Keeffe painting from Stieglitz. Maggie Johnson was a fashion model in New York before she married Robert Wood Johnson. During her summers at Ghost Ranch Maggie hiked and explored the Piedra Lumbre with friend Georgia O'Keeffe. (Photograph ca. 1936; collection of the Ghost Ranch History Archive)

The guest dining room in the main headquarters building, Ghost Ranch, ca. 1936. Pack, like Stanley, enjoyed frequent trips into the Four Corners country of the Hopi and Navajo, and he decorated the ranch rooms with the arts, crafts, and furniture indigenous to the region. (Collection of the Ghost Ranch History Archive)

Dancers from San Juan Pueblo were invited to perform at Ghost Ranch on Saturday afternoons throughout the ranch's summer guest season. Composer Leopold Stokowski was intrigued by the native rhythms and songs performed during his visits to Ghost Ranch in the mid 1930s. (Collection of the Ghost Ranch History Archive)

Pack invited his friends from Princeton to vacation at his ranch on the Piedra Lumbre: here David McAlpin, founder of the Photography Department at the Museum of Modern Art, stands behind one of the Ghost Ranch burros with Godfrey Rockefeller seated precariously on its back. (October 1936; collection of the Ghost Ranch History Archive)

Pack hired a tutor to live at Ghost Ranch and instruct his children and those of other ranch personnel and guests. In the warmer months school was held on the headquarters porch; in the winter, in an adobe casita named Cedar. (Carl Glock, 1936)

The isolation of Ghost Ranch and the poor quality of the roads through this section of northern New Mexico necessitated Pack's earning a pilot's license and buying a Fairchild airplane. The ranch runway was packed clay. Pack is standing on the wing. (Carl Glock, July 1936)

In 1936, with friend and rancher Charlie Belden of Wyoming, Pack caught and flew several planeloads of baby pronghorn antelope to New Mexico, where he successfully reintroduced a herd to the Piedra Lumbre basin. (Charles J. Belden; collection of the Ghost Ranch History Archive)

Interior of Ghost Ranch guest cottage, 1936. The cottages were built in traditional northern New Mexico style, with thick adobe walls and beamed ceilings, and were furnished with handmade furniture and locally produced arts and crafts. (Collection of the Ghost Ranch History Archive)

Guests returned season after season to the same favored cottage at Ghost Ranch, such as this one photographed in 1936. The pine table in the foreground was built by Pete Dozier. Dozier also built furniture for Mary Cabot Wheelwright's Los Luceros ranch in Alcalde. (Collection of the Ghost Ranch History Archive)

The ranch string of horses was kept in corrals near the bunkhouse where the Ghost Ranch cowboys lived. O'Keeffe often visited with the ranch hands at what came to be called the Corral Block, and the young men who came to Ghost Ranch for a summer of work between college semesters also lived in these austere but comfortable quarters. (Collection of the Ghost Ranch History Archive)

The ox skull that marked the road to Ghost Ranch, 1937. (Photograph by Ansel Adams. Copyright © 1992 by the Trustees of the Ansel Adams Publishing Rights Trust. All Rights Reserved)

O'Keeffe knocked on the door of the old Archuleta homestead — renamed Ghost House — to ask for a room in the summer of 1934. Carol Bishop Stanley lived in the old adobe casa until she sold and departed the Ranch of the Witches in the late 1930s. The famous hanging tree, where cattle thieves, local legend remembers, were punished for their deeds, stands to the right. (Photograph taken in 1936; collection of the Ghost Ranch History Archive)

From her car, O'Keeffe could see the cliffs of Ghost Ranch but, much to her frustration, could not find the gate and the road that led to the guest ranch during her first trip into the Piedra Lumbre basin in 1933. (© 1996 Kent M. Bowser)

The Ghost Ranch skull motif drawn by Georgia O'Keeffe and given to Arthur Pack in 1936. The skulls of the giant oxen that once belonged to Juan de Dios served as the model for this drawing, and one became the marker for the Ghost Ranch road in the Piedra Lumbre basin. The O'Keeffe drawing was used on the Ghost Ranch brochure cover, 1936, and has served as the Ghost Ranch motif and trademark ever since. (Collection of the Ghost Ranch History Archive)

The Garden Cottage located at the east end of Ghost Ranch's vegetable garden was O'Keeffe's summer home in 1934, '35, and '36. (Photograph taken in 1936; collection of the Ghost Ranch History Archive)

Olive M. Bennett sitting on the outdoor staircase to the roof of the newly completed Bennett house, 1937. O'Keeffe particularly enjoyed the view of the Piedra Lumbre sky from this same roof on evenings when the Bennetts were out of town. (Edward H. Bennett, Jr.; collection of the Ghost Ranch History Archive)

Ghost Ranch cowboy and guide Pete Dozier, who sat with O'Keeffe and watched the guests' children perform under the stars in the summer of 1937. O'Keeffe had met Dozier several years before in Taos when he worked at Mabel Dodge Luhan's Los Gallos ranch. (Carl Glock, 1937)

Norrie (holding a Hershey's bar) and Peggy Pack in their riding clothes, perhaps after an impromptu visit with O'Keeffe on the desert in the summer of 1936. The Pack sisters often spent a morning on horseback looking for O'Keeffe's open-air studio on the Piedra Lumbre. O'Keeffe gave them chocolate bars and then asked them to leave her alone. (Collection of the Ghost Ranch History Archive)

Carl Glock standing before Rancho de los Burros, the house Arthur Pack built for his family in 1933. Pack sold Georgia O'Keeffe this adobe house in 1940. (Carl Glock, 1936)

Two photographs of O'Keeffe's Rancho de los Burros house at Ghost Ranch. (© 1973 Todd Webb; courtesy Todd Webb and Museum of Fine Arts, Museum of New Mexico, Todd Webb Study Collection)

Georgia O'Keeffe and Orville Cox at Canyon de Chelly, fall of 1937. Cox guided a group that included Ansel Adams, David McAlpin, and Godfrey Rockefeller through the Four Corners region of New Mexico and Arizona.

This photograph by Adams of O'Keeffe and Cox, who is credited with taking the painter to the Black Place, was a favorite of Adams's. (Photograph by Ansel Adams. Copyright © 1995 by the Trustees of the Ansel Adams Publishing Rights Trust. All Rights Reserved)

The Indian Room in O'Keeffe's Abiquiu residence. This room was known as the Ute Room when it belonged to General José María Chávez before the turn of the twentieth century: Indian "guests" were placed here overnight. At that time the room had no windows and the door could be bolted from the outside. (Laura Gilpin, "Georgia O'Keeffe Residence, Abiquiu," 8×10 in. safety negative, 1960; Copyright 1981 Laura Gilpin Collection, Amon Carter Museum, Fort Worth, Texas, Nº AR 5019.3)

During World War II, Ghost Ranch was cleared by the FBI to serve as a weekend getaway for the scientists working on the atomic bomb in Los Alamos. Katherine (Kitty) B. White, standing on the porch of the ranch's main headquarters with Arthur and Phoebe Pack, was a nurse married to engineer Roger White (who was also a cousin of Arthur's); both were employed by the Manhattan Project. (Roger H. White, 1943)

Preeminent paleontologist Dr. Charles Camp (foreground) of the University of California, Berkeley, spent the summers of 1928–34 digging the badlands of the Piedra Lumbre. Rare fossilized remains were found on the Piedra Lumbre in the 1870s during the Wheeler Expedition, but Camp's crew found the first complete phytosaur skeleton on the Piedra Lumbre in 1928. Camp's notes of his summers under the Cliffs of Shining Stone—he is here shown working under the Puerto del Cielo—prompted other professional bone diggers to visit the region in the 1930s and '40s, eventually resulting in the discovery of the remarkable Coelophysis quarry in 1947. (V. L. Vander Hoof, 1928; collection of Samuel P. Welles)

A phytosaur skeleton like this one was found in the sands below Orphan Mesa in 1934, giving the local myth of Vivarón, the giant child-eating snake, at least a modicum of substance. (Arthur N. Pack, 1936; collection of the Ghost Ranch History Archive)

Edwin H. Colbert working at the Coelophysis quarry at Ghost Ranch, 1947. (Detail of slide; collection of Edwin H. Colbert, courtesy Ruth Hall Museum of Paleontology, Ghost Ranch)

Members of the Salazar family, owners of more than half of the Piedra Lumbre land grant until they sold to Arthur Pack in the 1930s. The local ranchers were wary of the paleontologists' unearthing of the bones, albeit fossilized, in the Piedra Lumbre's soil, and explained to Camp and his colleagues the region's infamy in regards to *brujos* and *brujas* (witches). The paleontologists became friends with the local populace, Anglo and Hispanic alike, and were often guests at their homes. (R. T. Moore, 1935; collection of Samuel P. Welles)

After six years of legal work that involved an act of Congress, the Ghost Ranch Conference Center cleared disputed titles for 125 tracts of land claimed by the U.S. Forest Service and gave the titles to their Hispanic owners. The land trade, in which the Presbyterian Church gave the Forest Service acreage in exchange for the disputed lands within national forest boundaries, involved 111 families and was officially held at Ghost Ranch on April 6, 1975: "It was a time when charity kissed justice." (Collection of the Ghost Ranch History Archive)

Bode had immigrated to the United States in 1914, and after working briefly at an uncle's store in southern New Mexico, had come to Española, where he worked as a stockman for Frank Bond and his large mercantile enterprise. By 1920, the twenty-nine-year-old Bode had moved to Abiquiu, where he was a boarder in the house of Miguel and Blanchek Gonzales. Bode worked as a salesman at the Gonzales Store and eventually became Gonzales's partner.[4]

The Gonzales and Bode store was located behind the church at the northern edge of the pueblo mesa. The store owned and operated the pueblo's power plant, from which five village families received electricity. Ten Anglo families had moved into the valley in the early 1930s—one of these, the Mortons of Texas, purchased most of the lands owned by the Gonzales family—and the three tractors in the community were all owned by the Anglo farmers.[5] Across from the mercantile was the once elegant home of General Chávez, now vacated and in disrepair. Although its orchards still bore fruit, its once beautiful courtyards were now used for chickens, pigs, and goats.

While still a remote and largely forgotten corner of the United States, Abiquiu and its neighboring villages were directly affected by the Great Depression. Although still a subsistence-level agricultural and pastoral community, the valley's economy had become increasingly dependent on the cash jobs found in the mines, timber industries, or beet and potato fields of neighboring states. In the 1920s as many as eighty-five percent of the men in a northern New Mexico village—one hundred or more individuals in a town like Abiquiu—left home to work six months or more in Utah, Colorado, Wyoming, Nevada, or Arizona. The Depression reduced the traditional opportunities for jobs in the Southwest, and by 1934, Abiquiu had only thirty-eight men working out-of-state. Many valley families were on direct government relief, with more than half of the valley farmers accepting government feed and seed loans.[6]

Cash-paying jobs were available from a limited number of sources in the Chama Valley: several Civilian Conservation Corps (CCC) camps employed several dozen men from the Abiquiu communities. The state highway department brought wage jobs to the valley when it began work on a new road between Española and Tierra Amarilla in 1933, and twenty men in Abiquiu were employed by a F.E.R.A. project building a new school in 1934.[7] The Anglo-owned cattle and horse ranch offered seasonal jobs, as did the Gonzales sheep ranch. And Stanley's Ghost Ranch employed thirty-five temporary and fourteen permanent workers by 1934.[8] But these cash jobs were hardly enough to bolster the historically marginal, and now nearly destitute, valley economy.

But it was only on government paper that Abiquiu and its extended community was called poor. Abiqueños never thought of themselves as destitute or anything resembling poor, even in the Depression years. They raised sheep, usually under the *partido* system of their forefathers, and cultivated small kitchen gardens of tomatoes, peas, chiles, sweet potatoes, cabbage, okra, pumpkins, squash, and melons.[9] The irrigated lands along the river produced wheat, barley, oats, corn, and alfalfa, and each family had chickens, goats, and a milk cow on the family plot in the village, with a few head of cattle and horses grazing on the communal meadows above the village.

Life was simple. Abiquiu was a place that was *entre verde y seco* (between green and dry), a village with neither too much nor too little, where the strong ties of family and the tested strength of tradition adequately fed the peoples' souls just as the small gardens, modest fields, and ancient orchards fed their bodies. However, the poverty brought on by the Depression, coupled with a devastating blizzard in 1931, tipped the village's delicate balance and quickly placed most local families in very serious straits.

The winter of '31 was the coldest, longest, and meanest held in the *pobladores'* collective memory. The snow was so deep the tips of fenceposts disappeared into the white, and families watched as sheep, pigs, and goats died in their pens and cattle and horses froze in the fields. Airplanes dropped hay to snow-stranded animals on the mesas and up in the sierras, but few stock animals survived the winter. Before the blizzard of '31, Abiquiu's residents had several hundred horses loose on the open range south of the village; after the spring thaw, only fifty pueblo horses remained standing.[10]

Upon the frozen heels of the blizzard came a withering drought that in the next few years would reduce the cattle and sheep herds of the valley from several thousand to several hundred animals. In the midst of the drought swarms of grasshoppers descended upon the Chama Valley region in the summer of 1934 and completely decimated the farm crops of several communities, especially Abiquiu's sister village of Barranco.[11]

The years of drought turned all of the Midwest and Southwest into the Dust Bowl; the land of northern New Mexico could no longer support any animals. Once-narrow stock trails had become gaping arroyos; a simple path across a mesa was now a thirty-foot-deep trench cut into the bare sand.[12] In the Chama Valley, the only water for range animals came from the Chama River itself, and the bottomlands of the river bosque were soon stripped bare of foliage by the desperate horses and cattle who sought its shade and what was left of its native grasses.

By the mid '30s the federal government, in an effort to save severely overgrazed land, implemented land use and grazing regulations that limited the number of livestock a rancher could place on the public domain now under the auspices of the U.S. Forest Service. Although the local ranchers did not like the general policies of the Forest Service, who they believed had wrongfully partitioned ancestral lands into the public domain, most valley residents sought the aid of, and cooperated with, the Soil Erosion Service in the reclamation of their stricken lands.

In 1934 the Taylor Grazing Act organized the remaining public domain not under the Forest Service into regulated grazing districts. The Taylor laws curtailed homesteading in the West, and thousands of acres between Abiquiu and the Piedra Lumbre not previously claimed by Spanish or Mexican grants, or by homesteaders under American law, were removed from public access. The Piedra Lumbre, divided between Stanley to the north and sheep rancher Manuel Salazar to the south, remained an unfenced fifty thousand acres of open grasslands. But the wide open ranges of the Chama Valley, the mountains behind and beside Pedernal above Abiquiu, and the Piedra Lumbre basin were disappearing before native eyes.

The Forest Service began fencing in the early 1930s. Local men in the Chama Valley were hired to string hundreds of miles of barbed wire up mesa sides, across the high sierras, and down steep canyon walls. The men worked in the summer heat and the raw cold of winter. Few Abiqueños had winter boots, and men used old inner tubes stuffed with straw for protection against the deep snow and freezing temperatures.

The fencing of the Piedra Lumbre and the Chama Valley heralded the end of the Piedra Lumbre's wild horses, who became entangled in the strange, shiny wire that suddenly stretched between them and their historic trails across the mesas and mountains. Fences and posts were found broken apart as the horses made a general mockery of the Forest Service's attempts to mark and control its territory. In light of the herds' healthy numbers and their defiance of all government grazing regulations and stock quotas, the Forest Service deemed it necessary to remove the wild horses from the valley.

Forest Service personnel first attempted to round up the herd. It is not known if the government riders were privy to the skills of Juan de Dios, or if the old *caballero* would have cooperated with the federal newcomers. But the Forest Service was unsuccessful in their wild horse corralling efforts. The craftiness of the historic herd made physical capture impossible. The only solution apparent to the frustrated authorities, whose basically moral motive was to save the valley's soil from further overgrazing, was to shoot the herd. And that is exactly what they did.

Sharpshooters with high-powered rifles waited near watering holes and alongside arroyos known to be frequented by the black stallion's herd. Locals remember that more than two hundred horses were shot in one day in the spring of 1934, with several hundred more killed in subsequent shootings. The loss of the wild herd was difficult enough for the local ranchers who had depended on their offspring for generations; but the government's action became an unforgivable crime when it was discovered that many domestic animals loose on the open range were also inadvertently killed.

"They killed all the horses, all at once," one valley old-timer, Dorthy Burnham Fredericks, remembers. "Many families lost their own teams. After the snows of the early '30s, with so few animals left alive, people depended on those horses for survival. There were no cars, so the loss of their horses was terrible. . . .

"Bones were everywhere and the countryside smelled of dead animals. For years after, every watering hole was littered with the skeletons of horses."

Ravens and turkey vultures joined the mountain lions who came down from the high country to feed on the carcasses of the horses. In a

valley barren of grass, sage, or cactus flowers, where the skeletons of
unnamed horses were bleached a ghostly white under a searing sun, dust
devils joined the old spirits of the Piedra Lumbre as the basin's dominant
life form.

Abiquiu was not a community given to giving up. In spite of debts mounting at the Gonzales and Bode store, in spite of the depleted horse, sheep,
and cattle herds and numerous villager deaths from diphtheria, malaria,
and typhoid, and in defiance of a sky that remained the same cloudless
blue day after day, month after month, the residents of Abiquiu decided to
build themselves a new church. This church, whose imagined facade was
disliked by General José María Chávez three decades before it became a
reality, was to be built upon the site of the first Genízaro church.

    Between 1932 and the mid 1940s, Abiquiu was part of the El Rito
parish under the administration of a young energetic German immigrant,
the Reverend William Bickhaus. A former ambulance driver in the kai-
ser's army, Bickhaus, upon reaching New Mexico, became involved with
regional clergy and laypeople interested in the preservation and restoration of the historic churches. Bickhaus was soon a vocal leader among
those in the valley who believed Abiquiu's old plaza deserved a new
church.

    Although Martin Bode did not teach his young children German in
the 1930s, he did share long conversations in his native tongue with the
young priest from El Rito, who became a frequent visitor to the large and
comfortably furnished Bode home on the old plaza. Father Bickhaus
quickly enlisted Bode's support of the new church, which was to be
designed by "Santa Fe Style" revivalist and architect John Gaw Meem.
After plans were completed by the renowned architect, demolition of the
old church began.

    The rich history of the pueblo was held not only in the arrow- and
hatchet-stressed adobes, but also in the sacred ground beneath and surrounding the old church. Bodies buried alongside the church's outer walls
were exhumed and properly reburied in the village cemetery in a meadow
southeast of the village. Many of these were the bodies of children lost to
illness and injury in times when medical help was unavailable to the

remote pueblo: the boys were found buried with *coronas de talco,* cardboard crowns decorated with chips of mica; the young girls had been buried with *coronas de flores,* crowns of flowers.[13]

Below the wooden boards of the old church floor were the coffins of many of the pueblo's historic VIP's. Ironically, perhaps fittingly, the last such person to be buried in the church was General José María Chávez. The general's remains had been placed beneath the wooden floor before the altar in 1902. Because the services of a priest were often hard to come by in Abiquiu during the early years of this century, the same day that General Chávez's funeral mass was held, the church also hosted two weddings.[14]

Meem's pueblo-style plans for the new Abiquiu *iglesia* were completed in 1935, and construction began the same year, with the massive church completed by the end of 1937. All of the labor for the new church was volunteered by village and valley men. The building of a new church gave the community something to rally around—something that recalled their ancestor's struggles and victories through different but no less challenging times.

The adobes made and laid by the Genízaros of the Pueblo of Abiquiu more than a century before were not reused, but the old ceiling vigas were saved for use as a new village dance floor. Bode himself could not volunteer his time, but the Gonzales and Bode store, along with the wealthier families of the valley, donated the lumber needed for the new church. Additional building materials came from the Society for the Preservation of New Mexico Mission Churches, and the forty-eight thousand new adobes were made with Abiquiu soil by Abiqueño hands and feet.

According to local lore, the only obstacle the building of the new Church of Santo Tomás encountered was a brief but bitter disagreement among the villagers as to which direction the new church should face: to the south, like the historic church of the Genízaros? Or to the east, the direction preferred and promoted by the archbishop, the clergy, and the Santa Fe architect?[15] The "easterners" or "neo-architects" consisted of the priest and his friends, "residents of the suburb of Barranco and the merchant element."[16] The "southerners" or "traditionalists" were most everyone else, and they were fervent in their desire that the new church entrance face exactly the same direction as that of their forefathers. The archbishop himself visited the divided pueblo and attempted to persuade the traditionalists that Church policy dictated that the new church should have an easterly entrance.

In true Genízaro force and style, the traditionalists stood their ground and withdrew their support of the new church, telling the archbishop he had best move to the village and begin adobe making with his own two feet, as they would not be volunteering their soles for the task. Although disgruntled, the traditionalists seemed to have accepted defeat, and the easterners proceeded with construction of the sunrise-facing church. The foundation was poured and the first of the almost fifty thousand adobe bricks were made and set out to dry in the sun.

But the traditionalists' acceptance of defeat was short lived: the will and determination of generations of New Mexico's most independent and resourceful natives—descendants of the persevering Spanish colonists and Genízaros whose bones and blood littered the very soil of the new adobes basking in the sun—rose from the dust and overcame twentieth-century complacency one dark night. A young traditionalist "in an embittered state of mind over the setback suffered by his side, rammed his Model-T again and again into the freshly laid foundation until it crumbled beyond repair."[17]

The following morning, work resumed on the new church, only now the volunteer work force included individuals from both sides of the controversy, and the foundation was repoured so that the double doors of the new Church of Santo Tomás faced south into the strong light of the not so far away, and never to be forgotten, past. Soon after completion, the wooden cross that had protected the former church and its parishioners from the activities of the local *brujas* was re-erected before the doors of the new church.

Although representative of the classic Pueblo-mission style in vogue among Santa Fe's artistic elite, the finished church deviated enough in design and structure from John Gaw Meem's blueprints to solicit the architect's disapproval. Meem chose not to be among those who attended the archbishop's mass in the new church, nor did he enjoy the community feast and *baille* (dance) held immediately after in the Bode living room.

Local oral historians recall that Meem disavowed that the Church of Santo Tomás was built with his plans at all. Like the first church built in the tenuous times of colonial New Spain, the new Church of Santo Tomás was built with that elusive, uniquely Abiqueño spirit that subtly but proudly defied the authority of church or state or famous Anglo architects in favor of its own multicultural orientation.

10

GHOST RANCH

By 1933, Ghost Ranch was open for at least limited guest business and was, like San Gabriel before it, a lunch stop for the Couriercars of the Southwestern Indian Detours. The tourist-dude business of the West was greatly diminished during the '30s. Only the very wealthy came West during the Depression—in 1934, a guest paid fifty dollars a week for room, board, and both horse and automobile transportation. Along with car tours into Indian country, horseback riding was still the primary pastime of ranch guests.

Overland pack trips to the Grand Canyon were rare; fencing prohibited easy cross-country navigation and forced horse travelers to share roads with automobiles. The popularity of automobile trips had left the once unspoiled desert crisscrossed with tire tracks. To those who remembered it when, the whole region now clamored with too many tourists. Mechanized civilization was creeping across the Southwestern landscape, and crushed beneath its wheels was the frontier that had both deterred and attracted human travelers for centuries: "The setting was wild, as Nature had made it, until civilization kind of moved in on it," dude rancher Dick Randall wrote of the vanishing frontier. "It was that wildness that appealed to folks."[1]

By 1933, Stanley lived full-time at Ghost Ranch. In the early spring of that year, she received a letter from her old friend Arthur Pack: Pack's youngest daughter, Peggy, had suffered several bouts of pneumonia, and under a doctor's orders, the family was looking for a home in a drier climate. Pack had learned of Stanley's move to the ranch near Abiquiu and asked if his family could come for a visit. Stanley wrote that they could, and in June, the Pack family—Arthur and his wife, Eleanor Brown (called Brownie); their ailing daughter, Peggy; an older daughter, Eleanor (called Norrie); and their son, Vernon—disembarked the Santa Fe Railway at Lamy en route to Ghost Ranch.

After loading up a considerable amount of luggage, Pack drove the family in a rented car north and west down the mountains out of Santa Fe to Española, where they turned onto the "narrow, lonely, dusty track" that was the road northwest up the Chama River Valley. When the Pack car reached Abiquiu plaza, the family disembarked for a brief rest at the Gonzales and Bode store. In a conversation with Martin Bode, Pack explained that they were headed for Ghost Ranch, where they meant to spend the summer. Bode must have worried about the Princetonian's ability to navigate the road out to the Piedra Lumbre because he volunteered to accompany the Pack family to their destination. After a dozen miles of "poorly graded clay" that finally reached "up and out across a sea of dry grassland dotted with juniper and pinon," the Pack car with its German guide reached the turn to Stanley's ranch, "a mere track marked only by a cow's skull propped against a rock."[2] They followed the rutted track north across the desert, "slid down an incredibly steep hill, crossed a creek on a narrow log bridge and wound up on the other side beneath a spectacular array of cliffs seen years before"—Ghost Ranch.[3]

The Packs' two-thousand-mile journey ended before the old Archuleta homestead, "a single low adobe building whose every door and window staggered crookedly," the Ghost House.[4] They were greeted by "a woman who spoke in cultured tones unmistakably Bostonian," Carol Stanley.[5] Stanley and her maid, Alice, gave the family a dinner of chili and beans. When dusk fell, candles were lit on the tables and over the gleaming piano that had followed the fifty-four-year-old expatriate like an only child through her adventures and misadventures in the Great Southwest.

The Pack family chose to sleep out under the stars that first night.

Their view included the arms of the giant cottonwoods where, Stanley told them, cattle thieves had once swung by the neck.

Pack was an extremely well known name in American conservation circles. Although the Pack empire was built in the late 1800s from the lucrative proceeds of logging in Canada and the United States, by the early years of this century, Arthur's father, Charles Lathrop Pack, had recognized the threat his family business posed to the forests of North America and had become a champion of reforestation and conservation. During the first world war Charles Pack was president of the National War Garden Commission. After the war Pack used his own money to send millions of American douglas-fir seeds and seedlings to England and France to help reforest the war-ravaged landscape. By the 1920s, Charles Pack was president of the American Forestry Association, which he helped found, and with son Arthur, he wrote and lectured about the need for tree conservation in the United States.[6]

Arthur Pack attended Williams College and then Harvard, where he received a degree in business in 1915. Young Pack began writing nature-related articles in the early 1920s, and his first book, *Our Vanishing Forests,* was published by MacMillan in 1923.[7]

With his father's financial backing, Pack co-founded *Nature Magazine* with Percival Sheldon Ridsdale in 1923. The magazine was devoted to articles about forestry and the preservation of natural landscape, as well as to educational writings about wildlife. Founded the same year as *Time Magazine, Nature* quickly had 100,000 subscribers and in the early years ran neck and neck in popularity with *Time* among American readers.

Nature Magazine was published in Washington, D.C., by the American Nature Association, but Pack and his family lived in Princeton. Their friends included the wealthy and noteworthy of their time: before their move to the country and the tragic kidnapping and murder of their baby, the Lindberghs lived on the same block, and Anne Morrow and Brownie Pack shared lunches and attended concerts together in New York. The Packs' trips into the American and Canadian outback included many Princeton and Washington friends: Robert Wood Johnson of the Johnson and Johnson medical empire was a frequent member of the Pack/*Nature Magazine* entourage, often with new Johnson and Johnson products included in his first-aid bag.

On one month-long expedition to photograph mountain sheep and caribou in the Canadian Rockies, Bob Johnson brought along his company's newest insect repellent. Johnson chose to test the product's abilities on his own body and upon reaching their mosquito-clouded campsite beside a roaring river, splashed it liberally onto his arms and neck: "A moment later I saw him dash frantically out into the icy water," Arthur Pack wrote of the incident, "and begin splashing himself with unusual enthusiasm. Several minutes passed before he was able to explain that the new solution not only removed insects but human skin as well."[8]

On this same journey into northern Canada, a young Princeton undergraduate, Lawrence Rockefeller, split open his foot with an axe while chopping wood. The group was days from a hospital or a doctor, and it was Bob Johnson's medical know-how and little black bag of state-of-the-art first-aid supplies that dressed Rockefeller's wound and enabled him to remain on the expedition.

Pack was still an editor of *Nature Magazine* when he brought his family to northern New Mexico in 1933, but he was ready for a dramatic change in lifestyle. His semiannual trips into the American outback were no longer enough to satisfy his need to observe wildlife and nature: "Literally and figuratively," Pack wrote in the early '30s, "those who live beyond the reach of cement pavement have their feet on the ground."[9]

After one night under the bewitched stars of the Piedra Lumbre, Pack told Stanley he wished to buy land and build a home under the cliffs of her ranch. Stanley was land rich but cash poor, and she agreed to sell Pack a piece of the Piedra Lumbre. Together they chose a site in the red and gold sand hills between the two rock chimneys that marked the northern skyline of the Piedra Lumbre. The surveyed parcel was 390 acres.

Pack left plans with Stanley's long-time builder, Ted Peabody, for a flat-roofed, U-shaped adobe hacienda whose enclosed portal would face Pedernal. The house was completed by the time of the Pack family's return to New Mexico, Christmas 1933.

Although Pack's ultimate gift to the Piedra Lumbre would be the strictly enforced soil and wildlife conservation practices that would keep the basin's ecosystem in a relatively balanced, semiwilderness state until the arrival of the U.S. Army Corps of Engineers and their earth-filled dam in 1963, Pack initially viewed the land of Ghost Ranch with eyes colored by the stories and images of the Mythic West: as potential cattle country. In spite of the drought that had depleted the basin's grasses, in 1934 Pack and Stanley became partners in the Piedra Lumbre Cattle Company. Although the Piedra Lumbre Cattle Company was to be a short-lived operation, some five hundred cows were moved onto Ghost Ranch's 32,168 acres, with plans to bring on more cattle and also to add purebred Palomino horses if the business proved successful.

Pack supplied the capital, and Stanley placed more than sixteen thousand acres of Ghost Ranch into the company holdings. By the mid 1930s Pack had purchased at least fifteen thousand additional acres of the Piedra Lumbre llanos on the south side of the Chama River from Cañones rancher Manuel Salazar, whose substantial sheep business suffered losses initiated by overgrazing and drought and was further diminished when livestock prices slumped during the Depression.

The first cattle herd was driven to the Piedra Lumbre from Lamy, southeast of Santa Fe. In the spring of 1934, in true western style, Stanley's seasoned cowboys, headed by Jack McKinley and Shorty Skelton and accompanied by one of the Pack family's young Princeton friends, Frank Hibben, pushed the herd north and west to the Rio Grande Valley. They drove the cattle without rest because there was no place to hold the herd overnight. The country was now marked and measured by roads, and the route between Santa Fe and Abiquiu taken 170 years earlier by the Martín Serranos was broken and dislocated by fences. The Ghost Ranch cowboys had to plan their cattle trail according to gates and gate keys, but to Princeton graduate Frank Hibben it was "the old trail days, you know. Of course, I got a big bang out of it!"

Trail boss Jack McKinley, his wife and three children, and Jack's brother, Marvin, had come to Ghost Ranch with Stanley from San Gabriel. McKinley was a highly respected cowboy, born in Oklahoma and raised in New Mexico. He was fluent in Spanish and was the renowned owner of an inexhaustible amount of energy and the frontier work ethic. Rugged and handsome, and endowed with the natural charm and unpretentious chivalry exhibited by the best dude wranglers, McKinley was greatly favored by the women guests at both San Gabriel and Ghost Ranch. His wife-to-be, Margaret, had first come to San Gabriel as a nurse to the children of a wealthy Boston family. Margaret met and fell in love with McKinley and never returned to Boston.

Jack McKinley may have turned the heads of the eastern dudettes who came to northern New Mexico. But he was not so popular among the Chama Valley ranchers: "Woe betide the careless neighbor who left a gate down," Pack wrote of McKinley, "for Jack would trail him for miles and then proceed to give him a thorough beating, no matter how many friends tried to come to the rescue. He was a top hand, admired and yet feared throughout our whole country."[10]

Jack McKinley was a mild-mannered gentleman when compared to his elder brother, Bill. Bill McKinley was the leader of a notorious ring of sheep, cattle, and horse rustlers who terrorized Rio Arriba County in the late 1920s and early '30s. McKinley's group included fifteen Hispano riders who rustled livestock from herds grazing in the northern mountains. The stolen animals were sold to buyers in Colorado. McKinley's gang also confiscated at gunpoint corralled sheep, goats, hogs, and horses, wagons and tack from sheds and barns, even household goods like sewing machines. The mountain *ranchito* of sheep rancher Manuel Salazar was raided and burned by the rustlers.[11] Villagers and ranchers from Alcalde to Tierra Amarilla were afraid of these *banditos,* known among Rio Arriba lawmen as the Night Riders.[12] The local population became so terrorized by this gang they refused to help the few sheriff's deputies trying to track the rustlers' activities.

It took the relentless pursuit of one Swiss-born detective, Bill Martin, to catch and arrest, one by one, the entire gang led by "the big gringo" he eventually learned was named Bill McKinley. Although the Night Riders were linked to the burning of the Sargent and Martin store in El Rito, it was for the robbery of Mary Wheelwright's Los Luceros home, in which thousands of dollars worth of Indian blankets and jewelry were stolen, that McKinley was finally convicted. Detective Martin succeeded in arresting all of the Night Riders, and his carefully gathered evidence sent McKinley and his colleagues to the state penitentiary.[13]

By 1934, Pack was at least a silent co-owner of Ghost Ranch, with most of Stanley's land heavily mortgaged to him. Pack had his own publishing business activities to attend to, but he kept a close eye on Ghost Ranch's books and operation.

The horse and dude wranglers at Ghost Ranch, like at San Gabriel and every other guest ranch in the West, carried very high profiles, and for this reason, Stanley brought with her as many of her San Gabriel cowboys as was possible. Among the newer cowboys at Ghost Ranch was José Pitman Guadalupe Dozier. Pete Dozier was a half-Pueblo, half–Anglo American guide and wrangler. Dozier's father had been a schoolteacher of French descent who had come to Santa Clara Pueblo with the Indian Service in 1893. Dozier married a young Santa Clara woman soon after, and Pete was born in 1898.

Before joining Stanley, Dozier worked as a guide and a dude wrangler at the new Bishop's Lodge in the 1920s. His younger brother, Tom, was a driver for Fred Harvey's Indian Detours and, like Pete, also became a popular guide in northern New Mexico. Pete and Tom knew the Four Corners Indian country and led pack trips from the Española Valley to the Grand Canyon. On separate expeditions in the early 1930s, both Doziers guided Pulitzer Prize–winning novelist Oliver La Farge and his wife, Wanden Kane, across Navajoland.

The full-time resident staff of Ghost Ranch also included a full-time gardener, Archie Galbraith, and his wife, Laverne, who oversaw an immense kitchen garden of vegetables as well as uncommon desert luxuries like melons and raspberries. Ghost Ranch had its own chickens and milk cow, and the ranch dining room menu reflected the cowboy preference for range-fattened beef instead of the regional favorite, mutton.

In the first years, guests and staff ate together in the dining room of the headquarters, where a wooden sign over the kitchen door gave first-timers an indication of the character of the ranch cook: "Reach and ask, reach and ask," the sign instructed. "What you can't reach, ask for."

The cook, known around the ranch as Irish Mary, was a robust, buxom, no-nonsense woman who enjoyed her ability to shock and intimidate the uninitiated dudes and dudines with her loud voice and blunt service, which was often accompanied by a forceful slap on the back, or an elbow nudged into the ribs of a delicate female visitor. Experienced guests exercised amused tolerance of Irish Mary because they knew her food would be impeccable, even if her manners and social skills left something to be desired.

Arthur Pack named his new adobe hacienda Rancho de los Burros, a word play on its sister, Rancho de los Brujos. The name was also a tribute to the children's pet burros that had been rounded up and captured with great difficulty by Jack McKinley, Pack, and young Frank Hibben from the wild herd that roamed Cañon del Cobre to the east of the ranch. The Copper Canyon burros were descendants of the pack animals used by the first Spanish miners, whose old copper mines—called Jimmie's and Pedro's on topography maps—were, by the 1930s, gaping holes in the upper canyon walls, their crumbling sides feebly supported by rotting timbers.

The same year Stanley sold Arthur Pack his homesite under the Cliffs of Shining Stone she sold an equally beautiful building site to architect and Chicago Plan developer Edward H. Bennett. Bennett first heard of Ghost Ranch, "the place where the scenery started," from a fellow Chicagoan, Arthur Cable.[14] Cable, like other wealthy easterners, had built a summer home and ranch complete with a polo field in the Tesuque hills outside of Santa Fe. After visiting Cable's New Mexico hideaway the Bennetts wanted their own vacation home in the Southwest.

Upon Cable's recommendation, the Bennetts drove the "forty miles of washboard road" from Española to Ghost Ranch in their Chevrolet, which "acted as though it had no wheels and we were being dragged along." When they reached Ghost Ranch, the exhausted family was "greeted by Carol Stanley, a person of great charm, and given some iced tea."[15]

The Bennetts purchased 212 acres from Stanley and drew up plans for a U-shaped, traditional portal-shaded adobe hacienda under the Puerta del Cielo ("gate to Heaven"), the name given the westernmost sandstone chimney that jutted from the cliffs on the Piedra Lumbre's north side. The Bennetts' house, completed in 1934, like that of the Packs, faced the vast llanos that stretched south across the historic basin to the Chama River and Pedernal.

Throughout the 1930s, eastern tenderfoots, usually friends of the Packs, came to work summers at Ghost Ranch. For most of these young men and women their coming-of-age experiences on the Piedra Lumbre remained among the fondest memories of their lives. Although they worked hard, often glamourless jobs for little money, they viewed their position as one of rare privilege. The summer college staff accompanied ranch guests on camping trips to Mesa Verde and Canyon de Chelly, on sightseeing journeys to local Pueblo and village events, and to fiestas and other events in Santa Fe and Taos.

Around Ghost Ranch itself, summer staffers were exposed to a variety of traditional sports and pastimes: square dances for both the dudes and the staff were held under the stars every Saturday night; at some time during the week the ranch cowboys were persuaded to show off their roping and riding skills in impromptu rodeos; Native American dancers and singers from San Juan Pueblo came regularly to Ghost Ranch to perform; and local Hispano singers shared their music on special occasions. Burro baseball, which relied upon the cooperation of burros with batters, catchers, and base runners—although on a par with squirrel wrestling among the ranch cowboys—was a favorite sport among the guests and seasonal staff.

One such summer tenderfoot was Texan Richard Wells, whose mother was married to Arthur's brother, Randolph. To reach Ghost Ranch from Española, the young Wells took the stage line (a station, not a horse-drawn, wagon) up the Chama River Valley. The stage took Wells up the narrow canyon beyond Abiquiu and out onto the Piedra Lumbre basin. After crossing the river at de Dios's River Ranch, Richard and his "please-don't-rain" suitcase of belongings was deposited beside a lonely gate graced by a cow's skull. The stage driver told Wells that this was the road to Ghost Ranch and that someone would be along "after awhile."

Wells sat down beside his bag on the hot, silent desert of the Piedra Lumbre, where he contemplated Pedernal's blue-gray form, and wondered how long "after awhile" might be in New Mexico. After several hours, just about when Wells began to contemplate how it would be to spend a night beside that bleached cow's skull, alone on what had to be one of the most forgotten stretches of sand and sky in America, the dust from a vehicle rose off the sand hills to the north. Soon the outline of a vehicle solidified in the high-desert air, and within minutes a truck with

"GR" painted on its door reached Wells's lonely perch. The driver, a summer worker like Wells, deposited the outgoing mail in a box beside the highway and told Wells to climb in.

Wells washed dishes, waited tables, made beds, dug ditches, lit and relit the coal heaters in each guest house, and gathered up the garbage every afternoon. Time off was usually spent on horseback, exploring the Piedra Lumbre and the mountains everywhere around it. Wells and the summer staff lived with the cowboys in Corral Block, where they learned how to play cards, knot lariats, and tell tall tales about horses, cattle, rattlesnakes, and women. Wells described it in a letter he wrote me: "I remember the coyotes yipping and howling out in the night. They sounded as if they were right beside us, but in the dry desert air they might be a mile away in the back of some blind canyon. A full moon was spectacular out on the Ghost Ranch. It would come up from behind a mesa, fire engine red and big as a balloon. Anybody with the spirit of adventure had to be impressed."

Carl Glock accompanied his father on a automobile trip through the Southwest that included a few nights at Ghost Ranch in 1936. Carl's father had attended both Williams College and later Harvard with Arthur Pack, and he stopped at Ghost Ranch to see how his old friend was adjusting to life in New Mexico. Young Carl fell in love with the ranch and stayed on as a summer worker. He worked around the corrals, cleaned the swimming pool fed by the cold waters of the Rito del Yeso, irrigated the gardens and fields, and filled in the prairie dog holes on Pack's airstrip. (With the closest telephone or telegraph—and doctor or other emergency help—more than forty miles downriver at Española, and with all supplies not grown or made at the ranch itself purchased in Española and Santa Fe, the benefits of airplane travel became obvious to Pack, and he obtained a pilot's license in 1934.) Glock was an able driver and was soon entrusted with the ranch checks and receipts, which necessitated weekly car trips into the Española bank. The return journey over the bumpy, arroyo-fed road to Abiquiu often included a satchel of cash for the ranch payroll, and young Glock was given a loaded pistol in case of ambush.

The Packs' old friends Bob and Maggie Johnson came to Ghost Ranch for refuge the summer of 1934. Earlier that year, two would-be kidnappers were caught climbing the vines outside the Johnson children's bedroom window at their New Brunswick home. The Lindbergh baby's kidnapping and murder was still fresh and horrifying in the minds of all Americans, especially among their friends and neighbors like the Johnsons. Following the Johnson family's brush with a similar tragedy, Bob and Maggie Johnson packed up their four children and headed to New Mexico.

Accompanied by a bodyguard/chauffeur named Clay Wolf, a former state policeman, the Johnsons spent the summer of 1934 in Ghost Ranch's secluded canyon. Bob Johnson purchased a small piece of land to the northeast of the Archuletas' old homestead where Carol Stanley lived and began construction of an adobe casa for his family. This house supposedly met with great disapproval from Pack and Stanley because it was two stories high, not the traditional unobtrusive single-story adobe style of the Pack and Bennett haciendas. Bob Johnson later admitted he had chosen the wrong building style. Ted Bennett remembers: "It [the Johnson house] was a square box as he [Johnson] wished. Later he came to my father [architect Edward H. Bennett, Sr.] and said he wished he had asked father to design it."

The Johnsons' summer on the Piedra Lumbre was uneventful. The only time Clay Wolf had to draw and use his gun was during an afternoon swim: the Johnson children were in the pool when a rattlesnake entered the cold water, and Wolf was forced to unholster his weapon and kill the reptilian intruder.

During their second summer in New Mexico, Bob and Maggie Johnson became interested in the plight of a neighboring family, the Burnhams, who had a homestead east of Ghost Ranch. Dave Burnham and his wife, Marie, lived with their two children, Bill and Dorthy, in a stone-and-timber house built partially underground in the rocky mesa country between the Piedra Lumbre's eastern boundary and the western rim of Copper Canyon. Dave Burnham often worked for Stanley and later Pack at Ghost Ranch as a fence builder and mender and as a blacksmith. Mr. Dave, as he was often called, was also the favored "squares caller" for the Saturday night dances held under the stars at Ghost Ranch.

The Burnhams' daughter, Dorthy, had suffered polio-like symptoms in her legs before she was three. After consultations with many doctors, Dorthy was placed in steel braces attached to heavy shoes and that reached up her legs to her torso. These braces seem to do the young Dorthy more damage than good. Her father, frustrated with her lack of progress, cut them off and discarded them before Dorthy was five.

Five-year-old Dorthy crawled or was carried by her older brother about their homestead east of Ghost Ranch until she was placed on top of a horse: horses became Dorthy's key to freedom and mobility, but she seemed doomed to a life that excluded walking. When Bob Johnson met Dorthy in 1935, he decided to do something for the thirteen-year-old. When the Johnsons left New Mexico on their private railroad car in the fall of 1935, young Dorthy went with them.

Dorthy spent the fall and winter in the care of the Johnson family, during which she received several operations from leading surgeons in New York. After months of rehabilitation, Dorthy Burnham returned to the Piedra Lumbre and her beloved horses. Dorthy could, finally, walk on her own and was even able to buy "ordinary" shoes. But Dorthy's love for horses and horse training continued to be her first love.

By the mid '30s, Ghost Ranch's remote facility was beginning to develop a popular reputation among the elite residents and visitors of Santa Fe and Taos. Bob Johnson's sister, Evangeline, and her husband, composer and "Fantasia" conductor Leopold Stokowski, began to include Ghost Ranch on their summer travel itinerary. "On Saturday night we imported a group of Indian dancers from San Juan Pueblo," Arthur Pack wrote. "Many of these men and women were most graceful experts in their tribal ceremonies, and performed around huge bonfires to the beat, beat, beat of their drums. Leopold Stokowski, several times one of our guests, appeared fascinated by the strange mixture of their musical time, which is unfettered by standard rules of music and yet produces a throbbing rhythm that seems to re-echo all night on one's dreams."[16]

Stokowski was often a visitor to Mabel Dodge Luhan's home in Taos, and the Packs were occasionally among the guests at Mabel's famous dinner table. Mabel and her circle of friends often drove across the Rio Grande Valley to visit Ghost Ranch. Ted Bennett remembers one such afternoon: "One day we were visited, to my amazement, by Tony Luhan and his entourage.... The group consisted among others of Mabel Dodge, Dorothy Brett, and a man who looked somewhat like the pictures of

Leopold Stokowski. They all had luncheon, and looked about for something to do. Meanwhile, I had Goodyear, my old friend from St. Mark's, with me and we decided to climb a mountain. I said to Goodyear, 'I'll bet that guy thinks he looks like Stokowski.'

"When we finally returned to the ranch, we were approached by Bob Johnson, who had been with the Luhans and said they had been looking for us since they knew how much I liked music and that they had had a clambake, with Tony playing his drums and Stokowski (for it was indeed he) tuning the piano. I wish I had stayed."

The overgrazed and drought-depleted grasses of the Piedra Lumbre proved to be too sparse and fragile to support Pack and Stanley's cattle company, and the herd was moved off the basin by the end of 1936. Those animals left on the Piedra Lumbre—the ranch string of horses—roamed nearly bald sand hills looking for the last of the basin's grasses. At Pack's request, the Soil Conservation Service established a sizable Civilian Conservation Corps camp on the Piedra Lumbre north of the Chama River where they hoped to demonstrate good soil conservation practices and to conduct experiments in artificial seeding. The camp employed two hundred men and was built of wood, adobe, and stone.

The federal ccc program of the mid 1930s provided the 3.5 million people who worked at one of its camps with job training, room and board, and a dollar-a-day salary. The ccc program was among the country's first official environmental efforts: its programs included reforestation, erosion control, and the reseeding of national grasslands. The corps also constructed some one thousand national parks and restored four thousand historic sites in the United States.

Conservationist Arthur Pack was all too happy to put on his boots and gloves and work alongside the corps' men. The Piedra Lumbre reseeding and erosion control experiments were initially hampered by a lack of mechanized equipment and rainfall, but eventually the projects of the ccc aided the basin's return to a grassy rangeland. The stone check dams and other erosion-slowing devices built by the hands of the ccc men can still be seen in the Piedra Lumbre basin.

From his friend and neighbor, old Juan de Dios, Pack learned of the long-ago abundance of antelope and mountain sheep in the Piedra

Lumbre basin. It was not feasible to bring mountain sheep back to the region, but with the help of Wyoming rancher Charles J. Belden, who bred pronghorn antelope, Pack decided to repopulate the basin with antelope. Accompanied by Frank Hibben, Pack flew his Fairchild to Pitchfork, Wyoming, where after tranquilizing the fawns they gently tied together their long fragile legs and placed the antelope in grain sacks. Pack brought over two dozen baby antelope to Ghost Ranch in two different flights. The antelope were kept in corrals near, and sometimes inside of, Rancho de los Burros, where they were fed and cared for until they were old enough to survive on their own on the Piedra Lumbre's llanos.

Pack and Belden also flew a planeload of antelope fawns to Los Angeles. Each of Pack's three wildlife expeditions through the skies of the Southwest elicited much attention from the regional press and instigated overtures from various nature and wildlife conservationists. By the late '30s, Pack and the lands of Ghost Ranch began to emerge as prominent examples of land conservation and wild animal preservation and protection. At that time Pack helped found the new Southwestern Conservation League, and he worked with state and federal officials developing the priorities and procedures that would implement the new Taylor grazing laws.

The Mythic West was preserved in its native state on the Piedra Lumbre, where man and nature seemed to have found a balance that was disappearing in much of the greater world. But Ghost Ranch was not a desert paradise, and its surreal landscape was often host to the very real, very human follies that followed the lives of men and women through every era of myth or history.

In 1935, two sets of riders rode off into the Piedra Lumbre sunset leaving broken hearts and fragmented families behind them. The first pair included Arthur's wife of sixteen years, Brownie, who departed Ghost Ranch with Frank Hibben. Brownie left her intentions to divorce Pack scrawled in a short letter that young Ted Bennett, Jr., unknowingly delivered to Pack one August morning with the day's mail.

During his senior year at Princeton, Hibben had joined the Packs on very nearly every wilderness expedition they and *Nature Magazine* had embarked upon. After the Packs' move to Ghost Ranch, Hibben also came to New Mexico, where he continued working on his graduate degree while also working odd jobs around the Packs' new ranch home. Pack's frequent absences for business left too much opportunity for the "mesmerizing Brownie" and the young, ambitious, and handsome Frank Hibben to fall in love. There had been danger signals for at least the last year, but Pack had convinced himself that Hibben, twenty years his junior, and twelve years Brownie's, posed no real threat.

Pack was devastated by the news found in the little note handed to him by young Ted Bennett. With his judgement impaired by emotion and shock, Pack foolishly climbed into his Fairchild and headed into the New Mexican sky: "Between Española and Santa Fe a layer of low stratus was hugging the ridge, but my need was desperate and, accordingly, when a fair sized patch of blue above me seemed to offer an invitation to climb up through and get on top, I foolishly seized the opportunity.... I welcomed the breath-taking beauty and aching loneliness of this airman's world.... Gradually, however, a further bitter realization forced itself upon me—I was trapped. The deck of cloud beneath me now seemed to extend in every direction to the horizon, and the hole through which I had flown had closed and was no longer visible. I had no radio, no way of asking for human help, and my supply of gas could not last indefinitely."[17]

Pack was flying blind in a valley where mountains reached more than ten thousand feet into the air. Disoriented and frightened, he attempted to fly down through the thick clouds, but a near brush with the top of a piñon tree sent him back into the blinding white. After prayer and verbal reminders to follow his instrument panels and compass, Pack again descended, knowing that the side of a mountain could become his final landing strip. A wet black ribbon finally emerged from the foggy white, and he followed a blacktop highway he believed led to the Santa Fe airport as closely as the telephone wires and poles would allow. Miraculously, Pack located the dirt airstrip of the small airport: "I was safely down, taxiing towards a small shack where a man stood beside a car in drizzling rain. He was there, he said, to meet an expected mail plane but he now felt sure it wouldn't be coming in this weather."[18]

The Pack marriage was not to be the last victim of the Piedra Lumbre's bewitching stars that summer: Jack McKinley left his wife and their three young children for a wealthy Ghost Ranch guest, Ardith Johnston. Mrs. Johnston was the same woman with whom Margaret

McKinley had first come to New Mexico from Boston. The Johnston family of five had come West for a family vacation, but before their visit to Ghost Ranch was over, Mr. Johnston was suing Mrs. Johnston for divorce and Jack McKinley had informed Margaret that he was leaving the Piedra Lumbre with the soon-to-be-single Mrs. Johnston.

McKinley and Johnston married, traveled throughout Europe, and then returned to New Mexico and built the Diamond K Ranch near Glorieta, New Mexico. Margaret McKinley and the children remained at Ghost Ranch. Margaret worked for Pack, who, after losing custody of his two daughters (he was given custody of his son, Vernon), became legal guardian for the three McKinley children.

Marriages were crumbling to dust all around her, but Carol Stanley decided to give matrimony another try and married her foreman, Lloyd Miller, a Texas cowboy and former horse jockey whom Stanley had known since their days at San Gabriel. The drought had forced Stanley and Pack to end their Piedra Lumbre Cattle Company, and Ghost Ranch, although a viable and growing guest ranch, was not bringing in enough capital to support Stanley's half of the partnership. In 1936, Stanley sold Pack the Piedra Lumbre for an undisclosed amount. With the profit Stanley made from the sale, she and Miller bought Cottonwood Ranch in Alcalde, where they planned to breed and train race horses. But the business proved too costly at the outset, and by the late 1930s Stanley and Miller were broke: "We all saw it coming," Dorthy Burnham Fredericks remembers. "Carol turned her money over to Lloyd just like she had to Pfaeffle before him. My dad was real upset about this. He'd say, 'Lloyd's going to break her with gambling and horses.' Carol began to avoid her old friends—never went to lunches at La Fonda or any social event where she might meet people who knew what had happened. Carol couldn't take the humiliation of being broke twice by men."

Cottonwood belonged to creditors by 1940, at which time Stanley and Miller left northern New Mexico with "one good quarterhorse stallion and a borrowed saddle."[19] Alice Pring returned to Boston, possibly to England, after forty years with Stanley. No one seems to know what became of Stanley's baby grand piano.

Stanley and Miller disappeared into oblivion in Arboles, Colorado, where they lived in a two-room adobe house behind a small store. Dave Burnham learned of Stanley's and Miller's whereabouts and went to Colorado to visit his old friends. Fredericks remembers her father's last visit with Stanley: "Carol's health wasn't good, but she was doing all the cooking and wearing patched jeans after a whole life with a cook and a maid and fine dresses and pressed shirts. My dad talked with them awhile and then he laid a twenty dollar bill across Lloyd's knee and left. Carol passed away soon after. She was buried somewhere near Pagosa Springs. All the cowboys showed up for her funeral. All of them."

The Western Myth seemed to have gone terribly awry. Or perhaps the myth was being rewritten by those who had spent their lives in pursuit of it?

In one year's time, Pack had lost his wife, his daughters, his business partner, his ranch foreman, and one of his most experienced wranglers. Few of Pack's friends would have questioned his decision to abandon the Ranch of the Witches, but Pack chose to begin a new life for the second time on the Piedra Lumbre.

During the winter of 1936, Pack toured the East Coast lecturing and showing movies of Ghost Ranch to old friends and to perspective dudes. It was a difficult task—maintaining an outward enthusiasm for a place that had splintered his family and shattered his dreams. But in spite of the failures associated with the ranch, Pack found he had sunk roots into the land of the Piedra Lumbre that ran deeper than drought or personal sorrows.

When Pack returned to New Mexico to prepare for the upcoming summer and guest season, he began his new life by moving everything he owned out of Rancho de los Burros. Pack moved into the Archuleta homestead, Ghost House, vacated by Stanley, choosing the spirits of someone else's painful past over the ghosts of his own tragedies.

With his gardener, Archie Galbraith, Pack dug an extensive irrigation system with holding ponds that brought the waters of el Rito del Yeso east of the ranch directly to the land surrounding headquarters. A lawn of grass, more fruit and shade trees, and a larger garden were planted by Pack and Galbraith. The water brought to the dry canyon floor made the little Yeso Canyon bloom with uncharacteristic fertility.

The channel of diverted water also inadvertently exhumed one of the canyon's secrets and unearthed at least one of the mythological burial grounds used by the rustlers thirty years before. Pack wrote: "I awoke one morning at dawn to the song of a meadow lark and the unaccustomed sound of tumbling water in this desert land. Stepping to my door I confronted a deep hole about seven feet in diameter which had not been there the night before. Into this hole poured water from our new ditch and there it disappeared from sight. . . . I recalled Carol Miller's story of an old well which cattle thieves had used to dispose of the bodies of unwanted visitors. Evidently such a well had been only loosely filled in and now our ditch water had found it out."[20]

Pack and Galbraith probed the well for human bones, but the deep water and the thick, tangled roots of the old cottonwood trees made excavation impossible. "The legendary mystery remained unsolved and we again filled in the hole."[21]

Among the close friends who visited Pack at Ghost Ranch during the difficult year following his divorce was Irene Finley of Oregon. Irene's husband, nature photographer William Finley, was on his annual winter lecture tour in the East, and Irene came to New Mexico with their daughter, Phoebe. Although Irene was not sorry that Brownie Pack had departed (years before there had been considerable tension between the two women while on a camping trip; according to Irene, during this trip Brownie had devoted too much of her flirtatious attention to her husband, "Big Bill" Finley), Irene was sympathetic to Pack's despair and, with Phoebe, did her best to cheer him up.

Phoebe Finley had recently graduated from the University of Oregon, and although Pack had met Phoebe at the Finley home in Portland, the young woman who came to Ghost Ranch that cold winter was not what he expected: "She [Phoebe] had changed from a fat little teenager into an attractive young woman graduate. . . . When she volunteered that she would like a part time job on the ranch for the summer to pay for her board and keep, I figured that if she was half as good a sport as her mother, she might be just what I was looking for as hostess."[22]

Irene Finley was not simply a good sport: she was a good friend, an experienced outdoorswoman, and with her husband, Bill, part of a widely known and greatly respected nature photography/writing team. By the

1920s and Arthur Pack's first encounters with the Finleys, Bill Finley's stories and photographs of birds and other animals had brought him considerable fame in American conservation and nature circles. His work was regularly featured in *National Geographic, Life, Atlantic Monthly, Colliers, Field and Stream,* and many other publications. By 1924, Finley had become *Nature Magazine*'s western field representative and Pack's close friend.

Bill Finley also lectured and campaigned for the establishment of bird and wildlife refuges in the early years of this century. After befriending Theodore Roosevelt, Finley convinced the president to designate Three Arch Rocks on the coast of Oregon a federal sanctuary, the first in the West, in 1907. Finley was also influential in Roosevelt's establishment of two more Oregon bird refuges a year later and was instrumental in the birth of the Federal Wildlife Refuge System, which included some fifty sanctuaries by the end of Roosevelt's years in office.[23]

Phoebe Finley needed no introduction to the outdoors—she had camped throughout the Northwest with her parents since childhood, was familiar with all variety of wild animals, and was an expert horsewoman. When she returned to work at Ghost Ranch in May of 1936, Finley stepped immediately and easily into ranch life. Her main duties included overseeing the children under Pack's care—his own three, who were visiting for the summer, plus the three McKinley children—and she also was cook on overnight guest campouts in the mountains.

On one such overnight with Pack and several guests in the Canjilon Mountains above Ghost Ranch, the group was caught in a mountain thunderstorm. Cold sleet chilled everyone to the marrow, and after warming their bones with a crackling fire, and their bellies with heated grapefruit juice and a bottle of rum "kept on hand for some such emergency,"[24] everyone but Finley and Pack retired to their tents and bedrolls when the skies cleared. Beside a smoldering fire, and surrounded by a ponderosa forest fragrant from a heavy rain, Pack asked Phoebe Finley to marry him. Finley was surprised, but she accepted Pack's proposal under the stars.

The guest season was about to begin, and Finley and Pack had no time for an elaborate wedding or a honeymoon. They drove several hours to a telephone in Santa Fe and called Irene and Bill Finley. Phoebe was fourteen years Pack's junior, but the Finleys were delighted by the news and came immediately to Ghost Ranch for the wedding.

Under the new portal recently added onto the headquarters building, Finley and Pack were married by an Española minister who "had to drive out forty miles over the rough road and he arrived over an hour late because of getting lost on the way.

"He appeared nervous and unhappy in a place said to be haunted by evil spirits and, no doubt, his peace of mind was not helped by Bill Finley's insistence on making a movie of the actual ceremony, so that solemn sentences were punctuated by the buzzing of the camera when it moved in for a close shot."[25]

The reverend fled the haunted canyon as soon as the ceremony ended.

Ghost Ranch seemed to have returned to happier days and to have exorcised the last of its demons. But the spirits of the Piedra Lumbre would forever and always find ways of reminding those who lived upon it of its basically untamable character. The very next evening following the wedding, the Pack children's nanny was killed by an antelope. Earlier that spring the antelope herd had its first crop of fawns, and the nanny, fond of the herd and especially the new babies, enjoyed driving her car out onto the llanos each evening, where she fed the baby antelope with a nippled milk bottle. Although the adult antelope were accustomed to people, the presence of newborn fawns had made several of the males protective and ornery. One of these bucks attacked the nanny when she approached that evening. Although bloodied and dazed from the buck's lunges and stabs, the nanny managed to drive herself back to Ghost Ranch, where she collapsed against her steering wheel near headquarters. Although she was severely wounded and bruised by the buck's attack with his horns and hooves, the doctor brought from the nearby ccc camp decided that the nanny had actually died of shock.

The summer season began in spite of the tragedy. Guests filled the cottages, and the Ghost Ranch string of horses was often gone on trips into the high pine forests above the basin. There were automobile expeditions into Indian country, day trips to Taos and Santa Fe, cowboy rodeos and Indian ceremonials, afternoon swims in the cold canyon pool, and square dances under the stars. Pack hired a professional photographer, T. Harmon Parkhurst, to take promotional photographs of Ghost Ranch—photographs that would show how the partially real, partially imagined Western Dream of horses and cowboys, adobe and sky, beauty and peace, yet existed in the timeless Valley of Shining Stone.

THE GOOD COUNTRY

The Piedra Lumbre's transition from a country of hardship and struggle to a land of mythic beauty and serenity is perhaps best embodied in the life of the valley's most famous immigrant, American painter Georgia O'Keeffe. On O'Keeffe's canvases, the contours and colors of the Piedra Lumbre's archaic body would become one of the most painted subjects in the world of modern art.

O'Keeffe first saw New Mexico in 1917. Although she would not find the skull that marked the road to Ghost Ranch and the land below the Cliffs of Shining Stone that would become her home until the summer of 1934, O'Keeffe steadily worked her way toward the "wonderful emptiness" of the Piedra Lumbre in the intervening seventeen years: "From then on," she said years later of that first trip onto New Mexico's special soil, "I was always on my way back."[1]

O'Keeffe spent the summers of 1929 and 1930 in Taos, a guest at Mabel Dodge Luhan's home, Los Gallos. By 1931, O'Keeffe wanted the New Mexican landscape but not the complex and often interruptive social life found around Luhan's household and among the artists and intellectuals who moved between Taos and Santa Fe: "The Taos country—it is so beautiful—and so poisonous," O'Keeffe wrote to Taos painter Dorothy Brett, "the only way to live in it is to strictly mind your own business . . . and relatively keep the human being as about the size of a pin point. . . . As one chooses between the country and the human being the country becomes much more wonderful."[2]

O'Keeffe spent the summers of 1931 and 1932 at the H & M Ranch, a neighbor of Stanley's San Gabriel Ranch in Alcalde. But even the tiny village, located as it was along the only road between Santa Fe and Taos, became busy with people who crowded in upon O'Keeffe's precious work time and space. When O'Keeffe returned to New Mexico in 1934, following a difficult year in New York during which personal and professional anxieties resulted in a nervous breakdown, the painter was conscious of her very real need for privacy and solitude.

O'Keeffe had visited Abiquiu and the Chama River Valley in 1929, and in 1931 she had begun painting the landscape with which she would soon be forever artistically and emotionally linked. O'Keeffe wrote a friend: "I spent it [the summer of 1931] all but two weeks driving almost daily out from Alcalde toward a place called Abiquiu—painting and painting. I think I never had a better time painting—and never worked more steadily and never loved the country more."[3]

Even the devastation brought to the land by the drought—dust billowed behind the wheels of a vehicle, and the hills and mesas were nearly void of vegetation—was attractive to O'Keeffe: "It was the shapes of the hills there that fascinated me. The reddish sand hills with the dark mesas behind them."[4]

O'Keeffe found that she could stop and paint in the back seat of her Model A, the canvas propped on the swiveled front seats, for about two days before the local ranchers and villagers of the Chama Valley communities began to show an interest in her. Vehicles of any kind were rare in the Abiquiu valley during the Depression; an Anglo woman in an automobile, studying and painting the barren countryside for days at a time, was enough to catch the attention of even the valley's most practiced introverts.

1931 was a summer of newfound freedoms, both artistically and emotionally, for the forty-three-year-old O'Keeffe. It was her third summer away from her husband, the renowned photographer Alfred Stieglitz, and although she was still very much bonded to him and their life in New York, O'Keeffe was finding a rhythm of work and personal satisfactions all her own in the New Mexican frontier. O'Keeffe felt completely at ease in the Abiquiu country, and she often left her car by the side of the road and wandered alone up the arroyos and into the mesa land, or climbed into the cool water of the valley acequias on hot summer afternoons: "It seemed as though no matter how far you walked you could never get into those dark hills, although I walked great distances. I've always liked to walk. I think I've taken a bath in every brook from Abiquiu to Española. Irrigation ditches are fine for bathing, too. They're just wide enough to lie down in."[5]

During her stay in Alcalde in the summer of '34, O'Keeffe's friend Charles Collier told her there was a beautiful piece of country beyond Abiquiu that she had never seen. With Collier as her guide, O'Keeffe drove the Chama Valley road beyond the old Pueblo of Abiquiu, past the village of Barranco, into the narrow river canyon and finally out into the Piedra Lumbre basin. O'Keeffe had already seen Pedernal's profile from the Taos plateau, but she had never seen the mountain's true size as it rose from the desert. Nor had O'Keeffe seen the remarkable cliffs that edged and surrounded the wide shining valley.

Collier and O'Keeffe had heard that there was a guest ranch called Ghost Ranch somewhere under the vermillion cliffs. Although they drove about the llanos for several hours, they could not find the entrance gate. Frustrated, but also excited by this first glimpse of a magical land, O'Keeffe returned to Alcalde without actually setting foot on her future home. It did not matter: the power of the Piedra Lumbre had placed a spell on O'Keeffe that would influence her personal and creative choices for the remainder of her life.

A few days later O'Keeffe spotted a car with "GR" on its door at the San Juan Pueblo Mercantile near Alcalde. She settled herself beside the parked vehicle and patiently awaited the driver's return: "I waited for the man to come out, and he told me how to find Ghost Ranch. He said there should be a horse's head on the gate. So I drove out the next day to look for it."[6]

O'Keeffe had learned of Arthur Pack's decision to build his family a home on the high New Mexican desert—"the best place in the world"[7]—

from New York friend David McAlpin. McAlpin was the grandnephew of John D. Rockefeller, and his interest in art and photography begun as an undergraduate at Princeton would one day lead him to start the photography department at the Museum of Modern Art. McAlpin and Pack had been neighbors in Princeton and had collaborated on various civic projects in the 1920s, including the Westminster Foundation, a Christian student counseling center. McAlpin was privy to the Pack family plans to move to New Mexico and in the winter of 1934 had told O'Keeffe about their discovery of what they called the most magnificent place on earth, Ghost Ranch.

After her first glimpse of the Piedra Lumbre O'Keeffe had no doubt that it was, perhaps, the most magnificent place on earth. But on the day O'Keeffe finally found the ranch gate and drove across the desert toward the cliffs, she had very grave doubts about the people she expected to find living there: "Ghost Ranch was a dude ranch, I was told—and I thought dude ranchers were a lower form of life. . . . I wasn't sure I could live with dude ranchers."[8] In spite of her dislike of dudes and dude ranches, O'Keeffe marched up to one of the little cottages, probably the Ghost House, knocked on the door and "asked if I could spend a night there sometime."[9]

It is generally assumed that it was Arthur Pack of whom O'Keeffe first inquired about a room at Ghost Ranch. But in the summer of 1934, Arthur and his family lived out at Rancho de los Burros. It was most likely Carol Stanley who met O'Keeffe in the crooked Ghost House doorway. Stanley had known O'Keeffe at Alcalde—Dorthy Burnham Fredericks remembers how O'Keeffe, Mabel Dodge Luhan, Dorothy Brett, and various other friends often met for lunch on the San Gabriel patio in the late 1920s. But O'Keeffe's time at Alcalde and in northern New Mexico was just beginning as Stanley's was ending, and if the two women knew each other, it was only superficially.

Whomever it was that O'Keeffe found in the adobe *casita,* he or she told O'Keeffe that although the ranch was booked full for the summer, a room would be available for one night the following day. O'Keeffe drove back to Alcalde, packed a bag, and returned to Ghost Ranch the next morning.

Fate, luck, or destiny—perhaps a combination of all three—made it possible for O'Keeffe to spend the remainder of the summer of 1934 at Ghost Ranch. During her first night at the ranch, "a family came, with a boy who developed appendicitis. They had to leave and I got their rooms. I went immediately to Ghost Ranch to stay. And I never left."[10]

The summer of 1934 heralded the beginning of an extraordinary relationship between an artist and her subject: although deeply personal, O'Keeffe's depiction of the landscape of Ghost Ranch, the Piedra Lumbre, and the Abiquiu country was so monumental in scope that the outside world would soon blend O'Keeffe and the region of Avéshu pije into one persona. In the next five decades, O'Keeffe would make the contours and colors, the sky, clouds, bones, red hills, and blue mountains of the Piedra Lumbre and the Chama River Valley of the "Faraway Nearby" her home, her land, her world. In doing so, O'Keeffe would make this ancient high-desert plateau among the most recognized and admired landscapes in all the world.

At Ghost Ranch, O'Keeffe found exactly what her heart and her hand were looking for: a raw, unspoiled, unpopulated country; a desert plateau untouched by the hands of civilization; a place "more sky than earth."[11] Her accommodations at Ghost Ranch were simple and sparse. O'Keeffe reveled in the knowledge that she was forty miles from a telephone or a telegraph and was sixty miles and more from the bustling, gossipy social centers of Taos and Santa Fe. There was a generator on the ranch, but electricity was used sparingly. Candles and kerosene lamps were the preferred lighting. The horse was still the better, and often the only, choice for transportation, especially in the summer monsoons. When O'Keeffe was not painting she was often seen walking into the Piedra Lumbre's barren hills where "even the rocks seem alive to me."[12] Weather, wild animals, and the spirits of former visitors to the rancho beside el Rito del Yeso held as much power as—and perhaps even a bit more than—flesh-and-blood humans in the canyon of the witches.

Georgia O'Keeffe was already a major figure in American art when she settled into her first summer at Ghost Ranch. Stanley's and Pack's guests that summer—wealthy and influential easterners, nearly all of them friends and colleagues from Boston, Princeton, and New York—

were very much aware of O'Keeffe's importance in the world of modern art. For the most part, O'Keeffe's desire that she be left alone to paint and to walk the Piedra Lumbre was honored. Most everyone gave O'Keeffe a wide berth, whether in the ranch dining hall or out in the "untouched lonely-feeling"[13] places of the Ghost Ranch country: "The moment anyone met her he or she knew that the tanned woman, often dressed in immaculate white cotton—her new summer color—was 'somebody.' "[14]

In the summers of 1934, '35, and '36 O'Keeffe stayed in one of the guest cottages near Ghost House, usually the Garden Cottage located at the east end of Archie Galbraith's enormous vegetable garden. O'Keeffe ate her meals in the ranch dining room, but she did not seek nor encourage conversation.

"When you got to know Georgia, she was a very, very nice person," British painter Dorothy Brett said. "But she had a rather cold front that made things a little difficult for her and for everybody else. It's a horrid thing to say, but I think she was bored with people."[15] If O'Keeffe spoke at all in public, it was never about what she was working on or anything about her personal life. We can imagine O'Keeffe's cool, poker-faced exit from the Ghost Ranch dining room in the summer of 1935 after opening a letter from her husband and finding that he had mistakenly sent her a letter intended for his lover, Dorothy Norman. O'Keeffe came to prefer the easy, unintrusive comradery of the ranch cowboys and often opted to dine with the hired hands, who ate before the guests. But in spite of her cool reserve, over the next few summers O'Keeffe was slowly and inevitably drawn into Ghost Ranch's daily life and into relationships and even friendships with both guests and resident staff.

Arthur Pack's first wife, Brownie, became acquainted with O'Keeffe her first summer at Ghost Ranch. Brownie Pack and O'Keeffe had at least one friend in common—David McAlpin—but the women's friendship was not based on social connections, but rather on a shared visceral reaction to their environment: Brownie was enthusiastic, intelligent, and well traveled, and she loved the outdoors as much as O'Keeffe did. Brownie's appreciation for the land transcended its beauty—Brownie had spent months in the outback on various expeditions with Arthur and his famous colleagues. She was thoroughly versed in the names and habits of plants, birds, and animals, having co-written numerous wildlife articles for *Nature Magazine:* "Name an animal," her daughter, Eleanor Pack Liddell, remembers, "and my mother had one as a pet."

Brownie Pack was a natural guide for O'Keeffe during her first months at Ghost Ranch. Brownie had already explored much of the Piedra Lumbre basin with Frank Hibben, and she shared with O'Keeffe the prehistoric ruins and Indian sites her young archaeologist friend was studying. Brownie could drive a car as well as she could ride a horse and was willing to test the limits of either on the challenging terrain of the Piedra Lumbre: "When O'Keeffe first came out to Ghost Ranch," Brownie Hibben recalled of her first summer with O'Keeffe, "we began to take picnics and to explore weird canyons. And, of course, we got stuck in the mud! Once in the car—the old Ford thing—we got stuck in the Chama River. Oh, we had all sorts of times!

"I had a lovely time with O'Keeffe. I was very fond of her. We were friends immediately and loved the same things. We'd go out and find beautiful places for picnics. Then she would go back and paint them if they appealed to her."

The isolation and hardships, both personal and topographical, of the frontier of the Piedra Lumbre forged unique friendships between those who shared its soil in the 1930s and '40s. Arthur Pack and O'Keeffe's friendship began slowly and lasted until the end of his life in 1975.

Pack was, however, often the reluctant go-between for O'Keeffe and the ranch guests and staff. Pack was also the recipient of some of O'Keeffe's most memorable rages. O'Keeffe admitted the malicious vehemence of one such tongue-lashing of Pack in a letter to a friend: "I gave him one of my best trimmings—I had been mad at him long enough to have it all very clear in my mind and in fine order and I spared him nothing—I drew all the blood I wanted to and wiped my knife clean on what was left of him. He didn't have a leg to stand on—In a way it was pretty awful but it was what I thought and felt and I hammered it in one nail after another."[16]

Whatever the details of this falling-out, we can assume O'Keeffe was not wholly without blame. Even so, Arthur Pack was the sort of person who immediately set about mending bridges, even those he was not responsible for destroying. The following day Pack sent the McKinley children and several of their friends on burro-back with a peace offering to O'Keeffe. O'Keeffe wrote to a friend about the children's visit with

carrots
16 beets
2 cauliflower
2 cabbages
3 large head of lettuce—
I had to laugh—[17]

O'Keeffe demanded distance and privacy. Even so, she came to accept and even expect Pack's paternal watchfulness during her summers at Ghost Ranch. During a rainstorm that O'Keeffe decided to enjoy from the inside of her car, she wrote to Stieglitz about the beauty of the storm, about the comings and goings of the ranch community she was inevitably part of, and finally about Pack, who was watching the same storm—and her—from the headquarters porch: "I must drive to the house. I see Arthur and several people standing on his front porch looking at me. He probably thinks I am stuck in the mud or something like that."[18]

Pack—who was often compared to the Prince of Wales (Edward VIII) "both for his appearance and demeanor"[19]—was not an aggressive or imposing person. Pack's friendships were forged while traipsing the wilderness, or while working for common causes, or during quiet evenings of shared conversation about nature and conservation, religion and theology, and his great new love, Ghost Ranch. Although O'Keeffe frequently bullied Pack and often disregarded his wishes when they interfered with her own, Pack's humble but honest energy, and his perseverance through decades of personal and professional trials and triumphs on the Piedra Lumbre, earned O'Keeffe's trust and respect.

Pack admitted that he was not drawn to O'Keeffe's paintings of the land he loved. O'Keeffe was well aware of Pack's lack of interest in art, especially hers: "He didn't understand art at all," his daughter Peggy Pack McKinley remembers. "And O'Keeffe knew this and accepted it. Still, one day she asked him to come over and visit her. She said, 'Arthur, I now have something to show you. And you're going to get this one.' She had painted this great big painting of the blue with the clouds in it. She said to

Arthur, 'Okay, what's that?' And my father said, 'Oh, Georgia, that's easy! That's clouds seen from an airplane!' He was so proud of himself!"

Pack and O'Keeffe loved and guarded the same land; they were *compadres*—neighbors, friends, companions—who shared the same less-traveled road for several decades of their lives. On the frontier of northern New Mexico, even in the twentieth century, these were the ties that bind and hold for lifetimes.

O'Keeffe rarely gave friends drawings, but after Brownie's abrupt departure, O'Keeffe gave Pack a drawing of a steer skull: "She [O'Keeffe] tried to be a friend," Pack wrote years later, "even bringing me one day as a gift a perfect drawing of a cow's skull which I then and there adopted as the insignia and trade mark of the Ghost Ranch."[20]

The now famous drawing was of a skull of one of Juan de Dios's prize steers.[21] O'Keeffe became friends with old de Dios in the last few years of his life. O'Keeffe joked with the elderly *caballero* about how she was waiting for one of his giant oxen to die so that she could have its skull. Upon the death of the first steer, de Dios cooked the meat—which, witnesses recall, had the consistency and taste of rawhide—but he gave the gigantic head to O'Keeffe. It was from the bones of this magnificent animal, who had towed countless reluctant wild horses across the llanos of the Piedra Lumbre to de Dios's corral beside the Chama River, that O'Keeffe sketched the simple yet powerful skull motif that became forever and always synonymous with and symbolic of both Ghost Ranch and its most famous resident.

During O'Keeffe's first summers in New Mexico she had begun collecting and painting bones. O'Keeffe had even shipped a barrel of New Mexico bones back to her husband's summer house at Lake George in New York: "When I came to New Mexico in the summer of 1929, I was so crazy about the country that I thought, how can I take part of it with me to work on? There was nothing to see in the land in the way of a flower. There were just dry white bones. So I picked them up. People were pretty annoyed having their cars filled with those bones. But I took back a barrel of bones to New York. They were my symbols of the desert, but nothing more."[22]

A bone-lover like O'Keeffe could not have come to New Mexico at a better time. In the mid 1930s, when the drought claimed countless wild and domestic animal lives, bones—bleached to a gleaming white, or still covered with tendons and bloodied fur—were as easy to find on the parched land as the ravens who fed upon them. And after the wild horses were shot, the Piedra Lumbre basin was a virtual boneyard: "The bones were everywhere," Dorthy Burnham Fredericks remembers. "Of course O'Keeffe painted them. They were everywhere."

O'Keeffe commented in letters about the almost surreal prevalence of bones on the Piedra Lumbre, especially of the large, hauntingly elegant horse and cow pelvis bones: "For years in the country the pelvis bones lay about . . . always underfoot—seen and not seen as such things can be. . . . I do not remember picking up the first one but I remember . . . knowing I would one day be painting them. . . . When I started painting the pelvis bones I was most interested in the holes in the bones—what I saw through them—particularly the blue from holding them up in the sun against the sky as one is apt to do when one seems to have more sky than earth in one's world."[23]

O'Keeffe's friendships with the Ghost Ranch cowhands afforded her firsthand knowledge of the locations of skeletal remains. Several ranch cowboys regularly brought her gifts of skulls and spines, pelvic bones, horns and antlers. Before his elopement with the wealthy socialite Ardith Johnston, Jack McKinley was a friend of O'Keeffe's. O'Keeffe was attracted to McKinley's old world cowboy charm and his understanding of horses and cattle and the Piedra Lumbre valley. McKinley's son, Henry, remembers their friendship: "O'Keeffe and my father got along real well. Dad used to go out and bring her skulls. She told me this herself—that he used to go and bring her skulls all the time. And O'Keeffe told me that Jack McKinley made a very dashing figure, you know, with his silk handkerchief around his neck, and his hat and his chaps. She thought the world of him."

Frank Hibben was studying mountain lions in the summer of 1934. O'Keeffe liked to question Hibben about the lions he had seen and studied, and Hibben was soon aware of O'Keeffe's preoccupation with bones. Like McKinley, Hibben soon began to bring O'Keeffe skulls and skeletons back from his expeditions into the New Mexico outback: "I had one deer skull that she admired," Hibben remembers, "and I gave her that.

And then I got her a cow skull, and then a couple more deer skulls. And a bear skull. . . . I don't think she ever painted that one.

"O'Keeffe was awfully nice to me, and I liked her paintings very much indeed. She was very interested in the mountain lion study, and I gave her several photographs I'd taken of lions, usually sitting in a tree or something. I thought she was going to paint a lion, but I don't think she ever did."

In retrospect, it is only fitting that in a land where centuries of inhabitants—human and animal—are remembered not by recorded words or stories, but by the crumbling remnants of their villages and the skeletal remains of their bodies, bones became integral to O'Keeffe's portraits of the Piedra Lumbre: "The bones seem to cut sharply to the center of something that is keenly alive on the desert even though it is vast and empty and untouchable—and knows no kindness with all its beauty."[24]

O'Keeffe had no real studio during her first two summers at Ghost Ranch, and she spent most of her work time on the desert in her Ford, or painting under the wide sky. Ghost Ranch encompassed some thirty thousand acres and was surrounded by privately owned range or national forest land on four sides. But even in such a vast and unpeopled place, ranchers, guests, and even children often stumbled across O'Keeffe, intentionally and not.

Dorthy Burnham Fredericks had first met O'Keeffe at Carol Stanley's San Gabriel Ranch in the 1920s. She met O'Keeffe again one morning while moving a herd of Ghost Ranch horses across part of the Piedra Lumbre. Fredericks did not wish to disturb the artist, but there was little she could do to avoid her: "I was running horses across the desert—you don't walk horses, like cattle, you get them running and then you don't stop them until they're where you want them to be. I came up and over a ridge at a hard run. And there was O'Keeffe, sitting in front of her canvas. I couldn't stop them: the horses just thundered right past her, around her, the whole herd, and left her sitting in a huge cloud of red dust."

The Pack children spent the summer days riding their burros around the desert. Looking for O'Keeffe became a summer pastime for Peggy and Norrie Pack after the sisters located the painter's plein air studio by accident. "Peggy and I were very conscious of O'Keeffe being around here in the summer because we were always searching for her," Eleanor Pack Liddell remembers. "We'd get our horses and just ride around and look for her car. We were bound to run into her. She wasn't very friendly—why should she be to us? We were really bothering her. She was trying to paint and we'd hang over her shoulder and look at what she was painting! She really didn't like that. One day, in order to get rid of us, she gave us a Hershey bar. That was a bad mistake: we searched all the harder the next day."

O'Keeffe never complained to Arthur Pack about his children's antics on the desert. Perhaps she was more amused by their uninhibited curiosity than they knew. The girls did not realize it at the time—nor react with the respect and adulation the American art world would later lavish upon them—but the eyes of the Pack sisters were often the first after O'Keeffe's to view some of the masterpieces she was painting out on the Piedra Lumbre. "I can remember one day coming upon her," Eleanor Pack Liddell remembers, "and she was doing one of her paintings with a skull in the sky . . . a skull in the sky! We saw her painting of that and we thought this was hysterical! We were just laughing ourselves to death! O'Keeffe was getting furious!"

The McKinley children—Henry, Wayne, and Barbara—came to know O'Keeffe in the late 1930s and '40s. O'Keeffe was living in Rancho de los Burros, and she often invited the McKinley clan in for juice and snacks. Some biographical accounts offer a different, less friendly version of O'Keeffe's relationship with the children, but Henry McKinley remembers an amicable woman who "served us all lemonade and cookies. One time Wayne had his horse tied to her fence and the horse set back and ran off and took her fence down. But O'Keeffe was always real nice to us. We were friends for years."

O'Keeffe was often criticized because although she was friendly to someone as a child, she would have nothing to do with them as an adult: "She'd find a seven-year-old child at her door and say, 'Why, where did you come from? Come on in,' " Phoebe Pack remembers. "But then years later, if that child returned as a grownup expecting to be welcomed in again, she'd slam the door in their face."

Young John Crosby's relationship with O'Keeffe would prove to be exactly the opposite. Crosby, a student at the Los Alamos Ranch School built by Ashley Pond on the Pajarito Plateau, came to Ghost Ranch with his parents and brother from New York for four weeks in June and July of 1941. The Crosby boys were cautioned by the staff not to ride their horses too near O'Keeffe's house under the cliffs "so as not to disturb her."[25] (Other youngsters were told by one of the cowboys that O'Keeffe had a gun and would not hesitate to use it.) Throughout their month at Ghost Ranch, the Crosby brothers steered their mounts clear of the artist's residence under the cliffs and avoided her car when they found it parked on the desert.

John Crosby was not one of those offered cookies and lemonade in O'Keeffe's kitchen as a child, but he was later welcomed into her home: in 1957, after receiving a degree in music theory and composition at Yale University, Crosby founded the Santa Fe Opera. Crosby and O'Keeffe became friends, and in the next decades, O'Keeffe's black-and-white-clad figure was frequently among those in the audience of Crosby's opera under the stars.

O'Keeffe's letters to Stieglitz often included stories about the guests and staff of the ranch that was slowly becoming her home: "All the people are very nice—They are all people with their children of all ages and they come for the outdoor things they can do."[26] O'Keeffe watched a play performed one evening by the children on the headquarters porch. She sat with Pete Dozier, the guide and wrangler from Santa Clara Pueblo: "Last night the children gave a play that the governess wrote and helped them with—It was given out on the porch after supper,—was very amusing. It was amusing to see the way parents are effected by their children's capers. After that they danced, I only looked on with Pete, one of the ranch hands—half Indian and half a very good French line—He was working for Mabel when I was in Taos and has been here for a couple of years. He is very handsome and a beautiful dancer when he dances but he sat by me most of the evening."[27]

Phoebe Pack was a bold and hard-to-impress young woman when she first met O'Keeffe in the summer of 1936. Through her parents, Phoebe had come to know famous conservationists, politicians, wildlife photographers, and filmmakers. Georgia O'Keeffe was a fascinating woman Phoebe looked forward to meeting, but Phoebe was not in awe of the famous painter. This was perhaps the singular most important reason their relationship was one of equality and mutual respect for the next fifty years: "When I first met Georgia, who I always called Georgia, I was with Arthur, and also the Johnsons and the Bennetts. They were all standing around and Arthur introduced me. He said, 'Georgia, I'd like you to meet my new wife.' Georgia stood looking at me for a minute. I reached out my hand and I said, 'Hi Georgia!' She came back with her hand and said, 'How are you, Phoebe?' She was absolutely floored that anybody would approach her on a man to man basis! She was so sure she was above with her talents.

"Georgia was a very unique person. There's no question about that. Her aim in life was art and her painting and so forth. Not people."

In the years that Phoebe Pack ran Ghost Ranch with Arthur she played diplomat and feather smoother between O'Keeffe and the ranch guests. It was not easy, keeping O'Keeffe and the guests happy, especially because Phoebe did not place O'Keeffe's needs above those of her guests. O'Keeffe and Pack had numerous disagreements which were often marked by several weeks of no communication: "Georgia was pretty difficult to be with. She would come and ask for two carrots. Or a ripe melon. The only ripe melon. And then Arthur had to take somebody off the garden who was working and say, 'Go down and dig two carrots for Miss O'Keeffe.' We felt this was kind of a drain. The people in the garden were all busy. She did that almost every day. And she'd take what she wanted, anyway, like no one else existed."

Among the most famous stories that demonstrate O'Keeffe's attitude toward the Ghost Ranch community is a quarrel over one of Phoebe Pack's homemade desserts. "I had just baked a cake for dinner," Pack recalls, "and Georgia saw it in the kitchen. Georgia told me it was her housekeeper's birthday and she wanted the cake. I said, 'No! What would my guests eat tonight?' Georgia said, 'Bake another one!' I said, again, 'No.' Georgia left very miffed. But she got over it in a couple of months! We remained friends!"

O'Keeffe took an immediate liking to the young Phoebe Finley, but she could just as quickly and irrevocably take a dislike to someone. Bob and Maggie Johnson were building their home at Ghost Ranch during O'Keeffe's first summer at the ranch. For Bob Johnson, O'Keeffe felt nothing but contempt. "There were certain people that Georgia just

couldn't tolerate," Phoebe Pack remembers. "She couldn't see Bob Johnson without making a crude or cruel remark. She'd say something like,
'Why don't you keep off this property and then I wouldn't be bothered or
annoyed by you.'"

But O'Keeffe's reaction to Bob Johnson's wife, Maggie, was the
diametric opposite. Maggie was not from a privileged family but she was,
like her friend Brownie Pack, athletic and beautiful—Maggie had worked
as a fashion model in New York for photographer Eduard Steichen—and
was full of enthusiasm for the culture and landscape of northern New
Mexico. Although O'Keeffe would never visit Maggie at the Johnson
house at Ghost Ranch, O'Keeffe frequently invited Maggie on hiking and
painting expeditions around the Piedra Lumbre valley.

Although O'Keeffe honored her friendship with Maggie Johnson in
a painting titled "A Sun Flower from Maggie," O'Keeffe's affection for
Maggie proved to be of no use when the Johnsons attempted to buy one of
O'Keeffe's paintings of a morning glory. O'Keeffe never handled business
transactions involving her paintings, even for friends, and so referred the
Johnsons to her husband, Alfred Stieglitz, who managed O'Keeffe's art
sales. All of Bob Johnson's business dealings, which were substantial in
light of his position as chairman of the board at Johnson and Johnson, had
not prepared him for Stieglitz's negotiation style. Stieglitz had learned
a good deal about the Johnsons' personal and financial situation from
O'Keeffe, and he intended to use this information to his advantage. From
his perch upon a large table in his New York studio/gallery, An American
Place, Stieglitz explained to the Johnsons that he knew exactly what the
couple wanted: "You want a baby! You cannot have one—I know these
things. But you can have an O'Keeffe painting. For this, you will give her
two years of creative life, which will need fifteen thousand dollars."[28]

This was more than twice the going price for an O'Keeffe painting
in the mid 1930s, and the Johnsons, wealthy as they were, asked for time
to consider the offer. Arthur Pack was given the details of this meeting
and was later shown the letter Maggie Johnson wrote Stieglitz some
weeks later that explained the couple's decision to pass on the painting:
"Dear Mr. Stieglitz," Maggie Johnson wrote, "You will be glad to know
that we have adopted a baby. Sorry about the O'Keeffe."[29]

It was with some relief that Arthur and Phoebe Pack settled

O'Keeffe into Rancho de los Burros for the summer of 1937. This decision placed the ornery artist at a distance from the rest of the ranch's guests, and it gave O'Keeffe a residence and studio in the middle of what, to her, constituted a refuge in paradise: an adobe casa in the middle of the empty red hills that gave her a studio, a patio, a roof, and a piece of sky beneath the Cliffs of Shining Stone, miles from the annoying interruptions of dudes and dudettes.

O'Keeffe had become familiar with the Pack family's former residence the previous summer, when she had used a room in Rancho de los Burros for a studio. Young Carl Glock and his father were housed in the Packs' former hacienda for part of the summer of 1936, and Glock remembers that O'Keeffe came out to the house to work each day. When Glock was not working in the ranch kitchen, or at the corrals, or driving the ranch payroll in and out of Española, he often chauffeured O'Keeffe out to the desert studio. Glock also served as O'Keeffe's driver on various excursions around the valley.

In 1937, after O'Keeffe arrived unannounced at Ghost Ranch with expectations that she would be somehow accommodated in the middle of a busy summer—she suggested the Packs move a guest out of a cottage so that she could be moved in—Pack offered her his family's previous house, Rancho de los Burros. "As soon as I saw it, I knew I must have it," O'Keeffe said years later of the house between the sandstone chimneys. "I can't understand people who want something badly but don't grab for it. I grabbed."[30]

The Packs had enclosed the patio with a fence to keep the deer and wildlife from their rosebushes, but O'Keeffe developed the habit of leaving the gate open, and she purposely never watered the rosebushes. As the summer passed, the floor and ledges of the portal became decorated with the polished stones, bleached bones, twisted cedar, and hollowed cholla branches dragged home on O'Keeffe's daily walks into the red hills.

Rancho de los Burros was a sprawling and generously sized house, but its interior space was of secondary interest to its exterior views: Pack had placed the house so that its U-shaped portal embraced the southern horizon of Pedernal. To the north of the house the cliffs were transformed hourly by the movement of the sun and the shadows of the clouds. O'Keeffe adopted the landscape surrounding Rancho de los Burros as rapidly as she did the adobe house itself: "All my association with it [the house at Ghost Ranch] is a kind of freedom," O'Keeffe said years later. "When I first came here, I had to go 70 miles on a dirt road to get supplies. Nobody would go by in two weeks."[31]

The profound isolation at Ghost Ranch afforded O'Keeffe long uninterrupted days of work, and evenings alone or with one or two carefully chosen companions. "I was up early—painted all day—out in the car from 7 till 11—then the rest of the day indoors," O'Keeffe wrote Stieglitz in August of 1937. "—at 5:30 I went out and walked—just over the queer colored land—such ups and downs—so much variety in such a small space. . . . Maggie Johnson was at the house for supper—back from their pack trip."[32]

That summer O'Keeffe adopted Rancho de los Burros for her own. Although the house would not be legally hers for another three years, O'Keeffe began a series of paintings of the house and surrounding land with titles like "My Backyard" and "The House I Live In." These were not mere portraits of Rancho de los Burros, but were paintings of O'Keeffe's wonderful new world—the sweeping desert and tablelands that began at the patio fence and stretched for miles across the Piedra Lumbre.

Cerro Pedernal was soon a frequent and familiar motif in O'Keeffe's work. From Ghost Ranch, Pedernal seems to be positioned so as to be quietly observing whatever and whomever moves on the desert between the great cliffs and the mountain. The longer one lives out on the Piedra Lumbre, the deeper one senses a shared intimacy, shared history, with the sacred cerro. "It's my private mountain," O'Keeffe said of the blue mountain. "It belongs to me. God told me if I painted it enough, I could have it."[33]

Pedernal's form was laced with the stories of powerful women— Changing Woman, Spider Woman. Now the old peak was being claimed by an American painter whose story would one day become, like that of her real and imagined predecessors on this land, part of the mythical fabric of the mountain.

O'Keeffe discovered that the view of the sky and the landscape from Rancho de los Burros's flat-topped roof, reached by a traditional hand-hewn wooden ladder, was greater than the view from the patio. And when the Bennett family was away, O'Keeffe was known to walk the half-mile across the red and gold sand to their adobe house, where, after climbing an outside adobe staircase, she pondered the sky and the horizon from their roof. O'Keeffe's painting "Ladder to the Moon" glorified the cherished view from her roof: the painting is more sky than land, and the slice of horizon is dominated by the dark, regal contour of Pedernal, with the old ladder that connected O'Keeffe to the humbling sky of the Piedra Lumbre floating between heaven and earth.

O'Keeffe had found her home. Although she continued to return to her husband's life in New York, when she left New Mexico, she wrote a friend, "I have left the good country."[34] O'Keeffe would be only a summer and fall resident until Stieglitz's death in 1946, but Rancho de los Burros was firmly and irrevocably O'Keeffe's home.

O'Keeffe shared her new wonderful world with a select few friends. Those who accepted O'Keeffe's offer and came to New Mexico usually stayed in one of the Ghost Ranch cottages three miles across the desert from Rancho de los Burros.

David McAlpin was a frequent guest at Ghost Ranch in the 1930s, and O'Keeffe and McAlpin spent many hours exploring the Piedra Lumbre on horseback. O'Keeffe described riding to "places that we could only get the horses to go by getting off and pulling several times—places I would never dare to go alone and cowboys wouldn't be much interested—perfectly mad looking country—hills and cliffs and washes too crazy to imagine all thrown up into the air by God and let tumble where they would."[35]

David McAlpin introduced O'Keeffe to photographer Ansel Adams in New York in 1936. Adams had visited Santa Fe and Taos and, like O'Keeffe, was enamored of the people and the country. They were soon good friends, and O'Keeffe urged Adams to visit her at Ghost Ranch. "By a miraculous sequence of circumstances and the kindness of David McAlpin"[36] Adams came to the Piedra Lumbre valley in the autumn of 1937. Adams photographed O'Keeffe out on her daily walks, often with her arms full of bones. She also allowed him to intrude on her outdoor studio and photograph her while she painted.

Adams enjoyed the landscape of the Chama River Valley and spent days alone on the Piedra Lumbre photographing the desert, the sky, even the clouds above the bleached steer skull that marked the Ghost Ranch road. Adams wrote Stieglitz about Ghost Ranch: "It is all very beautiful and magical here—a quality which cannot be described. You have to live it and breathe it, let the sun bake it into you. The skies and land are so enormous, and the detail so precise and exquisite that wherever you are you are isolated in a glowing world between the macro and the micro, where everything is sidewise under you and over you, and the clocks stopped long ago."[37]

Adams was not the aloof guest that O'Keeffe had been, but engaged himself in the life and people of Ghost Ranch. Phoebe Pack remembers that Adams "got along with everyone": "Adams had no personal prejudices. He was much friendlier than O'Keeffe and was interested in everything. He was a great fellow!"

Adams often borrowed one of O'Keeffe's two cars, kept at Ghost Ranch, and drove himself up and down the valley. "I scoot all over the country," Adams wrote his wife, Virginia, "on and off the roads. It's a grand place."[38] Adams happened upon O'Keeffe on one of these sojourns over the sands of the Piedra Lumbre: "She was painting in her station wagon, protected from the hot summer sun. She had folded down the back seats and was comfortably seated before an easel, working away at a luminous painting of fantastic cliffs and a beautifully gestured dead pinon tree. . . . She allowed me to photograph her as she painted."[39]

In the fall of Adams's first Ghost Ranch visit the Johnsons' two-story adobe house was closed up for the season. The house harbored the finest piano on the ranch, the Steinway used by Stokowski when he accompanied Tony Luhan's drums. O'Keeffe learned that Adams was a highly trained classical pianist, and one evening she asked the ranch housekeeper if Adams could play the Johnson piano for a few hours. O'Keeffe wrote, "After supper I got the key to the Johnson house from the housekeeper and we all went there—the sitting room—a good big room all done up for the winter—furniture all in the middle of the room covered with a vast piece of unbleached muslin—carpet all covered with newspapers—We dug out the piano—a very good Steinway Grand and Adams played for us—He plays very well—Dave and [Haniel] Long and I all stretched out on the floor on the newspapers."[40]

O'Keeffe, like McAlpin, often hired Orville Cox to drive her into

New Mexico's outback. Cox is credited with introducing O'Keeffe to the hauntingly beautiful landscape of dark hills ninety miles from Ghost Ranch in Navajoland O'Keeffe called the Black Place.[41]

The fall of Adams's visit, McAlpin arranged for Cox to take Adams, O'Keeffe, and Godfrey Rockefeller into the Indian country of New Mexico, Arizona, and Colorado. Several of Adams's photographs of this trip, especially those taken at Canyon de Chelly, became favorites of both the photographer and his admiring public: "Some of my best photographs have been made in and on the rim of the canyon. A favorite photograph from this trip was the one I made there with my Contax of O'Keeffe and Cox. The charm of O'Keeffe's expression is arresting, most obviously not posed, a true 'candid.' This was one special moment."[42] Adams's portrait of Georgia O'Keeffe and Orville Cox standing beneath a stormy sky, with O'Keeffe giving a mischievous and very nearly flirtatious glance to Cox, was of such candor that many who saw this photograph assumed Cox to be the painter's husband.

O'Keeffe did not come to New Mexico in 1939, but went to Hawaii for the Dole Company, which had commissioned two promotional paintings. The trip was not a successful one, and by the summer of that year when O'Keeffe returned to New York she was stricken with headaches and sinus trouble, weight loss and sleep disorders.

After a winter and spring of recovery in New York, O'Keeffe headed for the beloved land of New Mexico where she knew she would find the solitude and space she needed to paint and to smile again. As she had in previous summers, in 1940 O'Keeffe did not forewarn the Packs of her impending arrival and of her plans to spend the summer at Ghost Ranch. Rancho de los Burros was already rented when O'Keeffe arrived. After a confrontation between Arthur Pack and O'Keeffe, in which Pack reminded O'Keeffe that the house was, in fact, his to rent as he pleased, O'Keeffe suggested Pack sell the house to her so that they might avoid this misunderstanding in the future. Pack agreed. In the next few weeks, whoever was in Rancho de los Burros was moved into another cottage, and O'Keeffe was moved in.

The sale of Rancho de los Burros was finalized on the thirtieth day of October, 1940. Some accounts claim O'Keeffe paid six thousand dollars for the house and eight acres under the cliffs. But Phoebe Pack believes Rancho de los Burros became O'Keeffe's for the lesser sum of twenty-five hundred dollars.[43] The eight acres of land included the packed clay earth that was the Pack family tennis court south of the house, and the little corral and adobe shed where the baby antelope had once lived. O'Keeffe wanted more acreage so that she could have her own horse: "But Arthur wouldn't sell it to me," she told a friend years later. "All he'd sell me was enough for my sewer."[44]

Whatever the price and the final size of the property it was more than good enough. O'Keeffe finally owned a piece of the "far away country"[45] she had fallen in love with a decade ago.

Ghost Ranch seemed to be physically and emotionally removed from the greater world and its problems. However, the beginning of World War II brought challenges and changes to those living at Rancho de los Brujos. The New Mexico guest ranch business ended with the United States' entry into the war, as ranch hands joined the armed forces and moved into urban areas to contribute to the war effort. Visitors to Ghost Ranch were soon few and far between.

Among the last to visit Pack at his beautiful ranch were Charles and Anne Lindbergh, whom Pack had known years ago in Princeton. The Lindberghs were traveling across the Southwest en route home to Connecticut. Although Phoebe Pack did not recognize the famous couple when they drove their car up in front of the main ranch building, she knew they were somebody. "There are two people in a small car down by the steps," Phoebe told Arthur up at the house they lived in beside headquarters. "They didn't tell me their names and they are so brown that they might be Indians or artists, but they asked if you were here. Perhaps you better take a look yourself."[46]

That afternoon Arthur enjoyed a brief but pleasant reunion with his old neighbors, with whom he "shared much the same views about the war in Europe."[47] Phoebe was far more impressed with Lindbergh than she had been with O'Keeffe, and after serving everyone lemonade, she sat in awe of the famous pilot and his conversation with Arthur about planes and flying and "things I didn't understand at all."

The young actor John Wayne dropped in on the Packs just before the war, but visitors, famous and not, became infrequent after December of 1941. Pack served on the Española rationing board, which limited his, O'Keeffe's, and everyone in the valley's gasoline. Transportation returned to horse and wagon, and the winding dirt road between Española and Abiquiu looked very much like it had a hundred years before.

The traditional survival skills still used by their Hispanic neighbors became mandatory to those Anglos who lived at Ghost Ranch. O'Keeffe relearned childhood skills of baking and canning. Pack learned, for the first time in his life, the skills of a farmer, gardener, carpenter, plumber, and electrician. The Packs kept their own beef cattle, chickens, and hogs and maintained the fine Ghost Ranch vegetable garden, canning up to twelve hundred quarts in a single year. Milk and dairy products from Española were delivered to the Gonzales and Bode store but were brought no farther north than Abiquiu. The Packs invested in their own milk cow, Bessie, who at first would allow only an inexperienced and reluctant Arthur to milk her. After several months of dawn milkings by hands that "had never handled one of nature's bovine spigots,"[48] Pack insisted the McKinley boys take over the task.

If the mail went out at all, it was by horseback. Ghost Ranch still had no telephone or telegraph, and, like in the colonial days, neighbors depended on neighbors for news and information and for aid in time of emergencies.

O'Keeffe realized that for all their compassion and reliability, the Packs could not provide her with all of her food and supply needs. With help from Martin Bode, who put items aside for her, O'Keeffe was able to obtain some meats and fresh foods when they could be found. Even so, the 1940s were a time of making do. O'Keeffe remained ardent in her love of the simple, uncomplicated life found at Rancho de los Burros, but during the summers on the Piedra Lumbre, she missed fresh foods, especially garden-grown fruits and vegetables.

O'Keeffe attempted to raise a small garden of vegetables in the old antelope corral at Ghost Ranch, but the soil, made as it was from the eroding cliffs, was coarse and sandy. Water had to be pumped from the well, and whatever plants managed to root and sprout under the searing summer sun were quickly discovered by the desert animals—jackrabbits and chipmunks. It was evident that even a small vegetable garden at Rancho de los Burros would be impossible.

In 1943, with her companion and housekeeper Maria Chabot, the twenty-nine-year-old niece of Mary Wheelwright whom O'Keeffe had met at Los Luceros in 1940, O'Keeffe found and rented fifteen irrigated acres in Abiquiu. The two women planted beans, lettuce, corn, and other vegetables. It was a long journey down the river valley to the little village, and frequent summer cloudbursts rendered the narrow canyon road useless on many an afternoon. But the women persevered and raised a small crop that gave O'Keeffe the fresh vegetables she yearned for.

The difficulties of life on the Piedra Lumbre, combined with Stieglitz's decline into old age, forced O'Keeffe to reevaluate her future plans. She knew she would leave New York when Stieglitz died. But as much as she loved Rancho de los Burros and the cliff and desert country of Ghost Ranch, O'Keeffe realized she would eventually need a home in New Mexico where she could spend winters. And she very much wanted a garden outside her kitchen door.

The old adobe hacienda once owned by Abiquiu legend General José María Chávez had caught O'Keeffe's eye on one of her very first visits to the pueblo in 1930. At that time the house and grounds harbored the village chickens, pigs, and goats, and when O'Keeffe peered into the deceased general's silent, overgrown courtyard, she was met by a large white pig who stood just inside the patio, beside the old well. The great walls were beginning to disintegrate and crumble back to the earth, and the rooms of the house were being reclaimed by sand. But O'Keeffe's eyes saw past the decay to the wide view of the Chama River Valley beyond the garden wall. Her attention was drawn to the beauty of the wide *zaguán (saguan),* the double-doored entry that had impressed young Cleofas Jaramillo decades before. Partially dead, partially alive, to O'Keeffe the great old hacienda and its gardens were a magical place.

O'Keeffe inquired about the house in the early 1930s. The son of the general, J.M.C. Cháves, agreed to sell for six thousand dollars, but O'Keeffe thought this too much, and she did not buy the hacienda. Several years later when she reinquired about the house O'Keeffe learned that it was now owned by the Archdiocese of Santa Fe and that it was not for sale.

During the early 1930s Martin Bode had purchased the old house and land from its several owners, relatives of his wife's Taos family.[49] Bode had then given the house and acreage to the Archdiocese of Santa Fe with the stipulation that it be rebuilt and used as a parochial school. The church accepted the gift but had no funds with which to renovate the rambling adobe structure. The compound on the northern edge of the pueblo sat idle save for the comings and goings of pigs and chickens, seasonal apple and walnut pickers, and the village children who played throughout its walkways and overgrown portals.

The Archdiocese of Santa Fe would prove to be no match for O'Keeffe's relentless efforts to obtain the property once she decided she was going to own it. Bode insisted that the church stick to the terms agreed upon when he donated the property, and for a few years, the Archdiocese refused to sell the house to O'Keeffe. But O'Keeffe had been smitten by the house—by its undulating adobe walls, its garden and old wooden door hung on iron hinges built to protect its inhabitants from hostile visitors: "That wall with a door in it was something I had to have."[50]

Arthur Pack could have told his friend Martin Bode and the church fathers in Santa Fe that it was useless to fight: if O'Keeffe wanted the house, somehow, sometime, she was going to get it. According to O'Keeffe, she shamed the Catholic Church into selling her the house. O'Keeffe told a friend years later how. "She made an appointment to meet with the priest, and she said, 'I'm a successful artist, and as you know, I get my inspiration from this beautiful area around here, and I feel very connected to this land, and I feel that I see so much poverty around me and so many people that have so much less than me, and I'd like to do something to help out the village of Abiquiu. What can I do for you?' "[51] The church wanted to build a community center in the pueblo, and so Father Bickhaus, in his next-to-last year at the Abiquiu parish, accepted O'Keeffe's money for that purpose. When Bickhaus asked O'Keeffe what the village might do for her, "she told him to give her the house."[52]

Whether or not this is precisely accurate, O'Keeffe did manage to coerce the Archdiocese into selling the house and its three walled acres to her in December of 1945 for ten dollars. Martin Bode fought the transaction to the end, but his influence, which was substantial in the village, was not enough to hold back the tide of O'Keeffe's desire aimed at the house on the edge of the pueblo.[53]

Martin Bode never forgot how the church welched on an agreement. But in spite of Bode's irritation at the church, he did not hold a grudge against O'Keeffe. Bode and his wife, Tillie, formed a lasting friendship with the painter, whom they occasionally took camping. After O'Keeffe moved into the Abiquiu hacienda, she was often a dinner guest at the elegant Bode home in the old Grant Trading Post on the pueblo plaza. "They were two strong-headed people, my father and O'Keeffe," Elizabeth Bode Allred remembers. "At the dinner table they disagreed on politics, on the neighbor down the street . . . they disagreed on everything! And they always had a wonderful time of it!"

Although she had done very little to the Rancho de los Burros house, before O'Keeffe could occupy the old Chávez house she had to completely rebuild every room: "I wanted to make it *my* house, but I'll tell you the dirt resists you. It is very hard to make the earth your own."[54]

Maria Chabot, who had been given Wheelwright's Los Luceros ranch in Alcalde the same year, oversaw the renovation of the historic compound. The five oldest rooms of the main house, built around the patio with the well, were probably built in the late 1700s, and their viga-supported roof was caving in and adobe walls disintegrating. Additional rooms added by the general after the Civil War were also crumbling, as was the separate shed and carriage house on the northeast corner bluffs of the compound.

Chabot added no new walls, but repaired those already standing with adobe bricks made on the premises. Many large windows were knocked into walls. The carriage house became O'Keeffe's studio and bedroom. A corner window of wide plate glass framed the view of the Chama River Valley and Sierra Negra—Good Piñon Mountain—rising against the sky to the northeast.

The house's renovation was hampered by a lack of building supplies in wartime northern New Mexico, especially because of the construction of the secret city of Los Alamos just over the Jemez Mountains from Abiquiu. O'Keeffe had nails and building supplies sent to her by her architect brother.[55]

Chabot studied local architecture, both Hispanic and Native American, and duplicated traditional building styles such as *latilla* (rows of slender cedar sticks) ceilings and Hopi fireplaces. The tomblike "Ute room" where the general had placed overnight Indian traders, slaves, and visitors he did not completely trust was given an exterior window, and its *bancos* (adobe benches against the walls) rebuilt and freshly plastered. O'Keeffe renamed this room off the kitchen the Indian Room.

The walls and floors of the house were themselves a work of architectural art finished to O'Keeffe's exact specifications. Chabot hired local men to make adobes and to rebuild the walls, but as was traditional in northern New Mexico, women were hired to do all of the mud plastering.

Molly Martinez was a child when she watched her mother and other village women finish the interior walls: "The people in Abiquiu didn't see O'Keeffe very much, but she was very good to the people who had jobs with her. I remember how the rooms of her house were bare, even after they were finished. I walked into one finished room: there was no furniture, just a white sheet hanging against a wall. Just a plain white sheet. I never knew why."

The thick, high adobe walls that surrounded the house and garden and which gave the corner of the mesa a distinct measure of privacy from the rest of the village were also rebuilt. By the time the house was completed in 1948, nearly every square inch of it had been stabilized, rebuilt, reshaped, and replastered.

Alfred Stieglitz died in 1946. After O'Keeffe settled her husband's complex estate and financial affairs, which took nearly three years, she moved everything she owned to New Mexico. Summers were spent at Ghost Ranch, winters at the Abiquiu house. O'Keeffe had finally, completely, moved her life into the good country.

The only other Anglos in Abiquiu in the 1940s were the members of the Bode family, whose mother was a native New Mexican. Father Bickhaus departed the pueblo in 1946 and was replaced by a Hispanic priest, Father Placido Martínez. An Anglo like O'Keeffe remained a newcomer to the pueblo even decades after establishing a home in the village; full-fledged residency could take generations to establish in the old Genízaro community. "I'm a newcomer to Abiquiu," O'Keeffe admitted years after settling into the Abiquiu house. "That's one of the lower forms of life."[56]

O'Keeffe's skin became so tanned from exposure to the high-altitude sun that people often believed she was herself Indian. O'Keeffe enjoyed her aboriginal appearance, which intensified as her face aged and her skin creased, and was enhanced by her draped black-and-white clothing and her long hair tied at the back of her head under a wide-brimmed hat. Even in the '30s, Phoebe Pack remembers that O'Keeffe so resembled the Native American people of the valley that guests at Ghost Ranch often asked if the painter was part Indian. In the 1960s, Jim Hall, director of Ghost Ranch Conference Center, met O'Keeffe on the desert—he on horseback, she on foot—and after watching the dark-skinned seventy-plus-year-old painter stride effortlessly across the red hills toward him, told her that she "walked like a fourteen-year-old Indian girl."

Despite her growing physical resemblance to her adopted community in the Chama River Valley, O'Keeffe, until the end of her life, understood that there was something uniquely Abiqueño about her neighbors, something that she might never completely understand or assimilate: "Of course I am very close to my friends here in the pueblo and we all help each other. But the Indian mind is fundamentally different from ours. I have given up hope that we will ever really come to know each other. It is a reality that we Americans had better learn to accept in dealings with other peoples even more different in mentality from our own ways of thinking and doing."[57]

O'Keeffe was both friend and mysterious Anglo to the villagers, her black-and-white-clad form representative of both *patrona* and outsider. She depended on good relationships with the many men and women who kept her household and gardens running smoothly, and many pueblo families directly benefitted financially from jobs held for years at Miss O'Keeffe's. But her demand for privacy, and her sometimes eccentric treatment of neighbors and casual acquaintances—which could be casual neighborliness, or curt, even unprovoked hostility—made O'Keeffe an often feared village resident, always approached with caution.

Although she could be a forbidding adult to village children—one Abiqueño remembers watching O'Keeffe stride across the plaza in her black cape "looking like an apparition, or the devil himself"—O'Keeffe took an almost maternal interest in the pueblo youngsters. She financed the college educations of several Abiquiu teenagers and sought recreational activities for the younger children: "When I first moved here, the children had nowhere to go when it got dark. They'd play out in the street in front of the cantina until sundown and then sometimes they would come in here to see me. After a time, I took to sending them in my car when they had games with other schools. Once a week, I sent them to the movies in Española. The boys used to talk a lot about having a gymnasium, and eventually I had a gymnasium built."[58]

Floyd Trujillo was one of those small boys who benefitted from O'Keeffe's interest in the community's children. He told me, "A lot of the younger boys in the village used to spend quite a bit of time helping O'Keeffe in the garden. In return, she would give us some goodies, like homemade ice cream, cookies and stuff like that.

"We used to play baseball across the river from Silvestres—there was a big cottonwood tree for the backstop. We'd play teams from all the neighboring towns, even some from Conejos and Antonito, Colorado. O'Keeffe provided us with baseball bats and gloves for sports. We were the only team in small places like ours that had complete uniforms for both baseball and basketball."

At Christmas, Miss O'Keeffe, as she was called about the pueblo, gave the village children bags of nuts and fruit. Many of the pueblo children met O'Keeffe on her walks about the mesa, and she would stop and chat with them about rocks and plants. Although her gates were always closed and well guarded by her two Chow dogs, children did manage to find their way into O'Keeffe's studio, where she allowed them to use her paints to decorate their toys.

But O'Keeffe jealously guarded her privacy whether she was in the village or out at the ranch house on the Piedra Lumbre. Over the years, most of her involvement with the community was in the form of financial gifts that enabled programs or building projects: O'Keeffe donated money to build a gymnasium beside the church on the plaza, funded a water system for the village, and late in her life gave fifty thousand dollars toward the building of a new elementary school, as the old school in the village had small and poorly lit classrooms and was situated up a hill in a difficult location for the school buses to reach. In the early 1980s, when the old Ghost Ranch headquarters burned to the ground O'Keeffe offered Ghost Ranch, now a conference center owned by the United Presbyterian Church, fifty thousand dollars toward the building's replacement.

O'Keeffe lived to be ninety-eight years of age. Until the very last years of her life, she divided her time between Rancho de los Burros at Ghost Ranch and the hacienda on the edge of the pueblo. The house on the Piedra Lumbre was increasingly difficult for the aging O'Keeffe to negotiate, but the land of the shining stones was still the place that held her heart: "When I think of death I only regret that I will not be able to see this beautiful country anymore, unless the Indians are right and my spirit will walk here after I'm gone."[59]

O'Keeffe's ashes were scattered on the flat, narrow summit of Pedernal. But O'Keeffe's story in the valley did not end with her death. Like the legends of other real and imagined inhabitants of Abiquiu and the Piedra Lumbre, O'Keeffe's story magnified when she died. And like that of Changing Woman and Spider Woman, O'Keeffe's story and the story of the valley can no longer be separated.

12

BOMBS AND BONES

The events of World War II changed forever northern New Mexico's isolated hamlets and villages. Abiquiu's sons were drafted into the far-away battles of Asia and the Pacific, and their return brought the dreams, problems, and cash-carrying demands of the greater urban world into the rural homes of their parents and grandparents. The war effort particularly affected Española and the Chama River Valley because of their proximity to the secret city of Los Alamos built by the federal government in the Jemez Mountains above the Rio Grande.

In the early 1920s a young scientist named J. Robert Oppenheimer rode horseback across the Pajarito Plateau. This high mesa and canyon country on the lip of the Jemez range became the home of Ashley Pond's Los Alamos Ranch School and was the same country upon which Carol Stanley and Natalie Curtis spent the carefree summer of 1916. In 1941, when Oppenheimer was asked to advise the Army Corps of Engineers as to a site for a secret laboratory, he remembered this rugged landscape, whose canyons and mesa sides were dotted with the ruins of prehistoric pueblos, and he recommended the federal government consider the plateau for its secret laboratory. In 1942, after careful consideration, the U.S.

Government chose the Los Alamos Ranch School on the Pajarito Plateau to be the site of the top-secret Manhattan Project—the development of the atomic bomb.

The federal government quietly purchased fifty-four thousand acres of the plateau. And so it was that only a few dozen miles as the crow flies from the sacred peaks of Tschicoma, Polvadera, and Pedernal, on a pine and sage plateau marked with the ancient trails of the Tewa and the Navajo, where Hispanic shepherds had for generations pushed their herds each summer to the rich grasses of the high *valles,* a chapter of the most profound importance to the story of humankind—the making of the first atomic bomb—began to unfold.

The purpose of the project may have been unknown to the local residents, but that Los Alamos was a military operation of great significance was hardly a secret to anyone living in Santa Fe and up the Rio Grande and Chama Valleys. Although "the taboo on the mention of Los Alamos was final, complete . . . irrevocable and not susceptible to any exceptions,"[1] rumors about the nature of the activities on "The Hill" were rampant and imaginative: local speculation about the project's purpose included development of jet propulsion systems, death rays, gas warfare gadgetry, and submarine windshield wipers. "The Hill" was often the subject of talk over morning coffee in Santa Fe and upriver as far as Abiquiu, but newspaper writers and editors were forbidden to mention the words "Los Alamos" and operated under "what was probably the strictest censorship ever imposed upon the press of this state."[2]

The military's top brass came and went through the ancient capital of Santa Fe. Tightlipped outsiders disembarked the train at Lamy and came by bus into Santa Fe, where they were met by official but unmarked cars that whisked them from civilian sight, their place of residence cloaked under a common city post office box—number 1663. There was twenty-four-hour-a-day surveillance of the high sierras surrounding Los Alamos; armed soldiers patrolled the fenced circumference and warned shepherds and ranchers to make a wide circle of the plateau. Private pilots like Arthur Pack were instructed to steer their planes clear of the eastern slope of the Jemez or risk being shot from the sky. And night after night, lights twinkled against the black silhouette of the mountains where no one lived. "A whole social world existed in nowhere in which people were married and babies were born nowhere. People died in a vacuum, autos and trucks crashed in a vacuum and the MP's baseball team materialized out of a vacuum."[3]

Like every government that had feigned authority over this region before them, the United States government little understood even twentieth-century New Mexico. With the advent of the draft, Washington officials instructed local draft boards to sign into service the legions of "cattle guards" known to inhabit the state. Chama Valley sheep owners were expected to contribute to the war effort, and upon asking for more rations of kerosene to warm lambing tents in the cold weather of early spring, they were instructed to change the lambing season. A new rationing directive issued in the early years of the war placed New Mexico in a consortium with the Southern states, not with the Rocky Mountain states it was previously, and geographically, partnered with. This meant, among other things, that the residents of the state, which lay three thousand to thirteen thousand feet above sea level, received no rations of antifreeze.[4]

By 1942, following the departure of Ghost Ranch's cowboys, horse and dude wranglers, day laborers, and hired hands into various branches of the military, the ranch closed to paying guests. The only visitors to the adobe casitas clustered around the old Ghost House were invited guests of the Packs and friends of O'Keeffe's.

In the summer of '42, a young cousin of Arthur's, Roger White, came with his bride, Kitty, to honeymoon at Ghost Ranch. The Whites' honeymoon coincided with the first visits to Ghost Ranch by a new clientele at the ranch, which was otherwise closed for business: unknown to Roger and Kitty, the couple housed in one of the other ranch cottages were residents of Los Alamos. The Whites noticed that although friendly, the couple spoke little about themselves to the Packs, the cook, or the Whites. Arthur and Phoebe knew little more about them than the young honeymooners, but they did know that the couple was involved in some way with the government work of "The Hill."

Early in 1942, the Packs—and soon after, O'Keeffe—were visited by card-carrying FBI agents who wanted to know everything about everyone connected to Ghost Ranch. After divulging their entire lives in detail to the agents, Arthur and Phoebe were summoned into the FBI office in Santa Fe, where they learned that the federal government needed a restricted, secure, remote vacation site for men and women working "in the area." After thorough examination, Ghost Ranch was deemed spy-free, and the Packs were asked if they would allow Ghost Ranch to become an official rest and relaxation retreat for federally connected guests. Although the Packs were assured that everyone sent to Ghost Ranch would be of good character, they would not be told real names, and they were instructed not to ask personal questions of any sort. The Packs decided this would be their contribution to the war effort and, unbeknownst to them until after the war, opened Rancho de los Brujos' doors to the top nuclear scientists of the world.

Like Edith Warner and her tea room at Otowi Bridge, the Packs and Ghost Ranch became a refuge for those working on the first atomic bomb. Years later the Packs learned that the guests seated around the long wooden table on the supper porch facing Pedernal, with generic fictional names like Henry Farmer and Nicholas Baker, were people shouldering a weighty scientific and moral secret. Their real names included, among others, Enrico Fermi, Niels Bohr, George Kistiakowsky, Richard Feynman, Edward Teller, and J. Robert Oppenheimer.

"We would talk about homemade bread, and how many pounds of butter I had made during the week," Phoebe Pack remembers of those weekend encounters with the scientists of "The Hill." "You could talk about yourself, but you couldn't talk about them—ask where they were from or where they went to school—nor ask about anyone working up there. Not even their wives knew what they were doing, you know.

"The scientists came year-round. They were really at ease here; they knew they wouldn't be asked a lot of questions. And it was a beautiful place to spend a weekend with their families."

When Roger and Kitty White departed Ghost Ranch in early fall of 1942, they believed they were leaving to catch the train at Lamy that would take them back to Cleveland and to Roger's job at a tool factory. Roger was a mechanical engineer with a degree from Stanford. Kitty had completed her training at Presbyterian Medical Center in New York and was a registered nurse. Although sad to leave the beauty and peace of Ghost Ranch, they were anxious to begin their married life in Ohio.

Pack drove the Whites to Santa Fe and left them at La Fonda, where they were to catch the bus to the Lamy depot later in the day. Roger White remembers the afternoon that changed his life: "We were standing there on the corner at La Fonda waiting for the bus to show up and this perfectly strange woman walks up to me and says, 'Are you Roger White?' I said, 'Yes.' And she says, 'Dr. Bainbridge has come in to interview you.' And I said, 'I don't know what you're talking about.' She said, 'I think you better come with me.'

"She had me by the arm by that time. Kitty said, 'Go ahead, this sounds real exciting. I'll go over to La Fonda and have a drink.'"

The woman who had Roger White by the arm was Dorothy McKibben, who would manage the Manhattan Project's Santa Fe office for the next twenty years. McKibben had been told about the Whites by the young couple who had shared meals with them the previous weekend at Ghost Ranch. Mechanical engineers and registered nurses were both needed at Los Alamos. There was no phone at Ghost Ranch, and McKibben had been sitting in her office on East Palace Avenue wondering how to contact the Whites when she happened to look out her doorway and across the patio just as Pack's car, with the Ghost Ranch insignia on its door, drove past. McKibben frantically ran around the plaza, checking hotel lobbies and shops, and finally spotted Roger and Kitty, their bags piled on the curb, standing beside the recently arrived Lamy bus.

"This one little thing—Dorothy McKibben seeing the Ghost Ranch car go by—changed our whole lives," White remembers.

Dr. Kenneth Bainbridge, who interviewed Roger White that afternoon, was test director of the Manhattan Project and was in charge of the actual detonation of the first bomb exploded at the Trinity site in July of 1945.

"He was trying to find out what I was good for without telling me what the job was," White remembers. On that same day, Roger White accepted Bainbridge's offer for a job he could not give a name to at a place that did not exist. Kitty White was hired as a nurse. They returned to Cleveland where friends and family had been undergoing questioning by the FBI, gathered up their belongings, and, as Arthur Pack later observed, "vanished from the outside world into the secret behind the well-guarded gates of 'The Hill.'"[5]

The Whites were delighted that their new government jobs, although cloaked in secrecy—their movements restricted and regulated—included dinners down the hill at Edith Warner's tea room beside the Rio Grande and weekend getaways at Ghost Ranch on the Piedra Lumbre. "The ranch was used by a lot of the scientists—Kitty and I were here with Kistiakowsky, another time with Fermi, with Feynman and others. Not in big groups. But the scientists were all constantly together, talking physics. . . . 'How are we going to cope with this problem' . . . and I remember thinking, we're all here for a little r'n'r, why are we talking shop so much?!

"We were working six days a week. It was stressful, but there was so much excitement! It wasn't stress from worrying. You didn't worry about money, or about food. Everything was there. You'd just hold out your hand and you got it. It was just the stress of this constant drive to get the thing done."

The dropping of the atomic bomb on the city of Hiroshima on August 6, 1945, ended the press censorship concerning Los Alamos. Newspapers in New Mexico could finally acknowledge that there was, indeed, an entire city nestled on the Pajarito Plateau, and the villages and pueblos in the river valley below learned that they had a neighboring community of six thousand people nestled in the mountains above them.

The Packs learned exactly what their friends without names had been doing in-between their seemingly carefree days at Ghost Ranch. It seemed an incongruous partnership, Ghost Ranch's unspoiled wilderness a part-time think tank for the creators of the world's deadliest weapon. "Ghost Ranch had played a small accessory part in the making of the atomic bomb," Pack wrote years later. "We shared and understood some of the guilt that afflicted others."[6] He continued, "After the surrender of Japan, our atomic energy friends could talk a little more freely and philosophically about the future of the world. Here, on a Ghost Ranch evening, the utter incompatibilities and terrible contrasts inherent in man's warring natures stood out as starkly as did mountain, cliff and sky. The Hiroshima destruction, which one or two had actually witnessed, was a nightmare they might vainly wish undreamed."[7]

At least one of Pack's scientist friends became an organizer of those scientists who actively sought to outlaw atomic weapons. "Perhaps Ghost

Ranch had served to shape his world view for peace," Pack wrote, "but it was already too late. The problem was not the bomb, but man himself."[8]

After the war, the Packs did not reopen Ghost Ranch for guest business. But many friends of the Packs came and went, grateful for the ranch's clear skies and unscathed land. The Piedra Lumbre valley retained its pristine frontier facade, and many war-weary pilgrims returned to the Land of Shining Stone simply to bask in its emptiness and aura of innocence.

In early summer of 1947, a group of scientists—paleontologists, bone instead of bomb experts—drove a jeep across the Piedra Lumbre basin en route to Ghost Ranch. They were led by Dr. Edwin (Ned) H. Colbert, the curator of fossil reptiles at the American Museum of Natural History in New York. With George Whitaker and Thomas Ierardi, Colbert was ultimately bound for Arizona, where he had a permit to dig that summer in the Triassic badlands at the Petrified Forest. For years, Colbert had heard about the Triassic desert of the Piedra Lumbre valley, and before beginning his summer of work in Arizona, he wanted to spend a few days exploring the desert around Ghost Ranch.

Colbert and his colleagues entered the basin from the southwest. Their first view of the Cliffs of Shining Stone was from the flatlands below Mesa Prieta, where the Jicarilla Apaches had once camped and farmed: "I was completely unprepared for that first stupendous view of the Ghost Ranch cliffs," Colbert wrote. "Charles Camp [paleontologist, mentor and colleague of Colbert's] and his associates had been quite matter of fact when we talked about Ghost Ranch; I suppose because our conversations were along paleontological lines it never occurred to them to mention that Ghost Ranch is a place that almost rivals Zion Canyon in the beauty of its setting."[9]

After crossing the Chama River bridge they headed north on the newly paved road called Highway 84. As instructed, they looked for the fabled gate—in 1947, the Packs had placed a board painted with the silhouette of the cow skull and the Ghost Ranch logo at the ranch entrance—and upon finding the sign, drove up the rutted, bumpy dirt road to ranch headquarters. Arthur Pack invited Colbert and his colleagues to join Phoebe and the Pack children, Charlie and little Phoebe, for lunch. Colbert explained to Pack that although the findings of previous bone diggers in this region were important enough to warrant further investigation, Colbert, Whitaker, and Ierardi had only a few days to poke around the Triassic beds at Ghost Ranch before driving on to Arizona.

In previous decades, paleontologists had found skeletons of phytosaurs, a Triassic reptile, in the Piedra Lumbre basin. The first phytosaur (a water-loving, alligator-like reptile with long, dagger-toothed jaws) skeleton was discovered here in 1928 by Dr. Charles Camp from the University of California at Berkeley. Camp and his field crew camped several summers on various parts of the Piedra Lumbre, during which they uncovered several dozen fossilized phytosaur skeletons, as well as several Permian reptiles and a rare Typothorax reptile.

The Triassic layer of the Piedra Lumbre basin—represented by the lower red, sparsely vegetated hills of the Chinle Formation at the foot of the cliffs, whose barren contours captivated O'Keeffe's heart and were frequently the subject of her paintings—was known to hold the bones of the earliest dinosaurs. The Triassic in earth history was ruled by a reptilian species; dinosaurian reptiles were in their infancy, and mammals were still an insignificant element in the animal world. Fossils found in this layer were up to 225 million years old and represented the first dinosaurs.

At Ghost Ranch and on the surrounding perimeters of the Piedra Lumbre basin the Triassic lay exposed in talus slopes and sandy hills. The rapid erosion of the hills by wind and rain was constantly exposing new layers, and it was common for bone diggers to return to such a site that had previously yielded good finds.

The red hills of the Piedra Lumbre first caught a paleontologist's eye in 1874. Dr. Edward Drinker Cope of Pittsburgh came to New Mexico with the Wheeler Expedition that was mapping the American West. On that journey, Cope found fossilized bones on the Piedra Lumbre that identified a new fossil animal, Typothorax, a creature that had rows of bony plates down its back and resembled a giant horned toad.

Cope's journals and notes about the Chama River Valley and the Piedra Lumbre prompted other paleontologists to visit the region. In 1876, David Baldwin, a young assistant to one of Cope's fiercest competitors, Othniel Marsh of Yale, came to Abiquiu to prospect for fossils. Baldwin had also come to New Mexico with the Wheeler Expedition, and his fossil collecting for Marsh began in the San Juan Basin near Lindrith, New Mexico. Baldwin's bone prospecting soon included the Piedra Lumbre and Abiquiu region.

In the 1880s, Baldwin, who was now collecting for Cope, adopted the remote village of Abiquiu as his home, although he spent most of his time alone roaming the New Mexican outback. Contrary to most paleontologists' work habits, Baldwin preferred to hunt fossils in the winter, when he could melt snow for water and, as he wrote, "one or two men with jacks can prowl around the foot of the mesa and camp anywhere when there is snow."[10] Baldwin hardly knew his pueblo neighbors and saw little of his fellow paleontologists and geologists who regularly came and went in northern New Mexico. Baldwin's colleagues, although respectful of him professionally, came to regard him as an eccentric: "[He] was equipped like a Mexican with a burro, some corn meal, and a pickaxe," one eastern friend wrote of Baldwin.[11]

Baldwin did not resemble his Anglo contemporaries in the 1880s: he was not a trader or a merchant, not a lawyer, a land developer, or a soldier. Baldwin was not an intrusive or demanding man, and we can assume that regardless of his eccentricities and hermitlike demeanor, he became an accepted figure to those shepherds and ranchers who stumbled across his camp on some lonely mesa in the dead of winter.

Baldwin's fossil collecting was prodigious, and it set the stage for major paleontological finds in the next half-century, especially for those on the Piedra Lumbre. Among the fossils Baldwin boxed and mailed to Cope in Philadelphia from the tiny post office in the general store on the Abiquiu plaza in 1881 was a handful of small bone fragments found in the red hills below the Cliffs of Shining Stone. His note to Cope in February said: "Contains Triassic and Jurassic bones all small and tender. . . . All in this sack found in same place . . . Arroyo Seco. . . . No feet—no head—only one tooth. D. Baldwin, Abiquiu."[12]

Baldwin spent months exploring and digging the red hills of what is now Ghost Ranch, working his way up the narrow arroyos to the cliff face, and into the canyons that intersect the Arroyo Seco streambed as it works its way down from the Canjilon Mountains to the Chama River. Although Baldwin knew he was in an area that should yield rich Triassic fossils, he found only scraps. He apologized to Cope: "I am very sorry I could not find a single mammal to dig out. There ain't a foot nor skull in the entire lot. Abiquiu is my address all the time."[13]

The extent of the paleontological treasures of the Piedra Lumbre would remain buried for the next half-century, but among Baldwin's finds—the small handful of tiny bones "small and hollow, of reptile, and some so small they were almost microscopic"[14]—were bones of the little dinosaur Cope named Coelophysis (see-lo-fi'-sis). Baldwin's scant scraps of Coelophysis—a tiny dinosaur that would one day be recognized as among the oldest dinosaurs in the world, the great-grandfather of the colossal dinosaurs to come—were enough gold bits to a paleontologist's trained eye to precipitate additional expeditions to the Piedra Lumbre.

The Chama Valley was revisited by paleontologists in 1911. This expedition included scientists from the University of Chicago and the University of Michigan, as well as paleontology legend Professor Frederich von Huene of Germany. The discovery of fossils in various locales in Rio Arriba County of little-known Permian reptiles soon brought more fossil hunters to the area from the University of Chicago and from Harvard.

Camp's digging site on the Piedra Lumbre in the late 1920s yielded the skeleton of the Typothorax, the same rare reptile found here in the 1870s by Cope and the Wheeler Expedition. But Camp's crew also collected dozens of complete phytosaur skeletons. Wind and water erosion of the red cliffs and hills and talus slopes over the past fifty years had revealed the feet, skulls, and several complete skeletons whose apparent absence had frustrated David Baldwin in the 1880s.

Between 1928 and 1934, Camp and his field crew of four or five men returned in the summers to live in tent camps on different locations in the Piedra Lumbre basin. Camp and his colleagues became friends with the region's residents, new and old-timers alike. Carol Stanley, the crew's "guardian angel,"[15] often brought the crew a picnic lunch—on one occasion she sent the men four gallons of milk "that were most welcome,"[16] and she often brought the desert-parched crew fresh fruit. A highlight of each week was the paleontologists' visit to Stanley's Ghost Ranch casa, or to Pack's newly completed Rancho de los Burros, for supper and music. The fossil hunters learned of the local lore and legend that claimed the Valley of Shining Stone was haunted. Stanley told Dr. Camp that the site of their excavations in the summer of 1933 was called Spooky Gulch among the local ranchers. And she shared with the scientists Rancho de los Brujos' auspicious beginnings as a cattle rustling outfit and its lingering reputation as a playground for the spirits of those whose bones—human bones—lay in its sands.

Stanley and Pack also visited the bone diggers' camp for suppers and games of cards around their campfire: "Mrs. Stanley came over this evening, accompanied by Arthur and Mrs. Pack, Miss Seymour, Frank Hibben, and Lloyd," crew member Samuel Welles wrote in his journal on June 22, 1934. "We played hearts and bridge and had a fine time."

Camp and his crew also made their way down the valley to Abiquiu—a jeep trip that took one hour and twenty minutes each way—for supplies and to visit with Martin Bode: "Spent the evening in Abiquiu with Mr. Bode (owner of the general store) over several bottles of beer," Camp wrote in his field journal on July 23, 1933. "Bode spoke frankly and in detail of the Penitentes, the women, & the state of the country. Abiquiu he says is all Penitente except himself, Gonzales, Chavez & one or two others."[17]

Additional paleontologists often came to the Piedra Lumbre to visit Camp's sites. When Ghost Ranch's limited facilities were full, the visitors were housed with a family downriver at the pueblo. Martin Bode threw parties for these distinguished village guests, and Dr. Camp and his crew were invited into Abiquiu for summer dances in their honor. The lively music, food and drink, and the presence of young female dance partners from the community were a welcome respite from the monotonous rigors of bone digging on the dusty Piedra Lumbre desert.

Elizabeth Bode Allred watched the festivities from the shadows: "I remember moving all the furniture back in the living room for two different dances. I was just a kid, and I remember standing by the back of one of those chairs and watching. And I'd fall asleep and wake up again to see all this going on. Some of the local ladies were invited—you have to have partners to have a dance. I remember dad having a fine time, making the punch. This was something that mother had never done, but father made a wonderful punch with fresh strawberries and good things in it. They were fine evenings!"

In the summer of 1934, several bone diggers not connected with Camp and his crew knocked on Pack's door and asked if they could dig in the badlands near Rancho de los Burros. Pack knew it was considered bad etiquette for paleontologists to dig another's site, and, protective of Camp's prior claim, he steered the young men to the foot of Mesa Huerfano, where Camp had not worked. Pack told the fossil diggers there was good reason to dig below Orphan Mesa east of Stanley's ranch headquarters: he told them the local story of Vivarón, the giant child-eating snake, and with tongue planted firmly in cheek, Pack revealed that there had been several recent sundown sightings of the serpent's glimmering form:

> Descriptions of this supposedly twenty to thirty foot long snake-like creature given by badly scared shepherders had suggested that there really must have been something unusual to have occasioned a fright of such degree, and I half jokingly proposed that these young paleontologists might go over there to look around. Several hours later they came back in a frenzy of excitement, begging me to ride over and see what they had found. It was a hot summer day when direct rays from the sun reflected from the bare ground in shimmering waves. As my horse rounded the sharp bend of an arroyo a coiled skeleton, perhaps twenty feet long, uncovered by the vagaries of wind and storm suddenly appeared on the opposite slope, and in the dancing heat waves actually seemed to move from side to side.[18]

On that sizzling summer afternoon, the story of Vivarón stepped from legend into history, at least among Pack and the paleontologists. The fossilized creature that lay on top of the red sand below Orphan Mesa was identified as another phytosaur. In the next few days, the bones were carefully encased in plaster, and the skeleton, accompanied by fragments of the Piedra Lumbre myth of Vivarón, was shipped off for further study in Chicago.

Ned Colbert and his companions had several decades of reasons to return to the Piedra Lumbre and hunt for fossils in June of 1947. Back at Berkeley, Colbert had studied Camp's specimens collected from the basin. Camp, upon finishing his own work in Arizona and New Mexico, had given Colbert his "locality data," notes and site locations, of Ghost Ranch and the

Piedra Lumbre. Colbert was interested in seeing for himself the red hills and desert country that had yielded so many fine phytosaurs.

After their lunch with the Pack family, Arthur invited Colbert and his two colleagues to set up their tents near the ranch's swimming pool up the canyon beside the Yeso stream which filled the pool with clear, frigidly cold water. "This was an unusual piece of luck, considering how hot it gets in New Mexico during the summer," George Whitaker wrote of their campsite, which was, to his knowledge, the first and only fossil camp ever set beside a swimming pool.[19]

On their first morning at Ghost Ranch, Colbert, Whitaker, and Ierardi split up to explore the cliffs, talus slopes, and little red hills of the Piedra Lumbre's northern badlands. They did not look long for evidence of fossils: "On the first morning we found in a canyon a mile or so beyond our camp a very nice phytosaur skull," Colbert wrote. "It was too good to pass up, so we settled down to collect it."[20]

It took several days to uncover and safely encase the phytosaur in a plaster jacket. Colbert and his colleagues talked about departing the valley, but they were so thoroughly enjoying the scenery, the high-altitude air, the refreshingly cold swimming pool at day's end, and the obvious opportunities for more fossil finds that they decided to work a few more days at the luxurious Ghost Ranch camp.

Their second discovery came as effortlessly and swiftly as the first. "Again, on the very first morning of renewed prospecting there was another discovery. This time it was George Whitaker who stumbled onto paleontological pay dirt. We had all separated, as was our usual practice, individually to search the exposures . . . and shortly before noon George came running across a little arroyo with some bone fragments in his hand."[21]

Dorthy Burnham Fredericks was visiting "the bone-hunters, as we always called them" with her son, David, that particular morning: "George came running down the red hill yelling 'I found it! I found it!' He showed me what he had found and it looked like another red rock to me. But not to him!"

The bones Whitaker had found belonged to the ancient dinosaur Coelophysis. The scraps of fossils Whitaker held in his one palm equaled and maybe even doubled what was previously known about Coelophysis:

in 1947 the little dinosaur was known only from the fragmentary fossils collected by David Baldwin kept six decades in a single tray at the Museum of Natural History in New York.

Although Baldwin's notes claimed his Coelophysis finds were from the Arroyo Seco a few miles to the west of Whitaker's site, Baldwin was known to have been vague and inexact when describing his digging locales in northern New Mexico. The Rito del Yeso where Colbert and crew were working was a tributary of the Arroyo Seco: it was very possible that Whitaker had scooped these fossils from the same hill that had yielded Baldwin's fistful of rare Coelophysis bones more than half a century before.

Colbert and Ierardi followed Whitaker back to the sand slope and found more fragments belonging to Coelophysis. It was a momentous moment for Colbert: "Here was something quite unexpected that immediately changed my thinking about what direction our summer field program might take. . . . Within a few moments of scratching around on that talus slope we had found more materials of the little dinosaur than had previously existed."[22]

After a brief and excited lunch break, the three men returned to the talus slope wedged in the sand hills below the cliffs east of their camp. After following fragments of the little bones up the slope they found the rock stratum from which the fossils had been eroding. The three spent that afternoon and the next two days digging into the side of the little red hill. The more Colbert and his crew dug, the more bones emerged: "There before us was a bone bed of remarkable abundance, a layer of bones consisting of articulated [complete] and partially articulated skeletons—skeletons in which the bones were attached to one another more or less in their natural relationships—all belonging to Coelophysis. It was a paleontological treasure beyond one's wildest dreams!"[23]

Colbert was faced with a dilemma. He carried in his field bag a permit to work at the Petrified Forest, a permit which had been difficult and time consuming to obtain: "One had to go through channels all the way up to the secretary of the interior and back down again."[24] But at his feet were bones that could amount to one of the great paleontological finds of the century, "specimens that would furnish information of the most detailed nature about Coelophysis."[25]

The men dug in the talus slope for several more days, clearing away the earth at the rock ledge and eventually learning that the quarry extended over an area almost thirty feet long across the cliff face. The uncovered ribs, vertebrae, and finally jaw and skull convinced Colbert that what they were finding were the bones of the elusive, primitive dinosaur. And not simply one Coelophysis, but many. It was a site Colbert could not walk away from.

Even knowing that their withdrawal from work at the Petrified Forest would most certainly insult government officials in offices from Arizona to Washington, Colbert followed the paleontologists' creed "to gather ye rosebuds while ye may" and, throwing bureaucratic opinion to the high-desert wind, opted to spend the summer at Ghost Ranch. Colbert informed the Petrified Forest officials that he would not be using his permit. On June thirtieth, Colbert sent a wire from the Española telegraph office to his friend Carl Sorensen of the Vertebrate Paleontology Laboratory at the Museum of Natural History in New York, asking if he could come to New Mexico and help excavate the rich quarry at Ghost Ranch.

Pack had been enthusiastic about Colbert's and Whitaker's finds from the beginning: the initial discovery was celebrated with a party on the Packs' supper porch. When it was apparent that the paleontologists might be at the ranch for the entire summer, Pack insisted they move out of their dusty tents beside the pool and into the comfortable Johnson house which Arthur now owned.

Colbert and the others were more than a little grateful for the offer: "Camping out is all right for a vacation trip," Colbert wrote,

> but as a steady thing, week in and week out, when you're trying to get the job done, the outdoor life begins to pall. Moreover the business of writing up field notes at night, sitting on the edge of a canvas cot with a hot Coleman lamp as a source of illumination, and with the various local insects, attracted by the lamp, blundering into your face or onto the page where you are trying to compose your thoughts, can be at times an exercise in frustration.
>
> . . . Thus we changed our life style almost instantaneously from one of inconvenience to one of comparative luxury.

We had a dwelling where we could enjoy the comfort of a large living room in which there were shelves stocked with books, a modern kitchen, and two bedrooms, each with a full bath. It proved to be the most posh living in all my experience of fossil collecting.[26]

The treeless slope of the quarry was blistering hot during the day, and a wooden roof was built over the digging site to protect both the diggers and the fossils from the sun, from rain, and from rubble sliding down the slope above the excavation site. All of the excavating had to be done with picks and shovels, and the removal of the Coelophysis skeletons from the rock was a difficult and tedious job for Colbert, Whitaker, Ierardi, and Sorensen. They did not free each individual bone, but rather dug large blocks of rock that could be removed and taken to distant laboratories.

The Ghost Ranch Coelophysis quarry caused a national sensation: Colbert and crew were finding the bones of what was believed to be the oldest dinosaur in the world—Coelophysis roamed the earth 225 million years ago, some 30 million years before the great Jurassic dinosaurs like Brontosaurus and Stegosaurus.[27] And at Ghost Ranch, they had not just found a few bones, but had found complete skeletons, and not just several, but *dozens*. The skeletons ranged in age from those of the very young to those of the very old.

Few fossil sites in the world have ever yielded complete dinosaur skeletons: the Ghost Ranch quarry soon revealed at least one hundred complete Coelophysis skeletons. What Colbert and crew were pulling out of the red hills near the Rito del Yeso would offer paleontologists the rare opportunity to study the complete ancestry and evolution of this little dinosaur, thus illuminating the story of Coelophysis' great-grandchildren, the huge dinosaurs that followed a few million years later.

The quarry was obviously the location of a mass burial. But the how and why of so many Coelophysis—babies, young adults, adults, and elderly dinosaurs—perishing at once in one place plagued Colbert the summer of 1947 just as it does today. The bones are not chewed, broken, or battered in any way. Colbert's and other scientists' subsequent study of the Ghost Ranch quarry and skeletons led him to believe that their death was the result of a mass drowning followed by almost immediate burial: "When the various possibilities are taken into account it seems to me that the Ghost Ranch dinosaurs very possibly perished while they were attempting to cross a stream in flood. Perhaps they represent a single catastrophic occurrence, perhaps they represent an accumulation of skeletons from various attempted stream crossings through a succession of years."[28]

When the first block of Coelophysis-bearing plaster arrived in New York, the Museum of Natural History issued a press release that precipitated visits to the Ghost Ranch quarry by reporters, scientists, and writers from all over the world. Abiquiu and the Chama River Valley and their "embarrassment of riches"[29] were once again center stage for events that would be given lofty places in future history books.

On July 14, 1947, the *New York Times* front-page headline announced "Museum finds dinosaur 200 million years old." The story captured all of the excitement the paleontological world was experiencing, but it mistakenly placed the quarry in Lindrith, New Mexico, where Colbert's colleague, friend, and professional competitor Dr. George Gaylord Simpson was digging. The little dinosaur and its quarry at Ghost Ranch also made the front page of the *New York Herald Tribune,* and Colbert and crew were featured in major articles in *Life Magazine,* the *Saturday Evening Post,* and *Newsweek,* as well as numerous regional and national publications.

The Packs welcomed dozens of reporters and photographers to Ghost Ranch, which was temporarily turned into a bustling desert press village. Pack was generally a tolerant and helpful host, although he was amused by the comings and goings of big-city media people who pursued the dinosaur story into the red hills unprepared for the rough and tumble terrain of the quarry setting. One photographer particularly amused Pack: "Life magazine flew in their nearest cameraman, who happened to be in Hollywood specializing on *[sic]* movie actresses and 'cheesecake.' The young and shapely legs he was used to photographing were one thing, but small leg bones a million years old were something else again, especially when they lay embedded in red clay and the hillside was always sliding and filling the photographer's handsome sport shoes."[30]

Pack's cousin, Roger White, remained an employee of the laboratory at Los Alamos after the war and frequently visited Ghost Ranch with his family in the late 1940s. White had studied geology at Stanford and was as excited by the treasures found in the quarry as the paleontologists. During weekend visits to the ranch, White spent many hours at the Coelophysis site, where his mechanical skills and his keys to the vast tool shop at Los Alamos proved helpful to Colbert's crew: "During one visit, Ned was trying to chisel out a big chunk of rock with bones in it. He said, 'God, I wish we had one of those . . . things! And you can't buy one of those . . . things!' What he needed was a special kind of long chisel. I said, 'Ned, I can probably get you one.' I went back to the lab in Los Alamos—at that time we could go anyplace and do anything in the laboratory—and I got hold of some scrap tool steel and made a couple of these chisels and brought them back to Colbert. He was just elated!"

Georgia O'Keeffe was living at Rancho de los Burros that summer, and in spite of the clamoring journalists became a frequent observer of the diggers' tedious but rewarding work beneath the cliffs. O'Keeffe found kindred spirits among the paleontologists and often came and stood alone or with Pack in the shade of a nearby juniper tree, quietly watching the men brush away the debris covering the bones emerging before them on the rock ledge.

On one August visit, O'Keeffe brought four nuns to the quarry—two from Abiquiu and two from Ohio. "In spite of their long gowns," Ned Colbert wrote, "they piled into the jeep along with Georgia for the trip to the quarry, and a good time was had by all."[31]

Ned Colbert knew O'Keeffe's reputation as a distant and often unfriendly woman, and he also knew that the painter disliked being besieged by admirers. During O'Keeffe's visits to the quarry, or while sharing iced tea at her house, Colbert made a point of never asking O'Keeffe about her work. Their relationship was built, instead, upon O'Keeffe's interest in Colbert's work and his vast geologic and paleontological expertise. That summer, and during many summers to come, Colbert interpreted and identified O'Keeffe's rock and bone specimens collected on her walks around the badlands of the Piedra Lumbre: "O'Keeffe would come over from her house to visit the quarry, and we would on occasion visit her at her home. She and I became good friends, I suppose in part because we were both fascinated by bones. Although the bones she liked were recent and the ones I liked were very old, still they were bones—and that gave us common interests. Also, she had me describe to her what life was like millions of years ago, when Ghost Ranch was a tropical environment."[32]

The Ghost Ranch community, the scenery of the Piedra Lumbre, plus the remarkable fossil discoveries at the quarry made for a fine and memorable summer. Although their eyes were focused for hours at a time on the ground below them, the fossil hunters did find time to look up and enjoy the beautiful country surrounding them. For each of the men, it was a field camp and fossil site that would never be duplicated in the scope and importance of its paleontological treasures, nor in the extraordinary beauty of its setting: "So the summer days passed by all too quickly at Ghost Ranch, with much visiting among the members of our little group. Sometimes we would gather with Arthur and Phoebe at their house, sometimes we would all congregate at the old swimming pool. Always we would enjoy the distant view of Pedernal and the changing lights on the great cliffs behind us. Ghost Ranch in the days of the Packs was indeed a quiet and rather isolated haven."[33]

The amount of men and heavy equipment passing up and down the steep arroyos and small canyons near the fossil site necessitated the opening of a road between Ghost Ranch and the quarry. Pack offered the services of his foreman, Herman Hall, who bulldozed a road that jeeps could navigate and which was wide enough for the plaster blocks to be dragged down from the site on heavy wooden sleds originally built to move rocks and boulders.

Each block was between five and six feet long and equally wide, and weighed between fifteen hundred and six thousand pounds. The blocks were hoisted free of the quarry with a hydraulic tractor lift and a thick, heavy chain.

The paleontologists watched as Hall lowered their gigantic treasures onto the wooden sleds "more gently than a case of eggs."[34] Colbert wrote: "The American Museum of Natural History, and the science of paleontology, owes much to the cooperation from Mr. Pack and other people at Ghost Ranch who in various ways helped the Coelophysis quarry work."[35]

At the end of the summer, massive plaster blocks sat on the ground before the headquarters of Ghost Ranch awaiting transport to various locations. Four blocks were to be sent to the Museum of Natural History in New York where Colbert and Whitaker worked, and Herman Hall's father-in-law was brought in from Texas to drive the precious cargo. Upon arrival in New York and the safe unloading of the immense fossil-filled blocks, the driver admitted it was the heaviest load he had ever transported cross-country and that the trip was the crowning experience of his life.[36]

Other blocks pulled from the quarry in the red hills were shipped to the Peabody Museum at Yale, the Museum of Northern Arizona, the Museum of Comparative Zoology at Harvard, the Cleveland Museum, the University of Texas, the University of New Mexico, and the Connecticut State Dinosaur Trackway Park. It took skilled workers more than a year to separate the bones of a single Coelophysis from the plaster that encased their delicate and ancient bones.

Block Number One was given to Ghost Ranch. In 1958, after it had been prepared for exhibition at the American Museum of Natural History, the Ghost Ranch block of Coelophysis skeletons was returned to Abiquiu and put on display a few miles from its home quarry at the newly built Ghost Ranch Museum.

After two summers of digging, Colbert declared that science had unearthed enough material and ordered the quarry closed. Hall's bulldozer pushed the top off the red hill above the site, and the entire quarry disappeared under a landslide that would protect the bones from weather and from the damages that could be incurred from amateur "gophering."

The skeletons of Coelophysis returned to only partial oblivion in the sands of the Piedra Lumbre. In 1977, the scientific importance of the Coelophysis quarry at Ghost Ranch was officially recognized—Colbert's no-show at the Petrified Forest field camp in the summer of 1947 was evidently forgiven by the Department of the Interior—and the site was designated a National Natural Landmark. In 1981, the New Mexico Legislature chose Coelophysis to be the state fossil. The site was reopened that same year, with more blocks of Coelophysis skeletons removed for study. In 1986, the newly opened New Mexico Museum of Natural History in Albuquerque adopted the little dinosaur's running form for its logo, making it among the most recognized dinosaurs in the West.

Conclusion:

PROLOGUE TO THE NEXT CENTURY

People visit the American West because they believe in the realities of cowboys and Indians; they believe, too, in the possibility of encountering some whisper or vestige of the great bygone days.

Frederick Turner, *Of Chilis, Cacti, and Fighting Cocks*

Before the beginning of the second world war, the Packs bought seven acres of land northwest of Tucson and built a small winter home. Although they had tired of guest ranching in New Mexico, the Packs could not conceive of a home that could not accommodate family and guests, and their new retreat on the outskirts of the desert city soon included rental apartments. They named the new tourist court the Ghost Ranch Lodge. The Tucson lodge used the same logo designed by O'Keeffe for Ghost Ranch in New Mexico. The Ghost Ranch Lodge was among the first motels to become affiliated with the Best Western chain of tourist facilities.

In Tucson, Arthur Pack jumped into the center of civic and community life just as he had in northern New Mexico. With his old friend Bill Carr, the designer of the Bear Mountain State Park Trailside Museum on the Hudson River, Pack and some $100,000 from his father's foundation put into motion plans that turned the 30,000-acre Pima County Park in the Tucson Mountains into the Arizona-Sonora Desert Museum, opened in 1952.[1]

The success of the Arizona-Sonora Desert Museum prompted Pack and Carr to collaborate on a second, smaller trailside museum in New Mexico: the Ghost Ranch Museum and "Beaver National Forest" opened in 1958 near the paved highway that paralleled the Cliffs of Shining Stone.

In the '40s and early '50s, the Packs leased Ghost Ranch to friends who wanted to give western guest ranching a try, but even with wealthy Hollywood patrons and film crews as guests, the summers were financially unsuccessful. Liability insurance for guest ranches had begun to climb, and lawsuits against other dude ranch owners had resulted in expensive settlements that made all ranch owners nervous.

By the mid 1950s, the Packs were using Ghost Ranch only a few weeks out of each year. The ranch was overseen by a resident foreman and his wife, but each winter when the Packs departed the Piedra Lumbre for the warmer climate of Tucson, Arthur worried about the future of his beloved Ranch of the Witches. Pack wanted the wild cliff country and vast re-grassed and antelope-inhabited llanos of the Piedra Lumbre to be protected for future generations. Fearful that a property the size of Ghost Ranch, which constituted more than half of the Piedra Lumbre basin's private land, would eventually be subdivided by future owners, and that even those with the best of intentions might one day place financial considerations before ecological preservation, Pack decided to offer the land to a nonprofit organization rather than leave it to his children.

Pack began investigating various civic and religious organizations that might qualify for Ghost Ranch's next patron: the national YMCA and Boy Scouts were both candidates, but each already had substantial camps in the Southwest. The Archdiocese of Santa Fe was approached, but thought the property too remote to ever become a viable educational facility. Finally a minister friend in Tucson suggested Pack offer the ranch to the Presbyterian Church (U.S.A.). Pack approached the Presbyterians, and in 1955, after careful consideration, their Board of Christian Education accepted the gift of Ghost Ranch.

Any disappointment Pack's immediate family might have felt about Arthur's gift to the Presbyterians was minimal compared to O'Keeffe's outrage concerning his decision. During a meeting in the Packs' Ghost Ranch living room with several high-ranking Presbyterians, O'Keeffe marched up to Pack's house and without bothering to knock, entered Pack's house and cornered him: "Arthur, what's this I hear about your giving the ranch away?! If you were going to do that, why didn't you give it to me?"[2]

An embarrassed Pack explained to the irate artist that the men sitting about the living room were officials from the Presbyterian Church in Philadelphia. He assured O'Keeffe that they had only the best of intentions for Ghost Ranch. But O'Keeffe was not consoled: "Hmph! Now I suppose this beautiful place will be crawling with people and completely spoiled," she told Pack. "I never had any use for Presbyterians anyhow!"[3]

O'Keeffe exited the house in a huff, leaving behind a room full of red-faced dignitaries. Pack had forewarned them about their new neighbor, but nothing could really have prepared the Presbyterians for Georgia O'Keeffe. Others who witnessed this conversation between Pack and the outspoken painter claim that Pack's rendering of the exchange, as quoted above, is kind to O'Keeffe and does not actually capture the hostility of O'Keeffe's visit: "O'Keeffe was actually a good deal more vociferous," one witness remembers. "She was very, *very* angry with Arthur. She really believed he should have given her the ranch."[4]

In time, O'Keeffe forgave Arthur. The Packs continued to share supper and conversation with O'Keeffe at Rancho de los Burros in the ensuing decades before Arthur's death in 1975, at which time Pack's ashes were brought to Ghost Ranch and placed in the sandy ground of the mesa above the legendary homestead.

The Presbyterians and their plans for a conference center at Ghost Ranch would quickly prove to be the least of O'Keeffe's concerns as to the future uses of the Piedra Lumbre's lands. In 1957, with the blessing and legal approval of Congress, the U.S. Army Corps of Engineers began condemnation procedures that usurped hundreds of acres of privately held land in the Piedra Lumbre basin at $10.00 an acre for a flood- and sediment-control reservoir. Ghost Ranch lost 161 acres—the Chama River crossed the ranch for two miles and was its southern boundary for another six miles—and an additional 5,148 acres of Ghost Ranch were forcibly purchased at $2.50 an acre for perpetual easement rights. That same year, the corps began building Abiquiu Dam, an earth-filled structure that choked the deep crevice of the Chama Canyon north of Abiquiu where the Chama River departed the Piedra Lumbre basin. The dam's impact on the various natural habitats—human, animal, and vegetable—of the Piedra Lumbre basin would be substantial and irreversible.

Abiquiu Dam was completed by 1962. By 1965, 65 feet of water inundated several miles of the Chama River's ancient Piedra Lumbre cottonwood bosque, including numerous perching trees for bald eagles, and drowned the dams of the beaver that had thrived in the basin since the Paleo-Indians had journeyed to this valley for Pedernal's superior chert. Within a few years, the lake behind the flood- and sediment-control dam, now advertised for its recreational potential, was boasting a water level 6,220 feet above sea level. The flood-controlling waters inundated hundreds of historic and prehistoric habitation sites—the River Ranch of Juan de Dios lay below more than 150 feet of water—and washed away the last fragments of the various people who had come and gone across this basin for centuries.

The highway across the basin had to be relocated. A new roadbed was cut across Rancho de los Brujos: the old road to Ghost Ranch lost four miles to the reservoir, and the new highway brought cars and trucks and the clamor of civilization closer to the Cliffs of Shining Stone. The new roadbed was cut within a few yards of an old spring situated at the base of Mesa del Gato ("cat mesa"), so named for the mountain lions who once came to drink from the spring's cool water on hot summer afternoons. The mountain lions left the basin for higher, less civilized grounds. But other wildlife, along with the valley livestock, were forced to cope with the changes brought to the Piedra Lumbre by the unnatural lake that now cut the llanos in two: "We [Ghost Ranch and its neighbors] were losing burros and cows in the newly created quicksand," Jim Shibley, Ghost Ranch rangelands manager remembers, "and gone was the beauty of the river bottom. The beavers had to resort to the top branches of the tallest cottonwood trees for food. Some even walked three miles up rain-dampened arroyos looking for new homesites."

Old-timers generally avoided the lake, whose cactus-studded shoreline marked the boundaries of an invader they could not fight or ever hope to remove from the Piedra Lumbre. In spite of her anger toward the lake that had taken her beloved river and llanos, Dorthy Burnham Fredericks visited the lake during the first year of inundation: "I ventured out in a little boat, looking for the old River Ranch. Even floating on the water, I knew where I was . . . what mesa was here, what arroyo had been over there. I finally rowed to where I was certain the old crossing had been. I peered over the boat's side down into the water. Below I could see the tops of the great cottonwood trees. I couldn't see the stone house or the corrals. They were gone. There was just the branches of those old trees wavering in the water below me. . . . The arms of those drowned cottonwoods reaching up through the water have haunted me all my life."

By the early 1970s, the Army Corps of Engineers had begun aggressive expansion of the recreational facilities at Abiquiu Lake. In spite of continued community dissension, and unanswered questions about the placement of the dam on a major geological fault and the ability of the structure to safely hold a large permanent pool, the corps asked Congress to allow them to enlarge the lake's permanent pool. While the corps wrangled with the local community that opposed its desire to double the reservoir's size and develop Abiquiu Reservoir into a tourist site, the city of Albuquerque inadvertently gave the corps the leverage it needed to proceed with expansion plans.

In 1977, Albuquerque was looking for a site in which to store its surplus water imported to the Chama River through a tunnel over the Continental Divide from tributaries of the Colorado River. Abiquiu Lake, although legally a reservoir that would rise and fall according to flood needs, offered to store Albuquerque's water. In 1981, Congress passed a law that allowed the lake to permanently store 200,000 acre-feet of Albuquerque's surplus water. This meant a permanent lake that flooded thousands of acres of the Piedra Lumbre's privately owned rangeland. Ghost Ranch alone lost 3,570 acres to inundation; furthermore, if the reservoir were needed for flood control, the lake would be allowed to rise and inundate thousands more acres.

In 1985, after the melting of an abnormally high snow pack, the Army Corps of Engineers, instead of releasing water ahead of the anticipated thaw and subsequent high water, temporarily flooded an additional 1,800 acres of the Piedra Lumbre's private lands. The water was illegally held in the reservoir for ten months and finally precipitated a lawsuit by the State of New Mexico. The high waters receded, but hundreds of acres of the Piedra Lumbre's private rangeland were reduced to barren, silt-covered mudflats. The water had also backed into the Rio Chama Canyon west of the Piedra Lumbre, an area protected by the State of New Mexico's Scenic and Pastoral River designation, and had ruined valuable winter habitat for the bald eagle.

That same year, a grassroots coalition of Hispano and Anglo valley residents and northern New Mexico environmentalists began a "Save the Rio Chama" campaign. Years of meetings and hearings finally resulted in thirty miles of the Chama River Canyon to the west of the Piedra Lumbre receiving federal protection as a Wild and Scenic River in 1988. The federal designation protects the canyon and its wildlife and archaeological and paleontological sites from further inundation and means, at least until the law is changed, that Abiquiu Reservoir cannot rise above a certain level and threaten the Chama Canyon's natural ecosystem.

The protection of the Chama Canyon was one small victory for the valley residents. But once again, the future uses of the land of the Piedra Lumbre had been wrestled out of the hands of those who owned and lived upon it. Like in the days of Catron and the Santa Fe Ring, the dexterous legal maneuvers of outsiders in Santa Fe and Washington had resulted in substantial land loss to valley residents. It was an old and bitter story now shared by both the Hispano and the Anglo *pobladores* of the Piedra Lumbre.

The advent of grazing permits on national forest lands in the 1940s had cut into the local ranchers' ability to maintain even a subsistent herd of cattle. With each passing decade, the difference between the traditional villagers' view of land use and the Forest Service's—whose policies seemed to favor large-scale ranching and timber activities—widened. A simmering distrust toward government decisions and activities on their former *ejido* lands made the villagers of the Chama Valley region into adversaries of the Forest Service. By the 1960s, valley land use and rightful ownership was once again a hotly contested issue between the "natives" and the "outsiders" of the valley; and like in every era predating this time, the control of this land was an issue that would become the basis for regional unrest and even war.

In October of 1966, a group of armed men gathered at Echo Amphitheater, the large erosion-carved hollow in the walls of the white and yellow stone of Navajo Canyon on the Piedra Lumbre's northwest side. The men were led by Reies López Tijerina, "el Tigre" ("the tiger"), the charismatic leader of the Alianza Federal de las Mercedes—the Federal Alliance of Land Grants (also translated as the Federal Alliance of Free City States)—a Hispanic New Mexican political group that sought to reclaim Spanish-American ancestral lands in the Southwest. Echo Amphitheater, once favored by Pueblo orators who traveled miles to practice their skills below its reverberating bowl, and the lands surrounding it were part of the Kit Carson National Forest. Tijerina and his *valientes* (militants) challenged the legality of all national forest lands held by the federal government in New Mexico. Carrying rifles and wearing badges, the Alianza set up a tent village in the Echo Amphitheater campground. The Alianza had come, they stated to the press, to reclaim the 600,000 acres that had belonged to their ancestors, the lands once known as the San Joaquin de Rio Chama Grant, illegally seized, they claimed, by the United States government.

Forest Service rangers sent to diffuse the situation at the roadside picnic area were arrested by the Alianza, and their government trucks and radios confiscated. The two rangers were then put on trial below the sandstone cliffs. The Alianza charged the rangers and the Forest Service they represented with illegal seizure of Hispanic land grants and proclaimed the Alianza's sovereignty of the land upon which the United States was a trespasser.

Armed federal authorities moved into the canyon and evicted the Alianza. Tijerina and his followers were charged with assault of federal officials and illegal seizure of government property. The Echo Amphitheater confrontation, which Tijerina later admitted was ostensibly for publicity purposes, received wide regional press coverage. But what may have appeared to outsiders to be a minor skirmish in a small, disorganized battle was actually a significant step toward a major war.

The war had actually begun several years before, when an organization called the Abiquiu Corporation, forerunner of the Alianza, had begun posting signs in the region of the Tierra Amarilla Land Grant that informed "outsiders"—mostly Anglo ranchers with large tracts of land within the old land grant boundaries—that they were trespassing. The

Abiquiu Corporation, whose membership was predominantly men from the communities of Canjilon, Coyote, and Tierra Amarilla, began to assign armed border guards to the old grant and sent eviction notices to Anglo landowners of the region. Fences were cut, water tanks were shot up, haystacks and barns were burned, homes were vandalized, and irrigation ditches were wrecked. In the next few years, the night raider activities of the illegal Abiquiu Corporation, which was given a court injunction in 1964, had spread to ranches on the Piedra Lumbre. Both Anglo and Hispanic landowners were harassed and suffered substantial losses of stock and equipment, and miles of fence between the Piedra Lumbre's private lands and the national forest were snipped.

In tandem with the Abiquiu Corporation's bitter feelings toward private owners of lands once part of the ejido of the Tierra Amarilla and other northern New Mexico land grants was escalating resentment toward the U.S. Forest Service that oversaw and controlled all uses of what was now the public domain of northern New Mexico. The Forest Service was attempting to balance recreational and pasturage uses of the national forest with conservation of the land. But to local ranchers, Forest Service policies of land use favored large ranching and timber interests, not the traditional regional ranchers. In 1964, members of the Abiquiu Corporation, angry over increased grazing fees and decreased numbers of cattle permits issued by the Forest Service, returned to the same range war tactics used to drive off "outsider" ranchers in the early 1900s.

In the spring following the October 1966 armed takeover of the Echo Amphitheater campground, Tijerina's Alianza gathered five hundred men and women in the courthouse in Tierra Amarilla and established the Pueblo Republica de San Joaquin, the Free State of Tierra Amarilla. They elected a mayor, a sheriff, and a town council, and the villagers declared their independence from the State of New Mexico and from the United States of America.

The activities of the Alianza in Rio Arriba had resulted in much press speculation and rumor spreading, and by late May of 1967 it was widely believed that the Alianza was planning to take over New Mexico's national forests. The confiscation by local authorities of the Alianza's account books, lists of armies and generals, and area maps showed that the organization's primary target for seizure was Ghost Ranch on the Piedra

Lumbre.[5] Although sympathetic with the cause, Abiquiu itself was not a stronghold for Alianza membership, which the governor's office estimated to be at least two thousand.[6] But the old village, like all those along the Chama River north to Tierra Amarilla, was living on the warming edge of a smoldering fire whose flames were being fanned by the increased surveillance by county and state law officials of the valley's roads and villages. Everyone was suspect. Everyone was nervous. And far too many Rio Arribans were carrying guns.

A second Alianza meeting—in the form of a village barbecue—was scheduled to be held on June 2, 1967, at the town of Coyote on the southern side of the Piedra Lumbre. Tijerina planned to talk, and the Alianza would announce the details of their statewide campaign. The governor's office learned of the meeting, and the locals heard via radio announcements and word of mouth that anyone who attended this barbecue risked arrest. On Friday morning, the second day of June, the village of Coyote was surrounded by state policemen and local sheriff's deputies. The Alianza quickly cancelled their barbecue/rally, but ten members were arrested for unlawful assembly, anyway.

The ten who were arrested at Coyote were taken to the jail in the Rio Arriba County courthouse in Tierra Amarilla, where they awaited arraignment over the weekend. Between the Friday of the cancelled barbecue and the Monday arraignment of the ten villagers, twenty local farmers and ranchers (most residents of the village of Canjilon) were armed and deputized by Tijerina and the Pueblo Republica de San Joaquin. Their mission was to free the ten who had been wrongfully jailed in Tierra Amarilla and to arrest the district attorney, Alfonso Sanchez, who was held responsible for their unjust incarceration.

Just after three o'clock on Monday, June 5, the Alianza posse burst into the Tierra Amarilla courthouse. Gunfire from pistols and machine guns began immediately: one state policeman was shot in the chest; a judge and his staff scrambled into his chambers and locked themselves inside; several other court employees escaped the barrage of Alianza bullets through the courthouse windows, but deputy sheriff Elogio Salazar was shot twice before he managed to hurl himself through a window and crawl to safety on the ground below.

The Alianza posse searched the corridors, but district attorney Alfonso Sanchez was not in the courthouse. The Alianza deputies waited until dusk and then departed the courthouse with two hostages—a sheriff's deputy and a UPI reporter—with whom they fled by car into the Canjilon Mountains.

Two thousand lawmen that included National Guardsmen, members of the New Mexico Mounted Patrol, state policemen, sheriffs and deputies from all the northern counties, even officers of the New Mexico Game and Fish Commission, descended on Tierra Amarilla. M-42 tanks rumbled across the Piedra Lumbre en route to the mountains, and jeeps with mounted machine guns barricaded county roads. Rancho de los Brujos' adobe headquarters below the cliffs that formed the southern rim of the Canjilon Mountains, through which the fugitives might try to pass, became a National Guard operations center.

During the first night after the courthouse raid the National Guard herded thirty-nine men, women, and children into a sheep pen in the tiny hamlet of Canjilon where they were imprisoned overnight; "bait," the National Guardsmen said, for the "Mexican cat."[7] Like Kit Carson and the garrisons of U.S. soldiers who tracked fugitive Apache tribes in the ponderosa-thick mountains a century before, modern mounted patrols searched in vain throughout the high country of the Carson National Forest above the Piedra Lumbre for the twenty Alianza fugitives. (Their hostages had been released unharmed.) The national press joined the throng in the mountain village of Canjilon and watched as the Old West frontier of "good" guys and "bad" guys and gunslinging sheriffs returned to three-dimensional life.

John Dancy of NBC News, Los Angeles, arrived on the high-country fugitive search scene in the middle of the night: "It was very tense. There was a big search, with posses made up of men who looked like they had been taken right out of an Old West movie—guys in ten gallon hats, on horses, wearing six shooters. The courthouse raid was a very big story— NBC was there, and CBS . . . everyone.

"The guardsmen were going door to door. They had good reason to believe Tijerina was there somewhere. Our cameramen got very good pictures. It was a great story! But when we called in to New York the next day, the New Mexico story had been dumped: the seven day war in Israel had just broken out and NBC never ran the Canjilon footage!"

Tijerina was never found in the mountains above the Piedra Lumbre. After a week-long search, el Tigre was arrested north of Albuquerque where he was found sleeping in a car with his son and a friend.

Tijerina himself was eventually cleared of all charges stemming from the courthouse raid. But the work of the Alianza was not finished: two years later, in 1969, at the General Assembly of the Presbyterian Church held in San Antonio, Texas, the Alianza called for the lands of Ghost Ranch to be returned to the Hispanic people. Although the General Assembly did not give Ghost Ranch to the Alianza or any other organization, garbled news reports back to New Mexico gave the impression that the lands of the Piedra Lumbre were up for political grabs. At a rally in Coyote, Tijerina once again organized his people, this time calling upon them to join him in the reclamation of the old Rancho de los Brujos.

The Reverend Jim Hall, the conference center's director, was given advance warning of the impending takeover, by Hispanic friends not sympathetic with the Alianza. Hall and the staff at Ghost Ranch, as well as the state police and several judges in Española and Tierra Amarilla, prepared for Tijerina's late May visit to Ghost Ranch. Hall remembers: "Tijerina told his people at the Coyote rally to bring their dogs and chickens and pigs and together they would move in and occupy Ghost Ranch. In the days before their visit, the staff [at Ghost Ranch] had several meetings so that we could talk about what we were going to do."

Hall was a savvy Presbyterian minister, the son of a cowboy preacher who was as comfortable on a horse as he was in a pickup, a *patrón* who worked side by side with local ranchers. Hall had come to know the people and the stories of the Piedra Lumbre, and he well understood, and was even sympathetic to, the complaints of the Alianza. Rio Arriba County remained one of the poorest regions in the United States: the county unemployment rate was more than twenty percent and more than half of the valley families had an annual income of less than three thousand dollars. Even so, Hall had no intention of allowing Ghost Ranch lands to be handed over to the Alianza. However, he did recognize his and Ghost Ranch's position as a Rio Arriba patrón and the responsibilities inherent to that position, which Pack had passed on to the Presbyterians when they accepted the ranch.

In the days before Tijerina's arrival Hall wrote a statement that outlined Ghost Ranch's present community programs and its plans to further aid its neighbors. In particular, Hall promised that a section of Ghost Ranch land would be made available for a community program to be chosen and decided upon by the villagers. Fifty thousand dollars would be donated by the Presbyterians to augment whatever that program might be.

On Sunday, May 30, at 2:30 p.m., several hundred people in cars and trucks led by Tijerina began to arrive at the Ghost Ranch headquarters. Much to the Ghost Ranch staff's relief Tijerina's followers did not bring their livestock. The state police were on alert, close to the Ghost Ranch but out of sight of the actual meeting. Two local priests stood beside Hall and his staff, which included both Anglos and Hispanos from various local communities.

Hall's policy statement, written in both English and Spanish, was distributed to Tijerina and his people by the priests. The atmosphere was charged and tense, the ranch staff waiting and watching while Tijerina and the Alianza stood about reading over Hall's statement and talking among themselves. Finally, Hall walked down to where the Alianza had parked their cars and trucks and suggested that everyone come up to the main building, enjoy some cookies and coffee, and then sit down together and talk. Tijerina finally agreed—he initially wanted to speak alone with Hall—and the Alianza joined the Ghost Ranch staff in their convocation hall. "It was standing room only, probably a couple of hundred of people came," Hall remembers. "The meeting started off angry—the Alianza saying the ranch doesn't care about its neighbors or the poor. . . .

"Then Tijerina got up to speechify in English and in Spanish. He's quite an orator. He said, 'I'm the lion and I'm like a lamb but I can be like the tiger. . . . I'm for the poor but the church doesn't care about the poor. They lie and go back on their promises. I'm going to reclaim this land for the poor.' "[8]

After Tijerina sat down, Hall took the podium and disputed the Alianza's charges against Ghost Ranch and the Presbyterians that now owned it: "There are a lot of things that simply aren't true," Hall told the crowd. "We do care about the poor: we have a concern and you have our position in this statement. We intend to try to bend the ranch to serve the best interest of this broader community. But nobody's going to tell us what to do. We're not going to be threatened or occupied."

Ghost Ranch had already offered financial and professional assistance to various Rio Arriba community programs: in 1967, Ghost Ranch had initiated a winter grazing program that allowed neighboring ranchers to place cattle on Ghost Ranch lands after their herds were removed from summer grazelands in the national forests. Those ranchers who used Ghost Ranch lands were charged a minimal fee and were given free classes and instruction in animal husbandry and range management. Although the Ghost Ranch lands were still carefully monitored so that they were not overgrazed, as many as 1,200 cows were given winter pasture on the northern third of the Piedra Lumbre. The ranchers involved with the Ghost Ranch program had seen their average calf crops increase from twenty-five percent to eighty percent and even ninety percent a year.

Before the Presbyterians became an amicable patrón in the valley, Pack's money and influence had reached far beyond Ghost Ranch's private borders. In 1941, when Pack learned of the distance the young children of the Piedra Lumbre basin were bussed to elementary school, he funded the building of a school in the Piedra Lumbre community of Coyote. During the second world war, when his child, Phoebe, was born sixty miles downriver at a Santa Fe hospital, Pack pursued avenues to fund the building of the valley's first medical facility in Española. The Charles Lathrop Pack Forestry Foundation could not help build a hospital—its funds were for conservation, not humanitarian, purposes. However, Pack's father had given him a sizable stamp collection which had won many awards over the years. Pack put the collection up for auction in New York, and to his great surprise, the many rare and complete sets of stamps from all over the world brought in enough money to fund the building of a hospital.

The most recent Anglo owners of the Piedra Lumbre's lands actually had a long history of community-sensitive actions and efforts. Abiquiu priest Father Robert Kirsh spoke in defense of the ranch's gringo owners. Hall remembers: "Father Bob told the crowd, 'Let me tell you, it's been said that the Presbyterian Church doesn't care about the poor. Let me tell you about it: the Presbyterians have built hospitals and schools all through the valleys—the Chama and the Rio Grande—the Roman Catholic Church has been here a lot longer and it's a lot bigger but the Catholics haven't done anything like the Presbyterians have done for the poor.'"

The meeting ended peacefully.

Hall and Ghost Ranch received considerable private and public praise and publicity for their handling of this confrontation with the Alianza. The Presbyterians of Ghost Ranch even earned a modicum of the Alianza's trust, and the ranch later served as a meeting ground for Tijerina and the New Mexican governor, and for other meetings of the Alianza's council.

Ghost Ranch quickly made good on its land and program offer: in 1970, Ghost Ranch funds were donated to a new medical facility, La Clinica del Norte, in Tierra Amarilla. And within a year of the Alianza march on the old Ranch of the Witches, the Presbyterians and the local villagers established the New Mexico Producers and Marketing Cooperative—a feedlot coop. The coop organized eight sale days a year during which local ranchers sold their calves directly to national beef buying companies at the feedlot at Ghost Ranch. The feedlot coop today handles over a million dollars worth of sales, and on the land donated by Ghost Ranch for the facility are cattle scales, pens, and loading chutes used annually by ranchers from villages all over Rio Arriba County.

Although the Alianza was able to peacefully resolve its conflicts with the Presbyterians, one week after the Ghost Ranch incident, on June 8, Tijerina and his followers burned a national forest signpost near the town of Coyote. State policemen and forest rangers arrested Tijerina at gunpoint, saying he was a danger to the community. Tijerina was not held for this charge, but he was soon after sent to the federal penitentiary at El Paso when his bail for the charges stemming from the 1967 arrest of the Carson National Forest rangers at Echo Amphitheater was revoked.

The Alianza movement did, however, initiate positive changes in Forest Service policies affecting northern New Mexico. National media and political attention were focused on rural New Mexico's poverty and lack of agricultural development programs. The offices of the regional Forest Service responded with in-house evaluations and studies as to how the national forests might better serve the people of northern New Mexico. Federal budget allocations for northern New Mexico grazing and recreation requests soon doubled, and the Forest Service began to form new policies—especially in regard to grazing permits—that began to ease the local unrest over the uses of Carson and Santa Fe National Forests. The thrust of the new Forest Service land-use policies called for greater sensitivity and flexibility toward the local communities that needed the land and its resources to survive. Although none of the old land grants were returned to who the Alianza claimed were their rightful owners, the grassroots efforts of Rio Arriba's ranchers and farmers did force the United States government to listen to the grievances of Hispanic Americans, and to finally institute changes that directly benefitted rural New Mexicans.

The same year that the Alianza marched on the Ranch of the Witches, Hall and Ghost Ranch initiated a peaceful but often difficult legal process that eventually returned some national forest lands to their historic Hispanic owners: in 1969, Hall became aware of 125 tracts of land within the Carson and Santa Fe National Forests—both of which shared boundaries with the Piedra Lumbre basin—to which ownership was challenged by the Hispanic residents living upon them. Although the Forest Service had allowed these people to live on the disputed lands, the families possessed no clear title and could not sell or obtain mortgages or building loans for their homes and ranches.

The Ghost Ranch Museum and "Beaver National Forest" designed by Arthur Pack and Bill Carr had been leased to the Forest Service and used as a demonstration site for multi-use concepts since their beginnings in the 1950s. By the 1970s, to ensure the museum's future, it became necessary for Pack and Ghost Ranch to offer the museum land and facilities to the Forest Service. The Forest Service was delighted with the gift and asked what Ghost Ranch wanted in return. Much to the surprise of the Forest Service and the residents who were to benefit, Jim Hall and Ghost Ranch asked that clear title be given to the 125 parcels of disputed land within the Carson and Santa Fe National Forests.

It took nearly six years of hard work and red tape—the collective efforts of the U.S. Forest Service working with a panel of local representatives, the services of a lawyer and a surveyor (whose services were provided by Ghost Ranch), and eventually an act of Congress—but on April 6, 1975, deeds were distributed at Ghost Ranch to 111 families living on what was previously considered the domain of the U.S. Forest Service. Included in the trade were clear titles to half the village of Cañones, one Roman Catholic Church, two Penitente *moradas,* and one *campo santo* (cemetery).

The Ghost Ranch Museum—national forest land trade was one bright moment in a long and bitter story of land dispute and legal chicanery in New Mexico: "It was a time," one witness said of the small but significant battle won that April afternoon at the Ranch of the Witches, "when charity kissed justice."[9]

While out riding across the Piedra Lumbre one summer in the late 1930s, Juan de Dios told a young friend that someday in the not too distant future the huge grassy basin that stretched silent and shimmering before them would be full of people. Joe I. Salazar remembers the old Genízaro telling him, "I won't get to see it, but you're coming toward it. I see the tracks. . . . One of these days, you won't find a Mexican here. The gringos are going to run them out. Everyone. But there's only one thing: they're going to run them out with money." At the time, Salazar thought de Dios was talking nonsense. But today, himself an old-timer of the Piedra Lumbre, Salazar thinks the old Genízaro could see clearly into the future: where de Dios once chased wild horses there is a lake full of boaters and water skiers; on the llanos where there were once a few adobe *casitas* and *jacal* sheep camps beside rough lumber sheds and corrals there are now expensive subdivisions and gated housing developments.

The valley has become a land of contrasts: many descendants of the first *pobladores* have moved out of their ancestors' mud-and-wood casas into new trailer homes. The old dwellings built from the earth by subsistence-level settlers are now the renovated, even luxurious abodes of wealthy outsiders. Once the building material of the poor, adobe is today the high-priced material of choice among northern New Mexico's upper class. Mud-plastered walls and floors, *latilla* ceilings and hand-hewn *vigas*—these are the elements of Santa Fe Style, which carries a very high price tag. Among modern Anglo Americans, authenticity and history can be purchased at a price; but too often in a community like Abiquiu, those whose families lived that history are priced off the land they settled.

The Hispanic villages of the valley—Abiquiu downriver, Cañones, Coyote, and Youngsville in the basin itself, Canjilon in the mountains above the Piedra Lumbre—maintained a certain cultural integrity until well after midcentury. At that time, the numbers of outsiders flocking to the area, coupled with a growing interest in—even obsession with—the country and cultures of northern New Mexico, began to place financial and emotional pressures on these old communities that have threatened their historic identities and traditional land base.

The valley's population has tripled in the last decade: film directors, movie stars, bestselling authors, world-famous musicians, refugees from the urban chaos of New York, Chicago, and Los Angeles have moved in alongside Hispanic families whose daily lives include rural subsistence traditions hundreds of years old—the tending of kitchen gardens and fields of irrigated crops, and small herds of sheep, cattle, pigs, and horses. Pickup trucks parked beside the corrals and television antennas attached to the tin roofs may give Chama Valley *ranchitos* a facade of modernity, but in actuality, emotionally and culturally, many Hispanic families proudly maintain the ways of their pioneer ancestors.

As in the years following American occupation of New Mexico, the Penitentes of the valley have emerged as a strengthening and unifying faction within the Catholic Hispanic community. Both moradas in Abiquiu were closed and unused in the 1970s, but the Hermanos of the Morada del Alto on the edge of the Pueblo mesa today number more than twenty. Instead of cloaking themselves in secrecy, Abiquiu's modern Hermanos are outspoken advocates of Hispanic cultural and religious traditions. The Hermanos do not seek to factionalize the modern Abiquiu community, but serve as a bridge between the old ways and the new, inviting outsiders to some of their events and giving lectures and programs that explain northern New Mexico's past and present. When the old Morada del Alto was burned by vandals in 1992, the greater Abiquiu community, including the Presbyterians at Ghost Ranch and members of the new Dar al Islam Moslem community across the river from the pueblo, contributed monies to assist the Hermanos in the rebuilding of their morada. In addition, art and cultural foundations in Santa Fe, as well as individuals from all over the world who knew of and loved the old pueblo, raised funds to support the efforts of the new Penitente Brotherhood of Abiquiu.

The Ghost Ranch Conference Center receives ten thousand known visitors each year. The Ghost Ranch Living Museum of the U.S. Forest Service averages one hundred thousand visitors to its grounds each year.

And the Army Corps of Engineers claims that at least two hundred thousand people visit Abiquiu Reservoir's shoreline annually.

No one has ever counted exactly how many people drive up into the old Pueblo of Abiquiu hoping to glimpse the roof or the wall or a piece of the house that was once the home of Georgia O'Keeffe. But their numbers are enough to have spurred a no-cameras rule within the pueblo's village limits. Even painters have been asked to depart the pueblo grounds. It may seem like an unfair request to tourists who want to take home photographs of the historic town, and to artists who want to paint upon the same land that inspired O'Keeffe. But to some residents of Abiquiu the ban announces to the world beyond their mesa that the villagers still have some control over their community's present.

The pueblo's future, however, is threatened by a good deal more than *turistas* and plein-air painters: the ejido lands of the Abiquiu grant cannot be sold or used for any purpose without a consensus from the majority of the members of the Abiquiu Cooperative Livestock Association. But individual homes are outside of the association's jurisdiction, and there have been sales, albeit few, of historic pueblo houses to nonpueblo residents.

Partially due to the popularity of Santa Fe and its high cost of living, the population of villages like Abiquiu and its sister communities is burgeoning: between 1980 and 1990, the population of the community of Abiquiu, which includes the old pueblo and its satellite villages, increased by only 33 persons. But between 1990 and 1995, it is estimated that the Abiquiu community population jumped almost threefold—from 439 individuals to more than 1200. As in the rest of Rio Arriba County, most of these immigrants are Anglo—between 1980 and 1990, Rio Arriba's Anglo population grew by 86.9 percent, while its Hispanic population increased by only 14.5 percent.[10] Outsiders may be sensitive to and even protective of the valley's historic traditions, but they cannot, in such numbers, help but tread heavily across a culture whose members are being outnumbered, outmaneuvered, and outpriced in their own homeland.

Although the basin of the Piedra Lumbre is surrounded on four sides by national forest, civilization has spread housing developments across its interior, especially around the reservoir that floods the basin's middle. The valley of the Piedra Lumbre is commonly known as O'Keeffe

Country, at least among tourists and outsiders. Although the blue form of Cerro Pedernal is tucked safely within national forest boundaries, its traditional, multicultural identity is threatened by its modern role as the deceased artist's favorite mountain—some newcomers have even suggested that Pedernal be renamed O'Keeffe Mountain. O'Keeffe would probably have bristled at this proposed name as much as her native neighbors— surely Changing Woman and Spider Woman should be given historic priority before their twentieth-century sister—but even the suggestion of such a change is indicative of the region's simplistic, monothematic persona in the eyes of the rest of the world.

The private lands of Ghost Ranch, today reduced to 21,000 acres, protect the Cliffs of Shining Stone from the profit-hungry hands of developers. Except for the conference center's facilities, clustered in the canyon of the old Archuleta homestead, the lands of the Ranch of the Witches have been left in their primitive, undomesticated state. *Brujos* and flying cows, and a herd of phantom horses, continue to haunt the cliff country, and in the sierras above the basin coyotes and deer are still startled by the appearance of humans. It is a small, but significant, last frontier holding its own in a rapidly changing valley.

Although the wilderness has vanished from the valley, the idea of it has not. The Chama River and the high-desert country of the Piedra Lumbre have become the last frontier of the Mythic West perpetuated in Hollywood westerns: *Silverado, The Legend of the Lone Ranger, City Slickers,* and *Wyatt Earp* are among films whose Old West locations included the landscape of Abiquiu and the valley of the Piedra Lumbre. As civilization deepens its roots in the Chama Valley region people tend to idolize— mythologize—pieces of the land's history while obliterating others, to glorify some native traditions while ignoring other cultural attributes considered outdated, unglamourous, ultimately unprofitable.

The newcomers of the twenty-first century will alter and impact the flow of the valley's history just as the old-timers before them did, repeating a cycle that has patterned the human narrative of the region for eight hundred years. The decades will pass into centuries and the newcomers will become the old-timers. The only certainty in the story of this once faraway country is that it will be about change: the story will continue to be *entre verde y seco*—between green and dry, good and not so good. And the chorus of human voices joined by time and place will alternate between harmony and discord as the changes themselves, temporarily new in name and appearance, actually bring nothing to this old region that has not been seen and known before.

NOTES

Introduction

1. Crocchiola, *Abiquiu (New Mexico) Story,* p. 2.

Chapter 1. Avéshu Pije, "Up Abiquiu Way"

1. Wozniak, Kemrer, and Carrillo, *History and Ethnohistory along the Rio Chama,* pp. iii–v.

2. Kutsche and Van Ness, *Cañones,* p. 10; Foxx, *Ghost Ranch Nature Trail Guide.*

3. Tewa names taken from Harrington, *Ethnogeography of the Tewa Indians;* Harrington's spelling and accents corrected by Esther Martinez of San Juan Pueblo.

4. Reichard, *Navaho Religion;* Underhill, *The Navajos.* See also works by Clyde Kluckhohn.

5. Tiller, *Jicarilla Apache Tribe;* Opler, *Myths and Tales of the Jicarilla Apache Indians.*

6. Opler, *Myths and Tales of the Jicarilla Apache Indians,* p. 20.

7. Detailed in Warren, "Ancient Mineral Industries of Cerro Pedernal," p. 87.

8. Ibid.

9. Dougherty, *Archaeological Evaluation of Tsiping Ruin,* p. 9.

10. DeBuys, *Enchantment and Exploitation,* p. 23.

11. Harrington, *Ethnogeography of the Tewa Indians,* p. 37.

12. Ortiz, *Handbook of North American Indians,* vol. 9, p. 295.

13. Undated paper, Abiquiu File, Museum of New Mexico History Library; Córdova, *Abiquiu and Don Cacahuate,* p. 34.

14. Córdova, *Abiquiu and Don Cacahuate,* p. 9.

15. Harrington, *Ethnogeography of the Tewa Indians,* p. 152.

16. Jeançon, *Excavations in the Chama Valley,* p. 1.

17. Ibid., p. 20.

18. Taos Pueblo elder quoted in Ortiz, *Handbook of North American Indians,* vol. 9, p. 1.

Chapter 2. Abiquiu and La Tierra de Guerra

1. The spelling of P'efu is based upon Harrington's study of the Tewa language: initial *p* sounds like a medial Spanish *b, v* to English speakers; Tewa *f* sounded to Spanish ears like *qui, key* to English ears; the Tewa *u* was heard by the Spanish as a long *u.* Hence, the

Tewa name might be heard by English speakers as *Va-keyu*. The short *a* was added to the beginning of the name by the Spanish to facilitate pronounciation.

2. Kessell, "Sources for the History of a New Mexico Community: Abiquiu," p. 253.

3. Hodge, *Handbook of American Indians North of Mexico*, pp. 99, 100.

4. Adams and Chávez, *Missions of New Mexico*, pp. 331–32; Marc Simmons, "History of Pueblo-Spanish Relations to 1821," in Ortiz, *Handbook of North American Indians*, vol. 9, p. 190.

5. Harrington, *Ethnogeography of the Tewa Indians*, p. 136; modern San Juan Pueblo speakers say that Abiquiu's Tewa name is Phé shúu ú.

6. Ibid., p. 137.

7. Roberts, *Once They Moved Like the Wind*, p. 146.

8. Simmons, "History of Pueblo-Spanish Relations," p. 182.

9. George P. Hammond and Agapito Rey quoted in Simmons, "History of Pueblo-Spanish Relations," p. 180.

10. Twitchell, *Leading Facts of New Mexico History*, p. 341.

11. DeBuys, *Enchantment and Exploitation*, p. 51.

12. Ibid.

13. Simmons, "History of Pueblo-Spanish Relations," p. 186.

14. Alfonso Ortiz, in Anaya and Ortiz, *Ceremony of Brotherhood*, p. 10.

15. DeBuys, *Enchantment and Exploitation*, p. 53.

16. Frank J. Wozniak, "Ethnohistory of the Abiquiu Reservoir Area," in Wozniak, Kemrer, and Carrillo, *History and Ethnohistory along the Rio Chama*, pp. 59, 60.

17. Swadesh, *20,000 Years of History*, p. 10.

18. Quintana, *Pobladores*, p. 12.

19. Quintana and Snow, "Historical Archaeology of the Rito Colorado Valley," pp. 40–43; Quintana, *Pobladores*, pp. 14, 15, 16.

20. Quintana, *Pobladores*, p. 16.

21. John R. Van Ness, in Briggs and Van Ness, *Land, Water, and Culture*, p. 164.

22. Swadesh, *20,000 Years of History*, pp. 11, 12, 13.

23. Ibid., pp. 11, 12.

24. Ibid., p. 13.

25. Quoted in Quintana, *Pobladores*, p. 38.

26. Quoted in ibid., p. 18.

27. Twitchell, *Leading Facts of New Mexico History*, p. 442.

28. Wozniak, "Ethnohistory of the Abiquiu Reservoir Area," p. 34.

29. Quintana, *Pobladores*, p. 23.

30. Fray Angelico Chávez, "Genizaros," in Ortiz, *Handbook of North American Indians*, vol. 9, p. 198.

31. Ibid., p. 198.

32. Córdova, *Pedagogy of Missionization*, p. 58.

33. The term "Hispanic" is used here and throughout the remainder of the book to denote the culture and language of the Southwest's Spanish-speaking descendants of the seventeenth- and eighteenth-century colonial settlers. It encompasses people who are also referred to as Spanish American, Mexican American, Indo-Hispano, Latino, and

Chicano—terms used at various times by various groups to attempt to describe Spanish-speaking natives of northern New Mexico.

34. Quintana, *Pobladores*, p. 40.

35. Horvath, *Genízaro of Eighteenth-Century New Mexico*, p. 27.

36. Albert H. Schroeder, "Rio Grande Ethnohistory," in Ortiz, *New Perspectives on the Pueblos*, p. 62.

37. José Manuel Espinosa quoted in Córdova, *Pedagogy of Missionization*, p. 59.

38. Quintana, *Pobladores*, p. 23.

39. Córdova, *Pedagogy of Missionization*, pp. 118–19.

40. Ibid., pp. 35–36.

41. Ibid., p. 111.

42. Ibid.

43. Quintana, *Pobladores*, p. 25.

44. Córdova, *Abiquiu and Don Cacahuate*, pp. 63–64; Carrillo, *Indios de Abiquiu*.

45. Fray Domínguez in Adams and Chávez, *Missions of New Mexico*, p. 121.

46. Ibid., p. 126.

47. Ibid.

48. Ibid., p. 42.

49. Ibid., p. 12.

50. Escalante quoted in Bolton, *Pageant in the Wilderness*, p. 16.

51. Ibid., p. 17.

52. Ibid., p. 142.

53. Ibid., p. 140.

54. Ibid., p. 146.

55. Ibid.

Chapter 3. Pioneers of the Piedra Lumbre

1. Piedra Lumbre land grant papers, translated by John Ward, LGR reel #35, NMSRA.

2. Ibid.

3. Ibid.

4. Ibid.

5. Quoted in Bowden, *Private Land Claims of the Southwest*, p. 1083.

6. Ibid.

7. Ibid.

8. Piedra Lumbre land grant papers, translated by John Ward, LGR reel #35, NMSRA.

9. Lummis, *Land of Poco Tiempo*, 18–20.

10. Quoted in Carrillo, *Indios de Abiquiu*, pp. 159–60.

11. Quintana, *Pobladores*, p. 161.

12. Crocchiola, *Abiquiu (New Mexico) Story*, p. 12.

13. John R. Van Ness, in Briggs and Van Ness, *Land, Water, and Culture*, p. 170.

14. Information about the Pedro Ignacio Gallego family and Arroyo Seco ranch from Chávez, *Tres Macho—He Said*, and Carrillo, *Indios de Abiquiu*, pp. 140–46.

15. Kutsche and Van Ness, *Cañones*, p. 15.

Chapter 4.   The Fearing Time

1. Delaney, *Ute Mt. Utes,* p. 19.
2. Adams and Chávez, *Missions of New Mexico,* pp. 252–53.
3. Thomas, *Plains Indians and New Mexico,* p. 2.
4. Weber, *Taos Trappers,* p. 10.
5. Ibid., p. 26.
6. Frank J. Wozniak, "Ethnohistory of the Abiquiu Reservoir Area," in Wozniak, Kemrer, and Carrillo, *History and Ethnohistory along the Rio Chama,* p. 36.
7. Weber, *Taos Trappers,* p. 27.
8. Ibid.
9. Wozniak, "Ethnohistory of the Abiquiu Reservoir Area," p. 37.
10. Bailey, *The Indian Slave Trade in the Southwest,* p. 26.
11. Martinez, *Santa Cruz de la Cañada Baptisms 1710–1860; San Juan de los Caballeros Baptisms 1726–1870; Abiquiu Baptisms 1754–1870.*
12. McNitt, *Navajo Wars,* p. 12.
13. Weber, *Mexican Frontier,* p. 109.
14. Ibid., p. 216.
15. Quintana, *Pobladores,* p. 188.
16. D. W. Jones quoted in Hafen and Hafen, *Old Spanish Trail,* p. 268.
17. Quoted in ibid., p. 100.
18. Ibid.
19. Bailey, *Indian Slave Trade,* pp. 171, 416.

Chapter 5.   The Old Spanish Trail

1. Quintana, *Pobladores,* p. 51.
2. Details of Abiquiu land transactions from documents belonging to the late Georgia O'Keeffe: papers of José María Chávez, translated and graciously shared with the author by Frances Leon Quintana.
3. Weber, *Mexican Frontier,* p. 128.
4. Hafen and Hafen, *Old Spanish Trail,* p. 19.
5. Quintana, *Pobladores,* p. 43.
6. Hafen and Hafen, *Old Spanish Trail,* pp. 179–81.
7. Mexican newspaper, June 1830, quoted in ibid., p. 157.

Chapter 6.   Disenchantment and Disinheritance

1. Minge, "Mexican Independence Day," pp. 109–10.
2. Translated and quoted in ibid., p. 112.
3. Quintana, *Pobladores,* p. 66.
4. Minge, "Mexican Independence Day," p. 114.
5. Quintana, *Pobladores,* p. 189.
6. Aniceto Martínez, August 9, 1893, transcripts of the Court of Private Land Claims, *Aniceto Martínez et al.* v. *U.S.;* Piedra Lumbre papers held by White, Koch, Kelley, and McCarthey.

7. Ibid.

8. Quoted in Hafen and Hafen, *Old Spanish Trail,* p. 209.

9. Ibid.

10. From census, 1842–56, in Harley, *Agua Mansa Story,* pp. 22, 23.

11. Hafen and Hafen, *Old Spanish Trail,* p. 224.

12. Antonio José Martínez was born on January 17, 1793, in the Plaza de la Capilla de Santa Rosa de Lima beside the Chama River. His parents, Don Severino Martínez and Doña Maria del Carmel Santistevan, were a settler family of considerable wealth. Martínez became a champion of native education and with his own money brought the first printing press to Taos in 1835.

13. Ahlborn, *Penitente Moradas of Abiquiu,* pp. vi, 136. The Morada del Alto, until its destruction by fire in 1992, may have been the oldest surviving morada in New Mexico.

14. Weigle, *Brothers of Light, Brothers of Blood,* pp. 47–49.

15. Weber, *Taos Trappers,* p. 190.

16. Quintana, *Pobladores,* p. 161.

17. McCall, *New Mexico in 1850,* pp. 123–26.

18. Peters, *Kit Carson's Life and Adventures,* pp. 450–51.

19. Ibid., p. 511.

20. Frank J. Wozniak, "Ethnohistory of the Abiquiu Reservoir Area," in Wozniak, Kemrer, and Carrillo, *History and Ethnohistory along the Rio Chama,* p. 41.

21. Tiller, *Jicarilla Apache Tribe,* p. 37.

22. Ibid., p. 48.

23. Meriwether, *My Life in the Mountains and on the Plains,* p. 227.

24. Ibid., pp. 227–32.

25. Charles M. Carrillo, "Oral History/Ethnohistory of the Abiquiu Reservoir Area," in Wozniak, Kemrer, and Carrillo, *History and Ethnohistory along the Rio Chama,* p. 47.

26. Quoted in ibid., p. 131.

27. Smith, *Ouray,* p. 34.

28. J. M. Manzanares, quoted in Hafen, "Colorado Recollections of a Centenarian," 53.

29. Ibid.

30. Smith, *Ouray,* p. 38.

31. Ibid., p. 40.

Chapter 7.   A Land of Beauty and Evil

1. Van Ness and Van Ness, "Introduction," p. 10.

2. Ebright, *Land Grants and Lawsuits in Northern New Mexico,* p. 145.

3. George W. Julian quoted in White, Koch, Kelley, and McCarthey, *Land Title Study,* p. 33.

4. Van Ness and Van Ness, "Introduction," p. 9.

5. Robert W. Larson quoted in White, Koch, Kelley, and McCarthey, *Land Title Study,* p. 31.

6. DeBuys, *Enchantment and Exploitation,* p. 174.

7. Details of Abiquiu grant confirmation from Bowden, *Private Land Claims of the Southwest,* pp. 1103–7.

8. John R. Van Ness, in Briggs and Van Ness, *Land, Water, and Culture,* p. 196.

9. Pack, *We Called It Ghost Ranch,* p. 26.

10. Details of Catron and the attempted sale of the Piedra Lumbre from personal communication, John R. Van Ness to author; and Van Ness, *Land, Water, and Culture,* pp. 197–98.

11. Jaramillo, *Shadows of the Past,* p. 110.

12. Story told by Richard Valdez to Selena Keesecker.

13. Pack, *We Called It Ghost Ranch,* manuscript excerpted in "Historic Ghost Ranch Richly Deserves Its Name," *Rio Grande Sun* Special Historical Edition, November 8, 1962.

14. Story of Manuel Salazar family shared with author by his granddaughter Virginia Trujillo y Salazar.

15. Quoted in Twitchell, "Española and Its Environs."

16. "Gazetteer Lists Rio Arriba Merchants of 1884," *Rio Grande Sun* Special Historical Edition, November 8, 1962.

17. "Grant Boosts State," *Rio Grande Sun* Special Historical Edition, November 8, 1962.

18. Weigle, *Hispanic Villages of Northern New Mexico,* p. 156.

19. The Gonzales ranch, which came to embrace lands from both the Plaza Colorado and Plaza Blanca Grants, was later sold to a cattle rancher named Morton, who resold it to the Salmons. Rancho de Abiquiu, a cattle ranch, was bought by Alva Simpson in 1966. Today, the property is called El Sueño del Corazón and is owned by private individuals who maintain it as a residence.

20. Jaramillo, *Romance of a Little Village Girl,* p. 59.

21. Ibid., p. 60.

22. Ibid., p. 61.

23. Ibid.

Chapter 8.   Land of Beginnings and Endings

1. Athearn, *Mythic West,* p. 162.

2. DeBuys, *Enchantment and Exploitation,* p. 195.

3. *Milwaukee Sentinel,* April 6, 1876, quoted in Beck, *New Mexico,* p. 231.

4. *New York Observer,* March 9, 1876, quoted in ibid.

5. *Chicago Tribune* quoted in *Rocky Mountain News,* February 18, 1875, quoted in ibid.

6. Amy Lowell to D. H. Lawrence, quoted in Gibson, *Santa Fe and Taos Colonies,* p. 11.

7. A partial list of artists, writers, and photographers who frequented Santa Fe and Taos includes D. H. Lawrence, Carlos Vierra, Kenneth M. Chapman, Gerald Cassidy, Sheldon Parsons, Olive Rush, Gustave Baumann, Robert Henri, Alice Corbin, William Penhallow Henderson, Ernest L. Blumenschein, John Sloan, E. Irving Couse, Fremont Ellis, Victor Higgins, Dorothy Brett, Witter Bynner, Mary Austin, Georgia O'Keeffe, Ansel Adams, Willa Cather, Oliver La Farge, Robinson Jeffers, Thornton Wilder, Leopold Stokowski, and Aldous Huxley.

8. Corbin [Henderson], *Red Earth,* p. 13.

9. Wheelwright, *Journey Towards Understanding,* pp. 13, 14; all quotes used with permission of the Wheelwright Museum of the American Indian, Santa Fe, New Mexico.

10. Natalie Curtis returned several times to the Southwest. She married artist Paul Burlin in 1918. Curtis founded the Music School Settlement for Colored People in Harlem, organized a Carnegie Hall concert by Negro musicians, and lectured widely on Indian and Afro-American music. Her life was cut short when she was struck and killed by a car while visiting Paris in 1921. See Babcock and Parezo, *Daughters of the Desert;* see also *Who's Who in American Music.*

11. Definitions of the word "dude" from Borne, *Dude Ranching,* pp. 3, 4.

12. Ibid., p. 124.

13. Jack Lambert, quoted in Love, "A Cowboy Recollects."

14. Bennett, *Reminiscences of the Thirties.*

15. Wheelwright, *Journey Towards Understanding,* p. 8.

16. Lee, *Willa Cather,* p. 261.

17. Quoted in Love, "A Cowboy Recollects."

18. Pack, *We Called It Ghost Ranch,* p. 56.

19. Stanley's name is among those who met to discuss the formation of an organization whose purpose would be to preserve the traditions and cultures of both the Native American and the Spanish peoples of New Mexico, mentioned in the Museum of New Mexico's *El Palacio* magazine in the fall of 1923. (*El Palacio* vol. 5, no. 7 [Oct. 1, 1923].)

20. Wheelwright, *Journey Towards Understanding,* p. 8.

21. Ibid., pp. 8, 9.

22. Ibid., p. 17.

23. Ibid., pp. 17, 18.

24. Maria Chabot to author.

25. Details of Los Luceros history and restoration from National Register of Historic Places, Inventory-Nomination Form, Los Luceros Hacienda, 1984.

26. Wheelwright, *Journey Towards Understanding,* pp. 42, 43, 44, 45.

27. Pack, *We Called It Ghost Ranch,* p. 7.

28. Ibid., pp. 7, 8.

29. Quoted in Love, "A Cowboy Recollects."

30. Lambert's fourth and last wife was renowned anthropologist Marjorie F. Lambert, whom he married in 1950. Until his death at the age of 93 in 1991, Jack Lambert was a familiar and favorite Santa Fean, often seen riding his horse from his Garcia Street home down to the plaza where local shopowners and tourists alike enjoyed his authentic cowboy charm and lively stories and reminiscences.

31. Quoted in Love, "A Cowboy Recollects."

Chapter 9.   Between Green and Dry

1. Kane, *What Am I Doing Here?* p. 19.

2. There is great dispute as to de Dios's year of birth: the church record of his baptism (Archives of the Archbishop of Santa Fe, Abiquiu Baptisms 2, p. 86) does not give his age; such an omission is usually indicative that the baptized was an infant. But local historians say de Dios claimed he was twelve years old when he was brought to Abiquiu. In the 1870 census, de Dios is listed as a ten-year-old from "Pah-ute Indian Country" living in the Gallegos household in Abiquiu. This record would place de Dios's birthday sometime in

1860. The census taken in 1920 refutes the 1870 census and lists Juan de Dios as seventy years of age in that year. However, United States census records hold little validity among local historians, and valley old-timers are fervent in their unanimous insistence that Juan de Dios was at least ninety years of age when he died in the late 1930s.

3. Weigle, *Hispanic Villages of Northern New Mexico,* p. 154.

4. Martin Bode was ambitious and well educated, a scholar of Latin and Greek classics who eventually spoke Spanish and English as well as his native German. He remained at the Gonzales house until 1927, when he married Cleotilde (Tillie) Gonzales of Taos (the daughter of an old and prestigious Taos family), whose mother was a distant cousin of Amalia Chávez. They bought the abandoned trading post of Henry Grant on the Abiquiu plaza and refurbished it into their home, where they raised five children.

5. Weigle, *Hispanic Villages of Northern New Mexico,* p. 158.

6. Ibid., p. 146.

7. Ibid., p. 155.

8. Ibid., p. 165.

9. Ibid., p. 157.

10. Ibid., p. 156.

11. Ibid., p. 160.

12. Ibid., p. 159.

13. Poling, "Coronas de Talco y Flores."

14. Details of José María Chávez burial from Yuvonnia Owen interview with Rosana Suazo de Mansanares, July 16, 1977.

15. Córdova, *Abiquiu and Don Cacahuate,* pp. 55, 56.

16. Ibid., p. 55.

17. Ibid.

Chapter 10.   Ghost Ranch

1. Dick Randall, "Music, Saddles, and Flapjacks," quoted in Borne, *Dude Ranching,* p. 27.

2. Pack, *We Called It Ghost Ranch,* pp. 22, 23.

3. Ibid., p. 23.

4. Ibid.

5. Ibid.

6. Information about Charles Lathrop Pack from *From This Seed,* unpublished autobiography of Arthur N. Pack, graciously shared with author by Eleanor Pack Liddell.

7. Details of Arthur N. Pack's childhood from ibid.

8. Pack, *We Called It Ghost Ranch,* p. 89.

9. Pack, *Challenge of Leisure,* p. 81.

10. Pack, *We Called It Ghost Ranch,* p. 31.

11. Virginia Trujillo y Salazar to author.

12. This group is not to be confused with a second group of Night Riders, el Mano Negro ("the black hand"), a Hispanic vigilante group that burned and destroyed Anglo ranches and fences in the 1930s.

13. Martin and Martin, *Bill Martin, American,* pp. 132–217.

14. Edward H. Bennett, Jr., letter to author, April 9, 1992.

15. Ibid.

16. Pack, *We Called It Ghost Ranch,* p. 59.

17. Ibid., p. 42.

18. Ibid.

19. Dorthy Fredericks to author.

20. Pack, *We Called It Ghost Ranch,* p. 47.

21. Ibid.

22. Ibid., p. 46.

23. William Finley's reputation as one of the foremost photographers of birds began at the turn of the century, when he and photographer Herman Bohlman photographed the California condor. Their 250 black-and-white photographs of two adult condors and their baby became the most complete photographic record of this vanishing species. Finley helped organize Oregon's first Fish and Game Commission in 1911 and was appointed state game warden the same year. After Finley's death in 1953, a winter refuge for the dusky Canada goose in Oregon's Willamette Valley was named for William Finley. The Finley films that starred the family's many half-tamed wild animals may have served as prototypes for similar nature films produced by Walt Disney in later years. See Roger Tory Peterson, *William L. Finley.*

24. Pack, *We Called It Ghost Ranch,* p. 47.

25. Ibid., pp. 48, 49.

Chapter 11. The Good Country

1. Quoted in Tryk, "O'Keeffe," p. 19.

2. Quoted in Cowart, Hamilton, and Greenough, *Georgia O'Keeffe,* p. 201.

3. O'Keeffe to Russell Vernon Hunter, quoted in ibid., p. 204.

4. Quoted in Tomkins, "Rose in the Eye," p. 54.

5. Quoted in ibid.

6. Quoted in Tryk, "O'Keeffe," p. 20.

7. O'Keeffe quoted in ibid.

8. Quoted in ibid.

9. Quoted in ibid.

10. Quoted in ibid.

11. O'Keeffe quoted in Seiberling, "Stark Vision."

12. Quoted in Seldis, "Georgia O'Keeffe at 78," p. 14.

13. O'Keeffe, *Georgia O'Keeffe,* plate 60. Copyright, private collection.

14. Lisle, *Portrait of an Artist,* p. 276.

15. Quoted in ibid., p. 277.

16. O'Keeffe to Cady Wells, n.d., quoted in Robinson, *Georgia O'Keeffe,* p. 431.

17. Quoted in ibid.

18. O'Keeffe to Stieglitz, July 29, 1937, in *Catalogue of the 14th Annual Exhibition of Paintings,* p. 4.

19. Carr, *Pebbles in Your Shoes,* p. 19.

20. Pack, *We Called It Ghost Ranch,* p. 44.

21. Phoebe Pack claims that the steer skull drawing was in fact given to her and Arthur as a wedding present. In 1971, partially at O'Keeffe's suggestion, the skull motif she sketched for Pack became the official insignia for the Ghost Ranch Conference Center.

22. Quoted in Seiberling, "Stark Vision."

23. Quoted in ibid.

24. O'Keeffe in *Catalogue of the 14th Annual Exhibition of Paintings.*

25. John Crosby, correspondence with author.

26. O'Keeffe to Stieglitz, July 29, 1937, quoted in *Catalogue of 14th Annual Exhibition of Paintings.*

27. Ibid.

28. Pack, *We Called It Ghost Ranch,* p. 63.

29. Ibid.

30. Quoted in Janis, "Georgia O'Keeffe."

31. Quoted in Seiberling, "Stark Vision."

32. O'Keeffe to Stieglitz, August 20, 1937, quoted in *Catalogue of 14th Annual Exhibition of Paintings.*

33. Quoted in Wallach, "Georgia O'Keeffe."

34. O'Keeffe to Maria Chabot, November 1941, quoted in Cowart, Hamilton, and Greenough, *Georgia O'Keeffe,* p. 232.

35. O'Keeffe to Stieglitz, September 20, 1937, quoted in *Catalogue of 14th Annual Exhibition of Paintings.*

36. Ansel Adams to Alfred Stieglitz, September 21, 1937, quoted in Alinder and Stillman, eds., *Ansel Adams,* p. 98.

37. Ibid.

38. Ansel Adams to Virginia Adams, in Adams, *Autobiography,* p. 224.

39. Ibid., p. 225.

40. O'Keeffe to Stieglitz, September 20, 1937, quoted in *Catalogue of the 14th Annual Exhibition of Paintings.*

41. Maria Chabot to author.

42. Adams, *Autobiography,* p. 226.

43. Hogrefe, *Georgia O'Keeffe,* p. 192.

44. O'Keeffe to Jim Shibley, personal communication to author.

45. O'Keeffe to Ettie Stettheimer, August 1940, quoted in Cowart, Hamilton, and Greenough, *Georgia O'Keeffe,* p. 231.

46. Pack, *We Called It Ghost Ranch,* p. 76.

47. Ibid.

48. Ibid., p. 77.

49. Details of Bode's purchase of the hacienda and gift of the house to the Archdiocese told to author by Elizabeth Bode Allred and Karl Bode. At the time of O'Keeffe's first inquiry about the house, the general's son, J.M.C. Cháves, probably owned only part of the property. To have sold the house, clear title would have had to be obtained from the extended Salazar family, to whom José María Chávez was related through marriage.

50. O'Keeffe, *Georgia O'Keeffe,* unpaginated. Copyright, private collection.

51. Jerry Richardson to Jeffrey Hogrefe in Hogrefe, *Georgia O'Keeffe,* p. 208.

52. Ibid.

53. Martin Bode may have paid as much as $400 for the house and grounds. Previous owners traded the house for two cows, one with calf, and a bushel of corn in 1826 (see Tryk, "O'Keeffe"); the Trujillo family sold the house and land for $115.50 legal tender to the Salazars in 1874 (O'Keeffe papers of General José María Chávez); General Chávez lived in the house prior to 1874, but his claim to the hacienda was not through purchase, but through marriage. Upon releasing the church from its legal obligation to turn the donated property into a school, Bode insisted the Archdiocese reimburse him the $400 he had paid for the house.

54. Quoted in Seiberling, "Stark Vision."

55. Lisle, *Portrait of an Artist,* p. 326.

56. Quoted in Seiberling, "Stark Vision."

57. Quoted in Seldis, "Georgia O'Keeffe at 78," pp. 16–17.

58. Quoted in Tomkins, "Rose in the Eye," p. 62.

59. Quoted in Seldis, "Georgia O'Keeffe at 78," p. 14.

Chapter 12.   Bombs and Bones

1. William McNulty, in *Santa Fe New Mexican,* August 6, 1945.

2. Ibid.

3. Ibid.

4. Pack, *We Called It Ghost Ranch,* p. 80.

5. Ibid., p. 79.

6. Ibid., p. 80.

7. Ibid., p. 82.

8. Ibid.

9. Colbert, *Digging into the Past,* p. 285.

10. David Baldwin to Edward Drinker Cope, 1881, quoted in *Ghost Ranch Journal,* vol. 3, no. 2.

11. From "O. C. Marsh: Pioneer in Paleontology," quoted in Lucas, Rigby, and Kues, *Advances in San Juan Basin Paleontology,* p. 8.

12. David Baldwin to Edward Drinker Cope, quoted in Colbert, *The Triassic Dinosaur Coelophysis,* p. 5.

13. David Baldwin to E. D. Cope, October 24, 1881, quoted in *Ghost Ranch Journal,* vol. 3, no. 2.

14. Ibid.

15. Samuel P. Welles, unpublished journal, August 7, 1934.

16. Ibid., July 3, 1934.

17. Journal of Charles Camp, July 23, 1933, quoted in *Ghost Ranch Journal,* vol. 3, no. 3.

18. Pack, *We Called It Ghost Ranch,* p. 92.

19. Whitaker and Meyers, *Dinosaur Hunt,* p. 24.

20. Colbert, *Digging into the Past,* pp. 285–86.

21. Ibid., p. 286.

22. Ibid.

23. Ibid.

24. Ibid., p. 287.

25. Ibid.

26. Ibid., p. 290.

27. Coelophysis was about six feet long, with delicate, hollow bones, like those of birds. It was a very agile meat eater that ran rapidly on long, slender rear legs. Its forelimbs were small, with three-fingered hands and sharp claws that could grasp its prey. Coelophysis had a long tail, and its long jaws were filled with knifelike teeth.

28. Colbert, *Digging into the Past,* p. 298.

29. Colbert, *Little Dinosaurs of Ghost Ranch,* p. 51.

30. Pack, *We Called It Ghost Ranch,* p. 93.

31. Colbert, *Little Dinosaurs of Ghost Ranch,* p. 50.

32. Edwin H. Colbert, *Ghost Ranch Journal,* vol. 2, no. 2.

33. Ibid.

34. Pack, *We Called It Ghost Ranch,* p. 94.

35. Colbert, *The Triassic Dinosaur Coelophysis.*

36. Pack, *We Called It Ghost Ranch,* p. 94.

Conclusion: Prologue to the Next Century

1. Pack was Tucson's first "Man of the Year," was president of the Tucson Chamber of Commerce, and began watershed management departments at universities in Arizona and New Mexico.

2. Quoted in Pack, *We Called It Ghost Ranch,* p. 137.

3. Ibid.

4. Reverend David Sholin to author.

5. Nabokov, *Tijerina and the Courthouse Raid,* p. 63.

6. Ibid., p. 18.

7. Steiner, *La Raza,* p. 77. The American Civil Liberties Union later held hearings that claimed the civil rights of the thirty-nine individuals held overnight in the Canjilon sheep pen had been violated. See Nabokov, *Tijerina and the Courthouse Raid,* p. 110.

8. The recorded tapes of the speeches given by Tijerina, Hall, Kirsh, and others burned in the fire that completely destroyed the Ghost Ranch headquarters in March of 1983. All quotes from this meeting are from interviews by the author with Jim Hall, Father Kirsh, and several Ghost Ranch employees who witnessed the Alianza's May 1969 visit to Ghost Ranch.

9. John C. Purdy quoted by Jim Hall in *Ghost Ranch Journal,* vol. 1, no. 1, winter 1986.

10. Population statistics from Bureau of Business and Economic Research, *Census in New Mexico;* and from the U.S. Bureau of the Census, Pueblo, Colorado.

BIBLIOGRAPHY OF SELECTED SOURCES

Archival Sources

Archives of the Archdiocese of Santa Fe. Indexed by Fray Angélico Chávez, 1957; see also Martinez databases.

Law offices of White, Koch, Kelley, and McCarthey. Papers pertaining to the Piedra Lumbre Land Grant; Catron and Renehan files; Records of the Court of Private Land Claims. Santa Fe.

Museum of New Mexico History Library: files pertaining to Abiquiu, the Piedra Lumbre, Ghost Ranch, and Chama River Valley. Santa Fe.

New Mexico State Library: Southwest Collection, files pertaining to Abiquiu and Ghost Ranch. Santa Fe.

State Records and Archives: Records of the Court of Private Land Claims; Land Grant Records (LGR) pertaining to Abiquiu, Polvedera, and Piedra Lumbre Land Grants. Santa Fe. (Abbreviated as NMSRA.)

University of New Mexico: Coronado Room Special Collections, files pertaining to Abiquiu, Ghost Ranch, and the Piedra Lumbre. Albuquerque.

Published Sources and Memoirs

Abel, Annie Heloise. "The Journal of John Greiner." *Old Santa Fe Magazine* 3 (1916):189–243.

Adams, Ansel. *An Autobiography.* Boston: Little, Brown & Co., 1985.

Adams, Eleanor G., and Fray Angélico Chávez, trans. *The Missions of New Mexico, 1776: A Description by Fray Francisco Atanasio Dominguez, with Other Contemporary Documents.* Albuquerque: University of New Mexico Press, 1975.

Ahlborn, Richard Eighme. *The Penitente Moradas of Abiquiu.* Washington, D.C.: Smithsonian Institution Press, 1986.

Alinder, Mary Street. *Ansel Adams, an Autobiography.* Boston: Little, Brown & Co., 1985.

——, and Andrea Gray Stillman, eds. *Ansel Adams: Letters and Images, 1916–1984.* Boston: Little, Brown & Co., 1988.

Anaya, Rudolpho A., and Simon J. Ortiz, eds. *Ceremony of Brotherhood.* Albuquerque: Academia, 1981.

Athearn, Robert G. *The Mythic West in Twentieth Century America.* Lawrence: University Press of Kansas, 1986.

Babcock, Barbara A., and Nancy J. Parezo. *Daughters of the Desert: Women Anthropologists and the Native American Southwest, 1880–1980.* Albuquerque: University of New Mexico Press, 1988.

Bailey, L. R. *The Indian Slave Trade in the Southwest.* Los Angeles: Westernlore Press, 1973.

Bandelier, Adolph F. A. *Final Report of Investigations Among the Indians of the Southwestern United States, Carried Out Mainly In the Years From 1880 to 1885.* 2 vols. Papers of the Archaeological Institute of America. Cambridge, Mass.: John Wilson and Son, 1892.

——. *The Journals of Adolph F. Bandelier, 1880–1882.* Charles H. Lange and Carroll L. Riley, eds. Reprinted, Albuquerque: University of New Mexico Press, 1966. Previously published 1883–1884, 1970.

Beck, Warren A. *New Mexico, a History of Four Centuries.* Norman: University of Oklahoma Press, 1962.

Bennett, Edward H., Jr. *Reminiscences from the Thirties.* Unpublished memoir, Ghost Ranch History Archive.

Bolton, Herbert E. *Pageant in the Wilderness.* Salt Lake City: Utah State Historical Society, 1950.

Borne, Lawrence R. *Dude Ranching: A Complete History.* Albuquerque: University of New Mexico Press, 1983.

Bowden, J. J. *Private Land Claims of the Southwest.* Ph.D. dissertation, Southern Methodist University, 1969.

Briggs, Charles L., and John R. Van Ness, eds. *Land, Water, and Culture.* Albuquerque: University of New Mexico Press, 1987.

Bureau of Business and Economic Research. *The Census in New Mexico: Population and Housing Characteristics for the State and Counties from the 1980 and 1990 Censuses.* Albuquerque.

Carlson, Alvar Ward. *The Spanish-American Homeland: Four Centuries in New Mexico's Rio Arriba.* Baltimore: Johns Hopkins University Press, 1990.

Carr, William H. *Pebbles in Your Shoes.* Tucson: Arizona-Sonora Desert Museum, 1982.

Carrillo, Charles M. *Indios de Abiquiu: A Study of Abiquiu's Genizaro Past and Hispanic Present.* Unpublished paper, 1982.

Catalogue of the 14th Annual Exhibition of Paintings. New York: An American Place, December 27–February 11, 1938.

Chávez, Fray Angélico. *Archives of the Archdiocese of Santa Fe, 1678–1900.* Washington, D.C.: Academy of American Franciscan History.

——. *Origins of New Mexico Families in the Spanish Colonial Period.* Albuquerque: University of Albuquerque, 1973.

——. *Tres Macho—He Said: Padre Gallegos of Albuquerque.* Santa Fe: William Gannon, 1985.

Cleland, Robert Glass. *This Reckless Breed of Men: The Trappers and Fur Traders of the Southwest.* Albuquerque: University of New Mexico Press, 1976.

Colbert, Edwin H. *Digging into the Past.* New York: Dembner Books, 1989.

——. *The Little Dinosaurs of Ghost Ranch.* New York: Columbia University Press, 1995.

——. *Men and Dinosaurs.* New York: E. P. Dutton & Co., 1968.

———. *The Triassic Dinosaur Coelophysis*. Museum of Northern Arizona, Bulletin Series 57. Flagstaff, 1984.

———, and Stuart A. Northrop, eds. *Guidebook for the Fourth Field Conference of the Society of Vertebrate Paleontology in Northwest New Mexico*. Sponsored by American Museum of Natural History, New York, and the University of New Mexico, Albuquerque, 1950.

Corbin, Alice. *Red Earth: Poems of New Mexico*. Chicago: Ralph Seymour, 1920.

Córdova, Gilberto Benito. *Abiquiu and Don Cacahuate: A Folk History of a New Mexican Village*. Los Cerrillos: San Marcos Press, 1973.

———. *Pedagogy of Missionization: Reduccion and Hispanicization of Santo Thomas Apostoi de Abiquiu*. Ph.D. dissertation, University of New Mexico, 1978.

Cowart, Jack, Juan Hamilton, and Sarah Greenough. *Georgia O'Keeffe: Art and Letters*. Washington, D.C.: National Gallery of Art, 1987.

Crocchiola, Stanley F. L. [F. Stanley]. *The Abiquiu (New Mexico) Story*. Circa 1960.

deBuys, William. *Enchantment and Exploitation: The Life and Hard Times of a New Mexico Mountain Range*. Albuquerque: University of New Mexico Press, 1985.

Delaney, Robert W. *The Ute Mountain Utes*. Albuquerque: University of New Mexico Press, 1989.

Domínguez, Francisco Atanasio. *The Missions of New Mexico, 1776: A Description by Fray Francisco Atanasio Dominguez, with Other Contemporary Documents*. Translated and annotated by Eleanor B. Adams and Fray Angélico Chávez. Albuquerque: University of New Mexico Press, 1956.

Dougherty, Julia D. *An Archaeological Evaluation of Tsiping Ruin*. Albuquerque: USDA Forest Service, 1980.

Ebright, Malcolm. *Land Grants and Lawsuits in Northern New Mexico*. Albuquerque: University of New Mexico Press, 1994.

———. "Manuel Martinez' Ditch Dispute: A Study in Mexican Period Custom and Justice." *New Mexico Historical Review* 54, no. 1 (1979):21–34.

———, ed. *Spanish and Mexican Land Grants and the Law*. Manhattan, Kans.: Sunflower University Press, 1989.

Ellis, Florence Hawley. *From Drought to Drought*. Santa Fe: Sunstone Press, 1988.

Foxx, Teralene S. *Ghost Ranch Nature Trail Guide*. Pamphlet. Abiquiu: Ghost Ranch Service Corps, 1996.

Gibson, Arrell Morgan. *The Santa Fe and Taos Colonies*. Norman: University of Oklahoma Press, 1983.

Gillmor, Frances, and Louisa Wade Wetherill. *Traders to the Navajos: the Story of the Wetherills of Kayenta*. Albuquerque: University of New Mexico Press, 1952.

Hafen, Leroy R., ed. "Armijo's Journal." *Colorado Magazine* 27 (April 1950):120–25.

———. "Colorado Recollections of a Centenarian." *Colorado Magazine* 10 (1933):53–62.

———, and Hafen, Ann W. *Old Spanish Trail: Santa Fe to Los Angeles*. Lincoln: University of Nebraska Press, 1993.

Harley, R. Bruce, compiler. *The Agua Mansa Story*. San Bernardino County Museum Association no. 39. Redlands, Calif. 1991.

Harrington, John Peabody. *The Ethnogeography of the Tewa Indians*. 29th Annual Report of the Bureau of American Ethnology. Washington, D.C.: GPO, 1916.

Hibben, Frank C. *Indian Hunts and Indian Hunters of the Old West.* Long Beach, Calif.: Safari Press, 1989.

Hodge, Frederick Webb, ed. *Handbook of American Indians North of Mexico.* Bulletin 30. Washington, D.C.: GPO, 1907–10.

Hogrefe, Jeffrey. *Georgia O'Keeffe: The Life of an American Legend.* New York: Bantam, 1992.

Horvath, Steven M., Jr. *The Genízaro of Eighteenth-Century New Mexico: A Reexamination.* Santa Fe: School of American Research, *Discovery Magazine,* 1977.

Israel, Franklin. "Georgia O'Keeffe." *Architectural Digest* (July 1981):77–85, 136–38.

Janis, Leo. "Georgia O'Keeffe at Eighty-four." *Atlantic Monthly,* December 1971.

Jaramillo, Cleofas. *Romance of a Little Village Girl.* San Antonio, Tex.: Naylor, 1955.

——. *Shadows of the Past.* Santa Fe: Ancient City Press, 1972.

Jeançon, J. A. *Excavations in the Chama Valley, New Mexico.* Washington, D.C.: GPO, 1923.

Jenkins, Myra Ellen, and Albert H. Schroeder, eds. *A Brief History of New Mexico.* Albuquerque: University of New Mexico Press, 1974.

Kane, Wanden M. *What Am I Doing Here?* Palmer Lake, Colo.: Filter Press, 1979.

Keleher, William A. *Turmoil in New Mexico, 1846–68.* Albuquerque: University of New Mexico Press, 1982.

Kessell, John L. *Kiva, Cross, and Crown: The Pecos Indians and New Mexico, 1540–1840.* National Park Service. Washington, D.C.: GPO, 1979.

——. *The Missions of New Mexico since 1776.* Albuquerque: University of New Mexico Press, 1980.

——. "Sources for the History of a New Mexico Community: Abiquiu." *New Mexico Historical Review* 54, no. 4 (1979):249–87.

Kluckhohn, Clyde, and Dorothea Leighton. *The Navaho.* Garden City, N.Y.: Doubleday & Co., 1962.

Kutsche, Paul, ed. *The Survival of Spanish American Villages.* Research Committee, Colorado College, no. 15. Colorado Springs. 1979.

Kutsche, Paul, and John R. Van Ness. *Cañones: Values, Crisis, and Survival in a Northern New Mexico Village.* Albuquerque: University of New Mexico Press, 1981.

——, John R. Van Ness, and Andrew T. Smith. "Unified Approach to the Anthropology of Hispanic Northern New Mexico: Historical Archaeology, Ethnohistory, and Ethnography." *Historical Archaeology* 10 (1976):1–16.

Lee, Hermione. *Willa Cather: Double Lives.* New York: Pantheon, 1989.

Limerick, Patricia. *Desert Passages.* Albuquerque: University of New Mexico Press, 1985.

Lisle, Laurie. *Portrait of an Artist: A Biography of Georgia O'Keeffe.* New York: Washington Square Press, 1980; reprinted 1986.

Love, Marian F. "A Cowboy Recollects." *The Santa Fean,* December 1981.

Lucas, Spencer, Keith Rigby, Jr., and Barry Kues, eds. *Advances in San Juan Basin Paleontology.* Albuquerque: University of New Mexico Press, 1981.

Lummis, Charles F. *The Land of Poco Tiempo.* Albuquerque: University of New Mexico Press, 1952, 1975.

McCall, George Archibald. *New Mexico in 1850; A Military View.* Robert W. Frazier, ed. Norman: University of Oklahoma Press, 1968.

McNitt, Frank. *Navajo Wars: Military Campaigns, Slave Raids, and Reprisals.* Albuquerque: University of New Mexico Press, 1972.

Martin, Bill, and Molly Radford Martin. *Bill Martin, American.* Caldwell, Idaho: Caxton Printers, 1959.

Martinez, Thomas D. *Abiquiu Baptisms, 1754–1870.* Baptism database of archives held by the Archdiocese of Santa Fe and the State Archive of New Mexico. San Jose, California, March 1993.

——. *San Juan de los Caballeros Baptisms, 1726–1870.* Baptism database of archives held by the Archdiocese of Santa Fe and the State Archive of New Mexico. San Jose, California, January 1994.

——. *Santa Cruz de la Cañada Baptisms, 1710–1860.* Baptism database of archives held by the Archdiocese of Santa Fe and the State Archive of New Mexico. San Jose, California, 1993.

Meriwether, David. *My Life in the Mountains and on the Plains.* Robert A. Griffen, ed. Norman: University of Oklahoma Press, 1965.

Minge, Ward Alan. "Mexican Independence Day and a Ute Tragedy in Santa Fe, 1844." In *The Changing Ways of Southwestern Indians, a Historic Perspective,* ed. Albert H. Schroeder. Glorieta, N.Mex.: Rio Grande Press, 1973.

Nabokov, Peter. *Tijerina and the Courthouse Raid.* Albuquerque: University of New Mexico Press, 1969.

Nash, Gerald D. *Creating the West: Historical Interpretations, 1890–1990.* Albuquerque: University of New Mexico Press, 1991.

O'Keeffe, Georgia. *Georgia O'Keeffe.* New York: Viking Press, 1976.

Opler, Morris Edward. *Myths and Tales of the Jicarilla Apache Indians.* New York: American Folk-Lore Society, 1938.

Ortiz, Alfonso, ed. *Handbook of North American Indians,* vol. 9. Washington, D.C.: Smithsonian Institution, 1979.

——, ed. *New Perspectives on the Pueblos.* Albuquerque: University of New Mexico Press, 1972.

Owen, Yuvonnia. "A Preliminary Study of the Oral History of Santa Rosa de Lima de Abiquiú." Research paper, New Mexico Highlands University, August 1977.

Pack, Arthur Newton. *The Challenge of Leisure.* New York: MacMillan, 1934.

——. *From This Seed.* Unpublished autobiography.

——. *We Called It Ghost Ranch.* Abiquiu: Ghost Ranch Conference Center, 1979.

Peters, Dewitt C. *Kit Carson's Life and Adventures.* Hartford, Conn.: Dustin, Gilman & Co., 1873.

Peterson, Roger Tory. *William L. Finley: Pioneer Wildlife Photographer.* Corvallis: Oregon State University, 1986.

Poling, Lesley. "Coronas de Talco y Flores." *Youth Magazine* (January 1979):41–48.

Quintana, Frances Leon. *Pobladores: Hispanic Americans of the Ute Frontier.* 2nd edition of *Los Primeros Pobladores* (Notre Dame: University of Notre Dame Press). Self-published: Aztec, N.Mex., 1991.

——, and David H. Snow, eds. "Historical Archaeology of the Rito Colorado Valley, New Mexico." *Journal of the West* (July 1980):40–50.

Reeve, Frank D. "Early Navaho Geography." *New Mexico Historical Review* 31 (October 1956):290–309.

Reichard, Gladys A. *Navaho Religion: A Study of Symbolism.* Princeton: Bollingen Foundation, Princeton University Press, 1950.

Rio Grande Sun, Special Historical Edition, Española, November 8, 1962.

Roberts, David. *Once They Moved Like the Wind: Cochise, Geronimo, and the Apache Wars.* New York: Simon and Schuster, 1993.

Robinson, Roxana. *Georgia O'Keeffe: A Life.* New York: Harper and Row, 1989.

Seiberling, Dorothy. "Stark Vision of a Pioneer Painter." *Life,* March 1, 1968, pp. 40–53.

Seldis, Henry. "Georgia O'Keeffe at 78." *Los Angeles Times "West" Magazine,* January 22, 1967.

Simmons, Marc. *New Mexico: A History.* New York: W. W. Norton, 1977.

Smith, David. *Ouray: Chief of the Utes.* Ouray, Colo.: Wayfinder Press, 1987.

Steiner, Stan. *La Raza.* New York: Harper Colophon, 1969.

Swadesh, Frances Leon. *20,000 Years of History.* Santa Fe: Sunstone Press, 1973.

Thomas, Alfred Barnaby. *The Plains Indians and New Mexico, 1751–1778.* Albuquerque: University of New Mexico Press, 1940.

Tiller, Veronica E. Velarde. *The Jicarilla Apache Tribe: A History.* Lincoln: University of Nebraska Press, 1983.

Tomkins, Calvin. "The Rose in the Eye Looked Pretty Fine." *The New Yorker,* March 4, 1974.

Tryk, Sheila. "O'Keeffe." *New Mexico Magazine,* January/February 1973.

Turner, Frederick. *Of Chiles, Cacti, and Fighting Cocks: Notes on the American West.* San Francisco: North Point Press, 1990.

Twitchell, Ralph Emerson. "Española and Its Environs." *Harper's New Monthly Magazine* 70, no. 420 (May 1885):1–20.

——.*The Leading Facts of New Mexican History.* 5 vols. Cedar Rapids: Torch Press, 1911–1917.

Underhill, Ruth M. *The Navajos.* Norman: University of Oklahoma Press, 1956.

Van Ness, John R. *Hispanics in Northern New Mexico: The Development of Corporate Community and Multicommunity.* Ph.D. dissertation, University of Pennsylvania, 1979.

——, and Christine M. Van Ness. "Introduction." *Journal of the West* (July 1980):3–11.

Wallach, Amei. "Georgia O'Keeffe." *Newsday,* October 30, 1977.

Warren, A. Helene. "The Ancient Mineral Industries of Cerro Pedernal." In *Silver Anniversary Guidebook: Ghost Ranch, Central-Northern New Mexico,* ed. Charles T. Siemers. New Mexico Geological Society, 1974.

Weber, David J. *The Mexican Frontier, 1821–1846.* Albuquerque: University of New Mexico Press, 1982.

——. *The Taos Trappers: The Fur Trade in the Far Southwest, 1540–1846.* Norman: University of Oklahoma Press, 1970.

Weigle, Marta. *Brothers of Light, Brothers of Blood.* Albuquerque: University of New Mexico Press, 1976.

——. *Hispanic Villages of Northern New Mexico.* Santa Fe: Lightning Tree Press, 1975.

——. *Santa Fe and Taos: The Writer's Era, 1916–1941.* Santa Fe: Ancient City Press, 1982.

Westphall, Victor. *Thomas Benton Catron and His Era*. Tucson: University of Arizona Press, 1973.

Wheelwright, Mary Cabot. *Journey Towards Understanding*. Unpublished autobiography, 1957. Property of the Wheelwright Museum of the American Indian.

Whitaker, George, and Joan Meyers. *Dinosaur Hunt*. New York: Harcourt, Brace and World, 1965.

White, Koch, Kelley, and McCarthey. *Land Title Study*. Santa Fe: State Planning Office, 1971.

Wozniak, Frank J., Meade F. Kemrer, and Charles M. Carrillo. *History and Ethnohistory along the Rio Chama*. Albuquerque: U.S. Army Corps of Engineers, 1992.

INDEX

ABOUT THE AUTHOR

Lesley Poling-Kempes has lived and worked in New Mexico for more than twenty-five years. *Valley of Shining Stone: The Story of Abiquiu* is Poling-Kempes' third book. Her first book, *The Harvey Girls: Women Who Opened the West,* won the Zia Award for Excellence from the New Mexico Press Women. She is also the author of a novel about northern New Mexico, *Canyon of Remembering,* and her short stories have been published and anthologized in literary magazines throughout the West. Poling-Kempes lives near Abiquiu with her husband and two children.